Food Policies and Food Security under Instability

Food Policies and Food Security under Instability

Modeling and Analysis

David Bigman
The Hebrew University

Lexington Books
D.C. Heath and Company/Lexington, Massachusetts/Toronto

Library of Congress Cataloging in Publication Data

Bigman, David.
  Food policies and food security under instability.

  Includes bibliographies and index.
  1. Food supply—Government policy   Developing countries.
2. Agriculture and state—Developing countries.   3.   Natural
disasters—Economic aspects—Developing countries.   I.   Title.
HD9018.D44B54   1984   338.1'91724   82-48039
ISBN 0-669-05886-6 (alk. paper)

Published simultaneously in Canada
Printed in the United States of America on acid-free paper
International Standard Book Number: 0-669-05886-6
Library of Congress Catalog Card Number: 82-48039

To My Children

Contents

Figures

Tables

Preface and Acknowledgments

The instability inherent in agricultural production as an effect of erratic weather is perhaps the most important factor that distinguishes the analysis of the agricultural sector from that of all other sectors of the economy. It is also a crucial factor in the formation of agricultural production and food-distribution policies. Indeed, practically all countries are widely engaged in a multitude of programs at both the production and the distribution ends aimed at stabilizing the prices of agricultural produce; protecting farmers from default as a result of natural hazards, poor harvest, or a sharp price decline; and stabilizing the flow of supply to the population.

Despite its importance, the instability factor is often disregarded in the design of agricultural policies and development plans, and the analysis is still conducted mostly with deterministic partial or general equilibrium models or with programming models. Although its significance is always recognized, the analysis of the instability factor is largely nonquantitative and seldom lends itself to specific policy recommendations.

One objective of this book is to present a methodology for conducting a quantitative analysis of agricultural and food-distribution policies under instability. The book develops the analytical framework, gives the details of the simulation model that has been designed as the main instrument of analysis, and illustrates its application both in a prototype model of the food grains sector and in actual country cases.

The other objective of the book is to examine the effects of instability in agriculture and of alternative stabilization policies on producers and consumers, on international trade in agricultural commodities, on the fiscal budget, on the long-term growth prospects of the agricultural sector, and on the country's food self-sufficiency. Attention here is focused on the trade-offs involved in the policies and programs under consideration and on ways to determine their cost-effectiveness.

This book is in many ways an extension and expansion of my early work on this subject, summarized in my book *Coping with Hunger: Toward a System of Food Security and Price Stabilization.* (Cambridge, Mass.: Ballinger). In retrospect I think that my own early work—and, for that matter, most of the theoretical and empirical work on agricultural stabilization policies during the 1970s—has focused too narrowly on buffer stocks as the main instrument of stabilization. In practice, stabilization strategy is a complex package consisting of a large number of programs of which buffer stocks represent only one. An appraisal of any individual policy that does not take into account the economic environment in which it operates and the other policies already in effect is not only of very little practical value but may actually be misleading. A more general analytical framework which can examine the entire complex may have to be country-specific and thus lose its general validity. I believe that for an economic research work to be of any use in policymaking, this is a risk worth taking.

Many people helped me in writing this book. I would like to extend my thanks to Shlomo Reutlinger, Haim Shalit, Shlomo Yitzhaki, Edna Schechtman, Richard Burkrof, Pasquale Scandizzo, and Don Mitchell for helpful comments and advice. I would like to thank Miron Scheuermann, Ruti Steinberg, and Vinh Le-Si for their excellent research assistance. Special thanks are due to Jeanne Cummings, Nitza Sadeh, and Lynn Rosentzweig for their superb typing job and for bearing with my seemingly endless revisions.

The research was supported in part by a grant from the United States–Israel (Binational) Agricultural Research and Development Fund.

1
An Overview

I n *The Economics of Welfare*, Arthur C. Pigou asks whether anything
that is to the advantage of society as a whole can at the same time be to
the disadvantage of the poorer members of society. In different forms,
this question has concerned economists ever since Ricardo developed his
theory of rent. Hicks and Robinson, who laid the foundation for modern
production theory, have demonstrated that technical progress that raises
national income may at the same time reduce the relative share of labor—
sometimes even its absolute share.[1] In the agricultural sector, to take another
example, the Green Revolution has been accused of being biased in favor
of large farmers and against small farmers, who cannot afford to buy the
fertilizers needed for the new crop varieties.

The modern welfare state, which widened and deepened government
involvement in all aspects of life, raised another question, the exact oppposite
of Pigou's. Can anything that is to the advantage of the poorer members of
society at the same time be to the disadvantage of society as a whole? Can it
be so disadvantageous that ultimately even the poor themselves will not gain?

Today's global food problem raises these dual questions in their most
acute form. On the one hand, can faster growth rates of food production and
strategies concentrating on development and employment at the aggregate
level reach the poorer segments of society and reduce their food insecurity?
Can countries by promoting food production attain also levels of food consumption that will ensure adequate nutrition for even the lowest deciles in
their income distribution? On the other hand, can direct measures to amelio-
rate poverty and undernutrition through, among other means, cheap food
prices, be detrimental to the long-run growth of the agricultural sector and
ultimately to the food security of the poor themselves?

Ever since Malthus's days, the food problem has been seen as a race
between food production and mouths to feed. Efforts have been concentrated
on expanding the global food supply and increasing productivity in the agricultural sector. The evidence of the last two decades shows that these efforts
bore the desired fruits, disproving the Malthusian prediction that the world

population would grow to levels the earth would not be able to feed. During the period 1961–1977 the world staple food production increased at an annual rate of 2.6 percent, whereas the world population rose at an annual rate of 2.0 percent.[2] Even in the developing countries as a group, staple food production grew during these two decades at an annual rate of 2.7 percent, slightly above their population growth of 2.6 percent. Projections for the coming ten to fifteen years by both the World Bank and the Food and Agricultural Organization of the United Nations (FAO) forecast that per capita food consumption will continue to grow at a rate of 0.44 percent per annum, a marked increase from the growth rate of 0.3 percent during the 1960s and 1970s.[3]

Despite this impressive growth in food production, the number of undernourished people continued to rise, and diseases related to food deficiency are more prevalent today than ever before. According to FAO estimates, the number of undernourished people in the developing countries, which totaled over 400 million in the late 1960s, continued to rise in the 1970s.[4]

The crux of the problem is not an insufficient food supply but an inadequate distribution of the available supply. Lacking resources such as land, capital, skill, and even the sheer physical and mental capacity to work, the poor cannot command sufficient means or earn enough income to provide them with even the minimum amount of food necessary for living, even though there is no shortage of food in the market.

In normal times, poor subsistence farmers and urban workers may manage to provide adequate diets for their households. They generally participate in the economic development process, and some of its fruits are likely to trickle down to them and help improve their living conditions. But they remain highly vulnerable to market disruptions caused by supply shortages, sharp rises in food prices, or a decline in their income—any of which that can severely curtail their purchasing power and bring them to the brink of starvation.

The chronically undernourished may work when employment opportunities exist, but their incomes cannot buy enough food for their whole family. Children and women in these households are the first to suffer. (Indeed, it is estimated that children under five constitute over half of the world's malnourished population.) They are trapped in a vicious circle: They live in poverty marked by chronic undernutrition, poor health, unsanitary drinking water, large families, and crowded housing. These factors in turn increase their vulnerability to infectious diseases, hinder their motivation, and reduce their capacity for physical work—thus often dooming them and their children to remain in poverty. They share hardly at all in the fruits of economic development. For them, development at the aggregate level offers no relief. Even strategies of more equitable growth will not be very effective because, lacking the necessary means of production, they are unable to take part in the development process and share in its gains. Efforts to increase total food production in the country will not relieve their undernutrition unless they have enough income to afford the food they need.

The instability inherent in agricultural production adds another, often grimmer dimension to the food problem. Harvest failures due to bad weather conditions force subsistence farmers to cut their food consumption; the resulting increase in price and decrease in agricultural employment curtail the purchasing power of the rural landless and urban workers, for whom it may become impossible to maintain their normal level of food consumption, however small.

Local harvest failures are not the only source of supply instability and price gyrations. As the world grain market became increasingly integrated and the dependence of the less-developed countries (LDCs) on imports rose, instability in world prices became an important source of internal instability in many countries. Crop failure in one country raises the price on the world grain market, which in turn transmits the shock to all other countries. With the exception of the unusually stable conditions of the 1950s and 1960s, real cereal prices have fluctuated 50 percent or more at least once every half dozen years throughout the past 125 years (see Martin and Brokken 1983).

Volatile world prices are only partly the result of nature's caprice, however. Far more significant are the effects of trade policies. Many countries, in the pursuit of domestic price stability, impose barriers on trade that contribute to the instability on the world market. The developing countries are especially vulnerable to such disruptions. Foreign-exchange constraints often force them to cut their purchases on the world market if higher prices push their food imports bill beyond their means.

Government policies themselves are another significant source of instability. Food programs typically have a variety of consequences, some of which are unforeseen by policymakers, in part because of changes in the behavior of producers and consumers when these policies are implemented. All too often these programs have gone awry not from lack of good intentions but because their direct and indirect effects have not been adequately understood. Erratic price changes and ad hoc procurement and distribution programs, aimed at meeting special needs as they arise, leave producers highly uncertain about the price they are going to get or the quantity they will be able to sell, thereby inhibiting production and investments (see Thomas and Bhattagli 1983).

The poor are the most vulnerable to these market tides. Having relatively elastic demand for staple foods—a consequence of the large share of their budget allotted to food—they find the bulk of adjustments resulting from supply or price changes imposed on them (Mellor 1978). Production shortfalls and price hikes therefore both widen and deepen the circles of poverty and undernutrition. In India, for example, Mellor and Desai (1984) found that the proportion of the rural population living below the poverty line has fluctuated widely from 40 to 60 percent, largely because of the effects of changing agricultural production and prices. FAO (1977) estimated that in 1972–1974 the number of undernourished people increased by more than 50 million as a result of production shortfalls and price hikes that resulted in turn from adverse climatic conditions.

The immensity of today's food problem on the one hand, and the slow growth of food production and employment in the developing countries on the other, have raised serious doubts about the efficacy of development strategies concentrating on aggregate effective demand and employment. Some argue that these strategies have contributed to increasing the inequality of the income distribution instead of reducing it. Even if they were not to the disadvantage of the poor and the undernourished, however, their effects on these members of society have been too small and too slow.

Attention was then diverted to direct distributive and structural approaches to reduce poverty and fulfill basic human needs. In the late 1970s the basic-needs approach was adopted by aid donor countries and by international institutions such as the World Bank. In many developing countries strong political and humanitarian pressures have led to a direct attack on poverty and undernutrition through general or targeted food subsidy programs, rural employment schemes, supplementary feeding programs, targeted public investments, and agrarian reforms.

In the short run, these welfare programs play an extremely important political stabilizing role and offer rapid—though often temporary—relief for the poor and undernourished. Their widespread use, their high proportions in national budgets, and their effects on the balance of payments make these welfare programs the cornerstone of the food policy in most developing countries. The fundamental question for society as a whole is: What are the long-term effects of these short-term measures on food production and food self-sufficiency, on overall economic growth, and ultimately on the food security of the poor themselves? Johnston and Clark (1982) emphasize the opportunity cost of subsidies and other short-term welfare measures in diverting resources and attention away from long-run development programs to expand output and employment opportunities.[5] Lipton (1977) emphasizes the detrimental effects of the "urban bias" often revealed in the food policies of developing countries, as manifested by their cheap-food policies. Schultz (1978) argues that government exchange-rate and price policies in many developing countries, which have caused their relative food prices to be substantially lower than those in the developed countries, bear much of the blame for the poor performance of the agricultural sector in these countries. These arguments raise the question counterposed to that of Pigou: Can these measures to alleviate poverty and undernutrition be detrimental to the long-term growth of the economy as a whole? Can their adverse effects ultimately be to the disadvantage of the poor and the undernourished themselves?

One objective of this book is to highlight the trade-offs associated with food policies of developing countries: between short-term food needs and long-term production and employment goals, between stability and growth, between the general welfare and the nutritional status of different consumer groups, between the rural and urban sectors. Direct distributive and structural measures to alleviate poverty and undernutrition are primarily short-term measures. The study thus focuses on short-term needs, especially those arising from fluctuations in food production and prices, and on the specific policy measures implemented to meet these needs. For this analysis to be productive, it must go beyond the get-your-price-right nostrum into the details of the structural and institutional formation of food policies, into their adjustments to changes in the economic or climatic conditions, and into their stabilizing (or destabilizing) effects on food supply, on farmers' income, on the fiscal budget, and on the balance of payments. The analysis must also go beyond conventional stabilization programs such as buffer stocks into other intervention practices and alternative policy combinations aimed at stabilizing both the flow of supply and the price. On the consumption side, these interventions may consist of combinations of flexible subsidies to the general population, targeted subsidies or income transfers, variable export levies and import subsidies, direct public distribution, and the like. On the production side, they may consist of minimum price and guaranteed income programs to farmers, crop insurance, government procurement, variable import levies and export subsidies, and so forth.

The emphasis on instability adds two elements into the analysis that are seldom accounted for in a comparative static analysis. One is the effect of the policy on the probability distribution of the performance measures, in addition to its effect on their expected outcomes. Food insecurity, for example, would be measured not only by the average per capita consumption of consumers in different income groups, but also by the probability that their food consumption in any given year would fall below a certain critical level. The second element is the risk involved in production due to weather- or policy-induced variations in output or price, and its long-term effects on resource allocation and growth in the agricultural sector.

Before turning to the policy analysis, this chapter addresses several conceptual issues raised by the instability factor. The first section examines the effects of instability on food security in the context of a growing economy. It shows that if a choice must be made between more stable but less productive crop varieties, and less stable but more productive varieties, the selection of the latter is likely to offer *more* food security, not less, as has sometimes been argued. The second section illustrates the issues raised by instability with respect to the definition, identification, and measurement of food insecurity.

Policy analysis under instability has a number of unique characteristics that do not exist in a comparative static analysis. Most important, decisions in an unstable environment are likely to—indeed should—vary from year to year according to the prevailing climatic or economic conditions. The policy *rule* thus depends on the specific conditions in that year, or, in the current jargon, is contingent on the specific state of nature. An evaluation of the policy over all states of nature—that is, over the long run—may thus become considerably more complex. The third section reviews the issues involved in a theoretical analysis of government policies under instability. Finally, the fourth section groups the various policies examined in the book into categories according to which the subsequent analysis is conducted. This classification draws a distinction between the long-term effects of government policies on *trend* production, consumption, and distribution and their short-term effects on *variations* of these parameters around the trend.

Instability and Growth of Food Production and Their Effect on Food Security

Efforts to accelerate the growth of food production by developing improved crop varieties have been said to increase the variability of food production as well because of the narrower genetic base of the new varieties, the cultivation of marginal lands, and other factors. Hazell (1984) and Mehra (1981) found some evidence for an increase in instability in food grains production in India and in the United States.

The increase in production variability that accompanies the increase in average food production is not, however, in itself evidence that food security has declined. In fact, food security still may rise. Even when variability rises at a higher rate than production, so that the coefficient of variation of production is also rising, the severity of the food problem will actually *diminish* in most cases rather than increase. The following stochastic-dynamic analysis of different scenarios of world's food grain production and consumption over the coming twenty years further illustrates this point.

The severity of the food problem is measured by two indicators. The first of these is *food insecurity,* defined as the probability that in any given year actual food consumption will fall below a minimum level necessary for survival and adequate health. The minimum level itself is assumed to be equal to 90 percent of the 1984 level of average per capita consumption.

The second indicator is the *expected food gap,* defined as the *expected* gap between actual average consumption per capita in any given year and the 1984 level of average per capita consumption, when a gap exists. This measure is simply the probability that consumption per capita in the coming twenty-year period would fall below its 1984 level, multiplied by the size of the gap.

Table 1–1 summarizes the results of this analysis. In scenarios 2 through 4, the coefficient of variation in production rises by 5 percent over the twenty-year period. This assumption may be overly pessimistic at the global level, although it may be appropriate in certain regions. Nevertheless, the table shows that even a small rise in per capita production at an annual rate of 0.5 percent is sufficient to counter the effects of the growing instability, so that the severity of the food problem is reduced markedly. The reason is that the food insecurity measures are *absolute* measures. The frequency at which food consumption falls below the predetermined subsistence level would decline with the increase in mean production, even when its variablity rises. In scenario 5 the coefficient of variation rises by 1 percent each year, or by about 22 percent over the twenty-year period. Even then, however, food security would rise. The expected food gap would be reduced by 35 percent, and the probability of an extreme shortage (in excess of 10 percent of normal consumption) developing would fall from 8 to 3.8 percent.

The growing instability may, however, have adverse effects on farmers' income and hence on food security in rural areas. The extent to which farmers' income might be adversely affected depends largely on the price elasticity of demand for the product in the market; on the trade flows; on government policies; and on measures taken by the farmers to protect themselves against fluctuations in production and income through in-farm stocks, investments in cattle, and other forms of savings. These issues are taken up in chapter 4.

Food Security under Instability: Identification and Measurement

The common measure of food insecurity in a single country or in the world at large is the number of people who suffer from undernutrition. A person is defined as undernourished if his or her food consumption falls below an established minimum level. In most cases attention is focused on energy requirements and thus on the person's calorie intake. This measure is widely used by the World Bank and the FAO among others.

Controversy exists concerning the legitimacy of this measure and its usefulness as an aggregate measure of undernutrition. Nutritionists raise doubts about the notion that the energy intake required to maintain the body weight of an individual, which was determined by the World Health Organization (WHO) and the FAO as the minimum requirement, is indeed well defined and constant. They argue that a single standard of calorie needs fails to take into account interpersonal differences attributable to differences in age, sex, body composition, level of activity patterns, climate, and the like. They also argue that an inadequate intake of calories is not the only cause of undernutrition.[5]

Table 1-1
Food Insecurity under Different Growth Scenarios of Food Grains Production

| Average Annual Growth Rate | | | | 1985–2005: Period Average | | 1985 | | 2005 | |
| | | | | Food Insecurity[b] | | Food Insecurity[b] | | Food Insecurity[b] | |
Population	Mean Output	Output Variability[a]	Expected Food Gap[c]	10%	5%	10%	5%	10%	5%
1.8	2.0	2.00	1.4	9.0	21.0	10.0	21.9	8.0	19.3
1.8	2.0	2.25	1.5	12.0	25.0	10.0	21.9	17.1	27.4
1.8	2.5	2.75	0.7	5.4	12.8	10.0	21.9	2.6	5.9
1.8	3.0	3.25	0.3	2.7	7.0	10.0	21.9	0.0	0.8
1.8	2.5	3.50	0.9	6.3	14.2	10.0	21.9	3.8	12.1

[a] Rate of growth of the coefficient of variations.
[b] Probability that food consumption falls by more than the prespecified percentage below the trend consumption.
[c] Expressed as percentage of total world production.

Economists raise other objections. First, they argue, when the number of undernourished people is determined on the basis of the *national average* per capita calorie intake, this measure ignores large differences in food consumption between members of society. Such differences result from existing inequalities in the distribution of income and wealth and thus—to use Sen's (1981) terminology—in the entitlement to food. Second, this measure does not give information about the depth of the food deficiency of the undernourished people—the *size* of the gap between their actual consumption level and the minimum required level. Third, this measure smooths away information about temporary shortages that both widen and deepen the circle of the undernourished.

Recent estimates by the FAO and the World Bank have attempted to take into account the interpersonal differences in food consumption resulting from inequalities in income distribution. According to FAO estimates, the number of persons in developing countries consuming less than a "critical minimum energy intake" was about 400 million in 1969–1971. Reutlinger and Selowsky (1976), who also account for differences in levels of food consumption within countries associated with different income levels, estimated that as many as 1.1 billion persons had calorie-deficient diets in the mid-1960s.

FAO also publishes periodic calculations of per capita food availability derived from food balance sheets and based on national averages. Expressed as a percentage of the estimated energy requirements, the average per capita availability in the developing countries is estimated to provide 93 percent of defined requirements, compared to 115 percent of defined requirements for developed market economies (FAO 1976, 1982). Reutlinger and Selowsky have also estimated the food gap, but their estimate is based on the caloric deficiencies of the undernourished people only. These two measures still average out differences in the size of the food gap among the undernourished themselves, as well as variations in the food gap over time due to the instability in the availability of food.

Figure 1–1 depicts the issues involved in identifying the group of undernourished people when food consumption is unstable, and in providing an aggregate measure of food insecurity. The figure presents the Lorenz curve, which describes the distribution of food consumption in a country. On the horizontal line the population groups are ranked by their per capita income; the vertical line measures their share in total food consumption. The area under the main diagonal $\overline{OL}$ and above the Lorenz curve is the Gini coefficient, which measures the inequality of food distribution.

The diagonal $\overline{OA}$ describes a hypothetical distribution that endows every person with precisely the minimum required consumption. The distance $\overline{AL}$ thus measures the rate by which the average per capita food consumption exceeds the minimum. Measures of undernutrition based on the *average* per capita food consumption would identify people in that country as under-

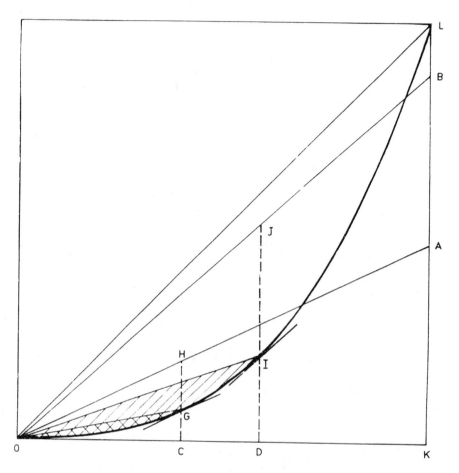

Figure 1–1. Food Distribution and Food Insecurity under Instability

nourished only if the diagonal $\overline{OA}$ intersects the vertical axis above point K. The distributional inequalities are recognized in the figure, however. The undernourished group can be identified by finding the point at which the tangent of the Lorenz curve is parallel to the diagonal $\overline{OA}$. On the vertical line, all persons ranked below that point have food consumption below the minimum. Hence the percentage of the undernourished in the population is given by the distance $\overline{OC}$. This is essentially Reutlinger and Selowsky's measure of the number of undernourished.

The food gap as a percentage of average per capita food consumption can be measured by the distance $\overline{GH}$. A third measure is required to demonstrate the size of the food gap in different subgroups among the poor. This is the Gini coefficient, which measures the inequality of food distribution among the undernourished only and is given by the shaded area under the $\overline{OG}$ diagonal and above the Lorenz curve.

All these measures are for a single year. In the following year food consumption may fall as a result of a production shortfall. In the figure, this can be illustrated by a rise of the minimum-requirement diagonal from $\overline{OA}$ to $\overline{OB}$. In other words, the rate by which the average per capita food consumption exceeds the minimum would fall as a result of the production shortfall from $\overline{AL}$ to $\overline{BL}$. Assume for the moment that neither the food distribution nor the rank of people by income would change from the first year to the next. Under these assumptions, the percentage of undernourished people has increased to $\overline{OD}$, and the food gap has risen to $\overline{TI}$.

Over time, therefore, both the number of undernourished and the size of the food gap varies with variations in food production, in food prices, or in income. The aggregate measure of food insecurity must take these variations into account. Chapter 5 reviews several measures of food insecurity under instability and examines their properties in comparison to a set of desired properties that these measures are expected to have.

Policy Analysis under Instability

In recent years government stabilization policies at both the macro, economy-wide level and the microsectorial level have attracted a large body of research. Sectorial studies of these policies within a partial-equilibrium framework have originated with the pioneering works of Waugh (1944); Oi (1961); and Massell (1969, 1970), who put forward the basic theoretical framework for analyzing price stabilization through buffer stocks. The simplicity and neatness of the Waugh-Oi-Massell model, which allows a rather thoroughgoing analysis and offers a clear performance measure for evaluating the desirability of these policies, have prompted a large number of studies, both theoretical and empirical. Hueth and Schmitz (1972) have extended the model to an open economy. Turnovsky (1973, 1976, 1978) extended the basic analytical framework to include more complex functional specifications such as adaptive expectations and multiplicative disturbances (see also Biery and Schmitz 1973; Bigman and Reutlinger 1979; Bigman 1982; Sabotnik and Houck 1976; Konandreas and Schmitz 1978; for other extensions and applications of the model). Nevertheless, the model suffers from a number of severe flaws that constrain its use so greatly that its results may sometimes be entirely misleading. These flaws have been discussed extensively in the literature and need no further elaboration here (see, for instance, Samuelson 1972; Hathaway 1976; Bigman and Reutlinger 1979; Cochrane 1980; Newbery and Stiglitz 1981; Bigman 1982).

More recently, attention has shifted from buffer stocks to trade and trade policies. Some of the studies that carried the analysis within a partial-equilibrium framework still adhered to the basic Waugh-Oi-Massell model, which proved helpful in a theoretical-illustrative analysis of these complex issues (see, for example, Desgupta and Stiglitz 1977; Young 1979; 1982). Others have concentrated on trade and trade policies under uncertainty, where the main concerns are the long-run *expected* results (see, for example, Mayer 1976; Batra 1975; Helpman and Razin 1978; Baron and Forsythe 1979). Newbery and Stiglitz (1981) offered an entirely different analytical approach to evaluting the welfare effects of stabilization—one that does not suffer from the weaknesses of the Waugh-Oi-Massell model. Their study focuses on two characteristics of a stochastic environment: the risk and uncertainty existing in this environment and their effects on production and consumption decisions of risk-averse economic agents;[6] and the structure of policies implemented in response to an unstable environment. In recent years numerous studies have focused on government policies operating under unstable internal or external conditions and have an explicit stabilization objective (see, for example, Sarris 1982; Driscoll and Ford 1983; Sarris and Freebairn 1983; Quiggin and Anderson 1979; Newbery and Stiglitz 1981; Bigman 1982).

The purpose of this section is to highlight the difficulties involved in an analysis of this type of policies and to examine possible ways to overcome them. Policies operating in an unstable environment and having explicit objectives are typically *state-contingent* and of the *feedback* type. They are state-contingent in the sense that the very decision whether or not to activate the policy in any given year depends on specific conditions existing in that year—on the state of nature. Thus, for instance, the decision whether to put into effect a minimum price support program for farmers depends on certain variables—a bumper crop harvest, a glut of cheap imports, a drop in foreign demand for the country's exports—that may make the implementation of this program necessary, given the government's stated objectives. Even decisions about the level or intensity at which to implement a policy depend on the state of nature. A government engaged in a subsidy program to consumers may raise the subsidy rate in years of high prices in order to moderate or even prevent a rise in the price to consumers.

Considerable analytical difficulty is involved in conducting a theoretical analysis of policies of this type that does not exist in an ordinary comparative static analysis. The reason is that these policies are both *nonlinear* and *discontinuous*. They are nonlinear because the policy control variables—the minimum price, the subsidy rate, and so on—assume different values at different states of nature, reflecting the government response to existing conditions by intensifying or moderating its intervention. They are discontinuous because they are activated only in certain states of nature—that is, when existing conditions make an intervention necessary—but remain inactive in other states of nature.

A large number of studies examined a rule of feedback policies whereby the control variable is proportional to the random term and thus varies from year to year according to the realization of the random event. One familiar example of this type of policy is known as leaning against the wind. Variable import levies or subsidies proportional to the deviation of the actual world price from its long-run level represent policies of this type. They moderate the rise in the domestic price in times of high world prices and the fall in the domestic price in times of low world prices. These policies would therefore be implemented in all states of nature, though possibly at different rates. This policy rule is, therefore, *continuous* with respect to the random term, in the sense that it is proportional to, or a continuous function of the random term and is active over its entire frequency distribution.

One assumption often made in these studies, mostly for analytical convenience, is that the policies are symmetrical—that is, that they are implemented at equal rates (though with opposite signs) along the two sides of the probability distribution. With variable import levies, for example, an import tariff in a year of low world price turns into a subsidy in a year of high world price. The following simple tariff rule can illustrate the modeling and the form of the analysis of this policy. Let the world price be given by

$$P_w = \bar{P}_w + u$$

where $\bar{P}_w$ is the mean world price and u a random term $E(u) = 0$, $E(u^2) = \sigma^2$. Let the domestic price be

$$P = P_w + t$$

where t is the tariff. A policy that leans against the tides in the world market with the objective of insulating the domestic market from disturbances in the world price can be formalized as

$$t = -\Theta u \quad : \quad 0 \leq \Theta \leq 1$$

The domestic price is then given by

$$P = \bar{P}_w + (1 - \Theta)u$$

and its variability by

$$\text{Var}(P) = (1 - \Theta)^2 \cdot \sigma^2$$

Hence the variability of the country price is smaller than that of the world. A departure from the assumptions that the policy rules are continuous and symmetric makes the analysis exceedingly difficult. Suppose, for instance, that in the foregoing illustration the government intervenes only when the import price rises above its mean. The policy rule will then have the form

$$t = \begin{cases} -\Theta u & : \quad u > 0, \quad 0 \leq \Theta \leq 1 \\ \\ 0 & : \quad u \leq 0 \end{cases}$$

t would now represent an import subsidy. This policy rule is neither continuous nor symmetric since it is activated only along part of the frequency distribution of u—that is, only in certain states of nature. The country's price is then given by

$$P = \begin{cases} \bar{P}_w + (1 - \Theta)u & : \quad u > 0 \\ \\ P_w & : \quad u \leq 0 \end{cases}$$

The mean price in the country is then given by

$$P = \int_{-\infty}^{0} (\bar{P}_w + u)du + \int_{0}^{\infty} [\bar{P}_w + (1 - \Theta)u]du$$

The variability of the price cannot be calculated without making simplifying assumptions about the structure of the frequency distribution of u.

Most of the policies considered in this book are neither continuous nor symmetric. A minimum-price program, for example, is activated only when the market price falls below the minimum price. Variable import levies, imposed to prevent cheap imports from being dumped on the domestic market, may be removed altogether when the import price rises above a certain level. Moreover, temporary fiscal or foreign-exchange constraints may introduce further discontinuities and asymmetries into the conduct of these policies.

Models of discontinuous and asymmetric policies are closely related to models of market in disequilibrium with bounded price variation. In his pioneering work in this area, Maddala (1983, p. 361) notes:

> There are many practical cases where some observations refer to equilibrium points. This is because trading in many markets is confined to some limits on price and the disequilibrium occurs only when these limits are violated. There are minimum wage laws in labor markets, usury laws in credit markets, and trading limits in commodity markets.

In all such cases, Maddala emphasizes, the markets are sometimes in equilibrium and sometimes in disequilibrium. Consider, as an illustration, a price-support program in which the government removes the excess from the market (to exports or storage) whenever the free-market price falls below a prespecified floor price, denoted by P_s. Assume that the instability derives from random variations in supply. When the market price P_t is larger than P_s, the market is in equilibrium and the price is determined endogenously through the equation $P_t = P_t(D_t, S_t)$, which specifies the market-clearing condition where D_t and S_t are the market demand and supply, respectively. When the free-market price falls below P_s, the price is fixed exogenously by the policy at P_s, and this in turn determines the quantities supplied, demanded, and procured by the government to extract the surplus. The expected price is therefore given by

$$E(P) = \int_{\Psi_1} P_t(D_t \cdot S_t) \cdot f(S_t) \cdot dS_t + \int_{\Psi_2} P_s \cdot f(S_t)dS_t$$

where $f(S_t)$ is the density function of supply, Ψ_1 is the set of values of supply for which the market is in equilibrium, and Ψ_2 is the set for which government intervention is required to support the price. The expected quantity procured by the government is given by

$$E(Q) = \int_{\Psi_2} Q_t(P_s, S_t) \cdot f(S_t)dS_t$$

A theoretical analysis of policies of this type is obviously quite complex and requires many simplifying assumptions. Alternatively, the analysis can be carried out by means of Monte Carlo simulation experiments with either a specific-country model or a prototype model. The advantage of the simulation analysis is that the model can assume any desired degree of complexity. The disadvantage is that the results depend on the choice of parameters. In a specific-country model, this deficiency is not very serious if the parameters can be estimated with a reasonable degree of accuracy. In a prototype model the simulation results can still serve two purposes: first, to illustrate the type of analysis that is possible and the issues that can be addressed by the simulation model in order to expose the methodology to potential users, and, second, to present results that are of analytical interest even when they are model-specific. Chapter 3, for example, shows that at a certain range of price elasticities of demand, free trade *can be* Pareto-inferior to no trade—a result that is in contradiction to established paradigms in international trade theory. In this book the theoretical analysis of each of the subjects examined is illustrated and extended with simulation results of a prototype model. The methodology is described in chapter 2, and its applications in country analysis are illustrated in chapters 6 and 7.

Food Policies under Instability

Food-policy analysis is concerned with practically all aspects of food production and distribution, ranging from agricultural production and marketing to the distribution and consumption of food products. It is also concerned with the mechanisms and institutions that have been or can be formed to address these issues. The analysis therefore deals with a wide range of policies and intervention practices that exist in one form or another in all countries.[7]

The diverse goals of these policies are often incompatible and sometimes even conflicting. On the production side, the main goals are to accelerate agricultural growth, achieve self-sufficiency in food consumption, secure the solvency of the farm sector, and protect the income of farmers and rural landless workers. On the consumption side, the goals are to improve the nutrition standards of the undernourished population, secure a stable flow of supply of staple foods to all consumers in all regions and at all income levels, and provide cheap food to consumers in urban areas.

Different countries may have different combinations of these goals and may rank them differently. Most developing countries, for instance, tend to emphasize consumers' needs by maintaining low food prices, with the goal of accelerating the intersectoral transfer of resources for industrialization. These policies, however, are detrimental to long-term agricultural growth, and conflict with stated goals for food production. Many countries also have political objectives—avoiding political disturbances and riots, or maintaining political support from powerful urban groups. The task for the policymaker is to reconcile these goals, to balance them where they conflict by weighing the trade-offs, and to choose a package of feasible and acceptable instruments that are mutually consistent.

In this book, the various food policies have been grouped into five categories. The analysis has been conducted first for each category separately and then for different policy combinations. The two main categories are price and income policies related to food consumption and distribution, and price and procurement policies related to food production and marketing.

Examples of the former are subsidy programs either to the general population or to target groups, income transfers, payments in kind, and the like. Examples of the latter are minimum product prices, guaranteed income to producers, crop insurance, government procurement, subsidies to output or factor inputs, and so forth. In practice, each policy affects both consumers and producers. A minimum-price program, for example, would encourage producers to increase production; and the additional supply would be beneficial to consumers. Nevertheless, most policies can still be identified as belonging to one category or the other according to the direct target and primary goal. One exception is a buffer-stocks scheme that assists both consumers—by stabilizing the flow of supply and the market price—and producers—by stabilizing their price.

A third category includes trade and exchange-rate policies, which directly affect—though often in opposite directions—both consumers and producers. An overvalued exchange rate, for example, lowers the market price of imported foods, thus effectively subsidizing consumers and taxing producers.

A forth category is that of so-called nonmarket policies. These are policies in which direct government activities effectively abrogate the free market and replace the price system as the main signal for economic activity by imposing a system of rationed quantities on consumers and producers. Forced procurement, which exists in different forms in many developing countries, is an example of such a nonmarket policy. Under this scheme, producers must sell some (or all) of their output to the government at a price lower than the market price. The food products thus procured are distributed by the government, through some form of rationing, at a subsidized price. Another example is the sale at a subsidized price or even the free distribution of agricultural inputs such as fertilizers and irrigation water to producers on an allocative basis.

A fifth category is that of nonprice policies, which include direct government activities in research and development, extension services, direct public investments, and the like. These are areas in which considerable externalities exist that would otherwise give rise to market failures.

In the analysis of each policy, a distinction can be made between its long-run effect on *trend* production, consumption, and distribution, and its short-term effects on *variations* about the trend. In practice, such a distinction may appear arbitrary since most policies have both long-term (trend) and short-term (stability) effects. A food-subsidy program, for example, is often designed both to raise and to stabilize the food consumption of the target population. When the market price rises, the subsidy rate is also raised in order to moderate the rise in the subsidized price to the target population. Even a so-called pure stabilization program such as a buffer-stock program may have a positive effect on the long-term trend of output by encouraging risk-averse producers to increase their production and investments.

The foregoing classification, though sometimes arbitrary, is nonetheless instrumental for analytical purposes and I have followed it in this book in the analysis of different groups of policies. Focusing on the short run, the book examines both year-to-year modifications of existing government policies in response to variations in economic and climatic conditions and to wide price gyrations in world commodity markets, and special policies aimed at countering or moderating their adverse effects. For each policy and program considered, its direct effects on the target population have been examined, along with its indirect effects on the other population groups or economic sectors; on the country's welfare, food security, and food self-sufficiency; on international trade and the balance of payments; on the fiscal budget; and on the long-term growth prospects of the agricultural sector. The main emphasis of the analysis is on the trade-offs inevitably involved in each policy and program, and on ways to determine their cost-effectiveness.

Chapter 3 examines government trade policies in agricultural products in general and food products in particular. The analysis concentrates on instability in food production; the resulting variations in the domestic and the world price; and the consequences for the country's trade, welfare, income distribution, and balance of payments. Much of the analysis is devoted to the policy of variable levies designed to buffer variations in the world price and to insulate the country from external instability. Variable levies or subsidies are also implemented to moderate internal price fluctuations by allowing compensating flows of imports or exports. The empirical study that concludes this chapter shows that in the late 1970s and early 1980s most countries, both importing and exporting, intervened much more aggressively than in the preceding decade in their wheat market by varying their import tariffs or subsidies considerably in order to counter variations in the world price. Variable levies thus have become perhaps the most important policy measure affecting world trade in wheat and most likely also in other grains and other agricultural products.

Chapter 4 analyzes policies targeted on the production side of the food equation. It evaluates alternative producers' support and stabilization schemes, including price supports, government procurement, buffer stocks, and guaranteed income. These policies affect farmers' production decisions and, through their income effect, also influence decisions about consumption, marketing, and in-farm stocks. Thus it is possible for agricultural output to rise as an effect of the policies but for the marketed surplus actually to fall, since more food is retained at the farm household. The chapter develops a behavioral model of farmers' production, consumption, marketing, and in-farm stocks decisions in order to determine the effect of price policies and various stabilization programs on income and food consumption in both rural and urban areas.

Chapter 5 analyzes policies targeted on the consumption side of the food equation. It evaluates alternative consumption and distribution policies, including a subsidy targeted on poor consumers, income transfer and transfers in kind, and buffer stocks. To assess the performance of these policies, the chapter continues the discussion of aggregate measures of food insecurity under instability and extends Sen's axiomatic approach (1976, 1981) to the derivation of food insecurity measures under instability.

In chapter 7, nonmarket policies are compared with the corresponding market policies with respect to their short- and long-term effects on food security, food production, the fiscal budget, and the balance of payments.

In practice, governments do not implement any one policy but, rather, different combinations of all these policies. This book examines the performance of different policy combinations in the cases of actual countries. Chapter 6 evaluates price-stabilization policies for grains in Turkey, and chapter 7 evaluates wheat procurement imports and distribution policies in Pakistan.

The analysis of government food policies in the short run requires an analytical framework that takes into account producers' risk aversion in order to examine their response to these policies as they affect both the average level of the price and its variability. It also requires a framework that can exhibit government decisions under different contingencies in response to varying climatic and economic conditions. The analytical tool that has been used in this study for the analysis of these policies is a simulation model of a subsector (food grains) of the agricultural sector. Chapter 2 provides the details of the model and describes the solution method in a dynamic-stochastic analysis. Each subsequent chapter provides further details on the specific policy rules examined in that chapter and on the parameter values in the simulation experiments.

Notes

1. The answer depends on the *bias* of the technical change and the elasticities of substitution between factor inputs.

2. In the developed countries, staple food production grew at an annual rate of 2.6 percent (3.0 percent) in the United States, compared with a population growth rate of 1.0 percent (see Mellor and Johnston 1984; see also FAO 1979; World Bank 1982).

3. See Bale and Duncan (1983); World Bank (1982); and FAO (1979).

4. Reutlinger and Selowsky (1976) estimate the number of people having calorie-deficient diets at 1.1 billion in the mid-1960s. See also Reutlinger and Alderman (1980); Reutlinger (1980).

5. See also Srinivasan (1977).

6. Although uncertainty is usually associated with instability, the two are not synonymous. Uncertainty is related to the ex ante behavioral response to contingent events (which may or may not be stochastic); instability is an ex post resort of the stochastic events.

7. See Timmer, Falcon, and Pearson (1983); Tolley, Thomas, and Wong (1982); Clay et al (1981); and Bale and Lutz (1981) for recent reviews of these issues.

References

Bale, M.D., and Duncan, R.C. 1983. Prospects for food production and consumption in developing countries. World Bank Staff Working Paper No. 596. Washington, D.C.

Bale, M.D., and Lutz, E. 1981. Price distortions in agriculture and their effects: An international comparison. *American Journal of Agricultural Economics* 63:8–22.

Baron, D.P., and Forsythe, R. 1979. Models of firm and international trade under uncertainty. *American Economic Review* 69:565–574.

Batra, R.N. 1975. Production uncertainty and the Heckscher-Ohlin theorem. *Review of Economic Studies* 42:259–268.

Biery, J., and Schmitz, S. 1973. Export instability, monopoly and welfare. *Journal of International Economics* 3:389–396.

Bigman, D. 1982.*Coping with hunger: Toward a theory of food security and price stabilization.* Cambridge, Mass.: Ballinger.

Bigman, D., and Reutlinger, S. 1979. Food price and supply stabilization: National buffer stocks and trade policies. *American Journal of Agricultural Economics* 61:657–667.

Clay, E.; Chambers, R.; Singer, H.; and Lipton, M. 1981. Food policy issues in low-income countries. World Bank Staff Working Paper No. 473. Washington, D.C.

Cochrane, W.W. 1980. Some nonconformist thoughts on welfare economics and commodity price stabilization. *American Journal of Agricultural Economics 62:* 508–511.

Council on Environmental Quality (CEQ). 1980. *The global 2000 report to the president.* Washington, D.C.

Desgupta, P., and Stiglitz, J.E. 1977. Tarrifs vs. quotas as revenue—Raising devices under uncertainty. *American Economic Review 67:975–981.*

Driscoll, M.J., and Ford, J.L. 1983. Protection and optimal trade restricting policies under uncertainty. *Manchester School of Economics and Social Studies 51:* 21–32.

Eaton, D.J., and Steel, W.J., eds. 1976. *Analysis of grain reserves.* U.S. Department of Agriculture, Economic Research Service 634.

Food and Agricultural Organization (FAO). 1976. *The state of food and agriculture 1975.* Rome: FAO.

———. 1977. *The fourth World Food Survey.* Rome: FAO.

———. 1979. *Agriculture: Toward 2000.* Rome: FAO.

———. 1982. *The state of food and agriculture 1981.* Rome: FAO.

FAO/World Health Organization (WHO). 1973. *Energy and protein requirements.* FAO Nutrition Meetings Reports No. 52. Rome: FAO.

Hathaway, D.E. 1976. Grain stocks and economic stability: A policy perspective. In D.J. Eaton and W.J. Steel, eds., *Analysis of Grain Reserves.*

Hazell, P.B.R. 1984. Sources of increased instability in Indian and U.S. production *American Journal of Agricultural Economics,* in print.

Helpman, E., and Razin, A. 1978. *A theory of international trade under uncertainty.* New York: Academic Press.

Hueth, D., and Schmitz, A. 1972. International trade in intermediate and final goods: Some welfare implications of destabilized prices. *Quarterly Journal of Economics* 86:351–365.

Johnston, B.F., and Clark, W.C. 1982. *Redesigning rural development: A strategic perspective.* Baltimore, Md.: Johns Hopkins University Press.

Knudsen, O., and Scandizzo, P.L. 1979. Nutrition and food needs in developing countries. World Bank Staff Working Paper No. 328. Washington, D.C.

Korandreas, P.A., and Schmitz, A. 1978. Implications of grain price stabilization: Some empirical evidence for the United States. *American Journal of Agricultural Economics 60:74–84.*

Lipton, M. 1977. *Why poor people stay poor: A study of urban bias in world development,* Cambridge, Mass.: Harvard University Press.

Maddala, G.S. 1983. Methods of estimation for models of markets with bounded price variation. *International Economic Review 24:361–378.*

Martin, M.V., and Brokken, R.F. 1983. Grain price historic perspective shows real weakness. *Freedstuffs 55:17–22.*

Massell, B.F. 1969. Price stabilization and welfare. *Quarterly Journal of Economics* 83:284–298.

———. 1970. Some welfare implications of international price stabilization. *Journal of Political Economy* 78:404–417.

Mayer, W. 1976. The Rybezynski, Stopler-Samuelson and factor-price equalization theorems under price uncertainty. *American Economic Review* 66:797–808.

Mehra, S. 1981. Instability in Indian agriculture in the context of the new technology. Washington, D.C.: International Food Policy Research Institute.

Mellor, J.W. 1978. Food price policy and income distribution in low-income countries. *Economic Development and Cultural Change* 27:1–26.

Mellor, J.W., and Desai, G.M., eds. *Agricultural change and rural poverty: Variations on a theme by Dharm Narion.* Forthcoming.

Mellor, J.W., and Johnston, B.F. 1984. The world food equation: Interrelations among development, employment, and food consumption. *Journal of Economic Literature* 22:531–574.

Newbery, D.M.G., and Stiglitz, J.E. 1981. *The theory of commodity price stabilization.* Oxford: Clarendon Press.

Oi, W.Y. 1961. The desirability of price instability under perfect competition. *Econometrica* 29:58–64.

Quiggin, J.C., and Anderson, J. 1979. Stabilization and risk reduction. *Australian Journal of Agricultural Economics* 23(3):191–206.

Reutlinger, S. 1980. Changes in the energy content of national diets and in the energy deficient diets of the poor: 1970–1980. Unpublished manuscript.

Reutlinger, S., and Alderman, H. 1980. The prevalence of calorie-deficient diets in developing countries. *World Development* 8:399–411.

Reutlinger, S., and Selowsky, M. 1976. *Malnutrition and poverty: Magnitude and policy options.* World Bank Occasional Paper No. 23. Baltimore, Md.: Johns Hopkins University Press.

Sabotnik, A., and Houck, J.P. 1976. Welfare implications of stabilizing consumption and production. *American Journal of Agricultural Economics* 58:13–20.

Samuelson, P.A. 1972. The consumer does benefit from feasible price stability. *Quarterly Journal of Economics* 86:476–493.

Sarris, A.M. 1982. Export taxes versus buffer stocks as optimal export policies under uncertainty. *Journal of Development Economics* 11:195–213.

Sarris, A.H., and Freebairn, J. 1983. Endogenous price policies and international wheat prices. *American Journal of Agricultural Economics* 65:214–224.

Schultz, T.W., ed. 1978. *Distortions of agricultural incentives.* Bloomington: Indiana University Press.

Sen, A.K. 1976. Poverty: An ordinal approach to measurement. *Econometrica* 44:219–231.

———. 1981. *Poverty and famines: An essay on entitlement and deprivation.* Oxford: Clarendon Press.

Srinivasan, T.N. 1977. Development, poverty, and basic human needs: Some issues. *Food Research Institute Studies* 16:11–28.

———. 1981. Malnutrition: Some measurement and policy issues. *Journal of Development Economics* 8:3–19.

Thomas, V., and Bhattagli, D. 1982. Price intervention analysis in agriculture. *The World Bank Research News* 3:3–15.

Timmer, C.P.; Falcon, W.P.; and Pearson, S.R. 1983. *Food policy analysis.* Baltimore, Md.: Johns Hopkins University Press.

Tolley, G.S.; Thomas, V.; and Wong, C. Mong. 1982. *Agricultural price policies and the developing countries.* Baltimore, Md.: Johns Hopkins University Press.

Turnovsky, S.J. 1973. Optimal stabilization policies in a market with lagged adjustment in supply. *Economic Record* 49:31–49.

———. 1976. The distribution of welfare gains from price stabilization: The case of multiplicative disturbance. *International Economic Review* 17:133–148.

———. 1978. Stabilization rules and the benefits from price stabilization. *Journal of Public Economics* 9:37–57.

Waugh, F.V. 1944. Does the consumer benefit from price instability? *Quarterly Journal of Economics* 58:602–614.

Young, L. 1979. Ranking optimal tariffs and quotas for a large country under uncertainty. *Journal of International Economics* 9:249–264.

———. 1982. Quantity controls vs. expenditure control in international trade under uncertainty. *Journal of International Economics* 12:143–163.

World Bank. 1982. *World development report 1982.* Oxford: Oxford University Press.

2
The Model for Policy Analysis and the Solution Method

Policy modeling and analysis in an unstable environment creates a number of methodological problems that were noted in the previous chapter. The dynamic model that describes this system is usually nonlinear and discontinuous, and its theoretical analysis requires a large number of simplifying assumptions that may severely constrain the generalizability of the conclusions.

Dynamic programming, for example, which was extensively employed for the determination of optimal stockpiling policy, requires a fairly simple mathematical model. Thus, for instance, the objective must be separable, the supply and demand functions must be well-behaved (for most algorithms they must be continuously differentiable), and so on. Most important, the ordinary algorithms cannot deal with nonlinearities resulting from state-contingent policy interventions. Consequently, these models have difficulty accommodating policies such as price support, consumers' subsidies, and various trade policies, all of which depend on the realized weather and economic conditions. Typically, the decision about each of these policies in any given year is jointly determined together with the stockpiling decision. Thus, for example, the decision whether and how much to import food grains depends on, among other things, the quantity in storage. Similarly, the stockpiling decision depends in part on the import and export opportunities. To take another example, in many countries minimum price and stockpiling are only segments of the government's overall price and procurement policy. Dynamic programming cannot accommodate this type of joint decision making.

In addition, the dynamic-programming approach cannot accommodate changes in the parameters of the model that result from the very policy measures implemented. This weakness is related to what has become known as Lucas's critique (Lucas 1976). Of particular significance in this context is the response of risk-averse producers to the increase in price stability and the reduction in risk resulting from the storage operations. Failure to take this response into account may lead to a consistent and potentially significant bias in the formulation of the storage rule. Consequently, the stockpiling policy emerging from this analysis may not be optimal.

To overcome these difficulties and permit a more thoroughgoing analysis, policy appraisal under instability is conducted here by means of simulation methods. Indeed, stochastic simulation models have been widely used for risk analysis or project appraisal under uncertainty, their key virtue being their flexibility and the ease of incorporating virtually any stochastic considerations or other relationship that may be desired.

This chapter provides the details of the simulation model and the solution method described. The decision rules themselves and the parameter values are described in subsequent chapters as needed. The chapter presents also an algorithm for integrating the simulation analysis with numerical optimization in order to determine the optimal value of certain policy variables, such as storage capacity or tariff rates. The final section reviews the development of the simulation model, its past applications at the World Bank and in academic and research institutes, and future extensions of the model. Before turning to the description of the simulation model, the first section reviews the methodological problems involved in modeling supply in a stochastic-dynamic environment and their solution in this study.

Supply Analysis under Instability: Stochastic Yields, Expectations, and Risk Response

Agricultural producers operate in an environment where both their yields and their output prices are uncertain. Farmers typically make most of their production decisions at the beginning of the season, knowing neither the market price for their products at harvest time nor the weather conditions during the season that will determine their yields. Past analyses of aggregate supply schedules for agricultural products have generally applied the Nerlov (1956, 1958) model of supply response via distributed lags. The adaptive expectations specification in this model manifests the fact that production decisions are made on the basis of anticipated prices.

This specification has several flaws. First, since both prices and yields are stochastic, their distributions are statistically dependent as a result of market-clearing conditions. Output decisions will therefore depend on their *joint* distribution. Hence, even under risk neutrality, supply should be a function of the expected price *and* the covariance of price and yield. Second, the adaptive expectation is ad hoc, arbitrary, and possibly inconsistent with rational behavior of economic agents. Third, this formulation does not manifest the risk involved in production and farmers' aversion to it.[1] These issues are discussed in this section.

Supply Analysis with Stochastic Prices and Yields

Hazell and Scandizzo (1975, 1977) have shown that when yield variations are multiplicative and supply decisions are based on anticipated prices only (ignoring the joint distribution of prices and yields), then competitive markets would be socially inefficient. If, however, decisions are based on anticipated unit *revenues* (thereby accounting for the joint distribution), the social inefficiencies and all distortions would vanish.

To examine their argument, consider a market for an agricultural product in which the quantity demanded is related to its price in a deterministic way as

$$D_t = f(P_t) \tag{2.1}$$

Producers are confronted by stochastic variations in yields, and thus a risky production function of the form

$$Q_t = h(Q_t^{\text{exp}}, \epsilon_t) \tag{2.2}$$

where Q_t^{exp} is planned or anticipated output and ϵ_t is the stochastic yield, assuming the disturbances to be multiplicative. Planned output is a function of the anticipated (or the certainty equivalent) price P^{exp}, and the aggregate supply function has the form

$$S_t = \epsilon_t A_t$$

$$= \epsilon_t g(P_t^{\text{exp}}) \tag{2.3}$$

where A_t is the area allocated for cultivation. After normalization, we can assume that $E(\epsilon_t) = 1$ and $\text{Var}(\epsilon_t) = \sigma^2$. It is further assumed that $\text{Cov}(\epsilon_t, \epsilon_{t-1}) = 0$ and $\text{Cov}(P_t^{\text{exp}}, \epsilon_t) = 0$, implying that producers, in forming their expectations about the price, have no knowledge about the eventual realization of the yield.

Hazell and Scandizzo determine the marginal revenue by differentiating the total revenue $P_t S_t$ with respect to planned total output (or the quantity supplied) S_t^{exp}, as

$$\frac{\partial(P_t S_t)}{\partial S_t^{\text{exp}}} = P_t \cdot \frac{\partial S_t}{\partial S_t^{\text{exp}}}$$

Profit maximization requires the expected marginal revenues to be equated to the marginal costs. The expected marginal revenues are thus given by

$$E\left[\frac{\partial(P_t S_t)}{\partial S_t^{\exp}}\right] = E(P_t) \cdot E\left(\frac{\partial S_t}{\partial S_t^{\exp}}\right) + \text{Cov}\ \left(P_t, \frac{\partial S_t}{\partial S_T^{\exp}}\right) \tag{2.4}$$

But the foregoing assumptions imply that $\partial S_t / \partial S_t^{\exp} = \epsilon_t$, so that $E[\partial S_t / \partial S_t^{\exp}] = 1$. Hence

$$E\left[\frac{\partial(P_t \cdot S_t)}{\partial S_t^{\exp}}\right] = E(P_t) + \text{Cov}(P_t, \epsilon_t)$$

$$= E(P_t \cdot \epsilon_t)$$

$$= E(r_t) = r_t^{\exp} \tag{2.5}$$

where $r_t = P_t \cdot \epsilon_t$ is the unit revenue, standardized by mean yield.

To illustrate the implications of this result, consider a simple market structure with linear demand and supply functions, given by

$$D_t = a - bP_t$$

$$S_t = cr_t^{\exp}\epsilon_t \tag{2.6}$$

Market clearing conditions yield the following equilibrium price:

$$P_t = \frac{a}{b} - \frac{c}{b}r_t^{\exp} \cdot \epsilon_t \tag{2.7}$$

By multiplying the two sides of equation 2.7 by ϵ_t and taking the expectations, we get

$$E(P_t\epsilon_t) = \frac{a}{b} - \frac{c}{b}r_t^{\exp}\mu_2 \tag{2.8}$$

where $\mu_2 = E(\epsilon_t^2) = (\sigma^2 + 1)$ is the second moment of ϵ_t and $r_t^{\exp}$ is the antic-ipated revenues per unit, as forecasted by producers. $E(P_t \cdot \epsilon_t) = E(r_t)$ is the expected realization of this forecast in the market. If expectations are rational in the sense of Muth (1961), then $E(P_t \cdot \epsilon_t) = r_t^{\exp}$. Solving equation 2.8 under the rational-expectations assumption yields

$$E(P_t\epsilon_t) = r_t^{\exp} = \frac{a}{b + c\mu_2} \tag{2.9}$$

Inserting the latter result to the price equation and taking the expectations yield

$$E(P_t) = \frac{ab + ac \cdot \sigma^2}{b[b + c(\pi^2 + 1)]} \qquad (2.10)$$

It is easy to verify that $\partial[E(P_t)]/\partial\sigma^2 > 0$, implying that the higher the yield variability, the higher the expected price and the smaller therefore the area allocated for cultivation even when producers are risk-neutral.

If supply was a function of the expected *price*—that is:

$$S_t = c \cdot P_t^{\exp}\epsilon_t$$

then the expected price would have been

$$E(P_t) = \frac{a}{b + c}$$

and this price is lower than the one based on supply with revenue expectations.

The presence of stochastic variations in yields also requires a calculation of the producers' surplus that is out of the ordinary in that it distinguishes between planned resource allocation and realized revenues and thus takes into account windfall profits or losses. The *anticipated* producers' surplus is given by

$$G_P^E = P_t^{\exp} \cdot S_t^{\exp} - \int_0^{P_t^{\exp}} g(P)dp$$

and the *realized* surplus is given by

$$G_P^R = P_tS_t \cdot \int_0^{P_t^{\exp}} g(P)\,dP$$

$$= (P_t \cdot S_t - P_t^{\exp} \cdot S_t^{\exp}) + \left[P_t^{\exp}S_t^{\exp} - \int_0^{P_t^{\exp}} g(P)dP \right]$$

This surplus would generally differ, sometimes by wide margins, from the ordinary ex post surplus given by

$$G_P^P = P_tS_t - \int_0^{P_t} g(P)dP$$

This latter measure would not, however, be appropriate for an analysis of stochastic supply (see Scandizzo, Hazell, and Anderson 1981).

Expectations in a Simulation Analysis

Planned supply in a country is a function of expected price and technology. (In the multicommodity specification it is also a function of other product prices and of input prices.) The expected price itself is not known when the production decisions are made. Predictions can therefore be made on the basis of a system of explanatory variables, the most important of which are likely to be past prices. The common hypothesis about the formation of price expectations in aggregate supply analysis is the Nerlovian (1958) adaptive expectations specification

$$E_t(P_{t+1}) - E_{t-1}(P_t) = \beta[P_t - E_{t-1}(P_t)]$$

where P_t is the actual price and $E_t(P_{t+1})$ the expected price at time $t + 1$, predicted at time t. $E_t(P_{t+1})$ represents the conditional expectations of P_{t+1}, given the knowledge of all past prices up to time t. The parameter β represents the speed of adjustment. This specification implies that the expected price can be expressed as a geometrically weighted average of past prices.

$$E_t(P_{t+1}) = \beta \cdot \sum_{j=0}^{\infty} (1-\beta)^j P_{t-j}$$

A special case of the adaptive expectations is the naive so-called cobweb model in which the expected price in the current year is simply last year's price. This would mean that expectations are adjusting rapidly, with an adjustment parameter β equal to one.

From a theoretical point of view, a more appealing hypothesis is that of rational expectations, which removes the ad hoc nature of the extrapolation rule in the adaptive-expectations formulation and offers a rule that is in line with the premise of individual rationality that underlies neoclassical economic theory. Indeed, for utility- and profit-maximizing individuals, operating in a world of perfect and costless information and pure competition, the only utility- and profit-maximizing forecasts are the rational ones. The rational-expectations hypothesis, as defined by Muth (1961), avoids the potential contradiction to this premise existing in other expectations formulations that may imply that traders are consistently wrong in their predictions.

Expectations are rational in the sense of Muth if producers' subjective probability distribution of future prices is identical to the objective probability distribution of prices conditional on the true model of the economy. Hence rational expectations yield predictions of future prices that differ from the corresponding eventual outcomes only by purely random errors—that is, errors that are serially uncorrelated and independent of the variables used to generate the predictions.

In a simulation analysis, the rational-expectations hypothesis presents a difficult problem. The reason is that a rational prediction rule is model-specific and must change with changes in the economic environment. In particular, the prediction rule must change with changes in the policy rules. If, for example, the government is engaged in a buffer-stocks program, producers would take the effect of this policy into account in forming their predictions about future prices, and the prediction rule must reflect this response of producers. The problem is especially difficult when the model is nonlinear, because for nonlinear models the reduced form expressing the expectation variables as a function of the structural parameters cannot be calculated explicitly. This section examines possible solutions for determining the rational prediction rules.

A thorough method of finding numerically the rational-expectation solution in *nonlinear* dynamic models is the one presented by Fair and Taylor (1983). Their solution method applies an iterative procedure designed to ensure numerical convergence to the rational-expectations solution. Their method can be applied as part of the simulation analysis, as follows:

The simulation analysis of a stochastic-dynamic system proceeds from one period to the next until a prespecified end period (see the details of the solution method in the following section). Each period, before introducing the stochastic term that represents the weather event, the model is solved dynamically for arbitrary values selected for the expected endogenous variables, setting future disturbances equal to their expected values (usually zero). At the beginning of the simulation analysis, these initial arbitrary values of the endogenous variables can be equal to their unconditional mean values, which are usually input parameters in the model. In later periods these values can be the average values of the endogenous variables in past periods. The solution provides a new set of forecasts for the endogenous variables. The model will be solved again for these new values of the expected endogenous variables—again setting future disturbances equal to their expected value—and another set of values for the endogenous variables will be generated. The process continues for several cycles, until the difference between two successive estimates of the expected endogenous variables does not exceed a certain tolerance level.

Predictions determined in this way are indeed rational in the sense of Muth, since they take into account the specific economic environment and policy intervention rules examined in that experiment, along with all other parameters and the relevant past values of endogenous variables, such as carry-in stocks. Nevertheless, this algorithm may not be practical when the simulation model is relatively complex because the computation costs necessary to obtain this solution are likely to be very high. In practice, however, it would not be necessary to solve the rational-expectations forecast for every period over the entire time horizon of the simulation analysis. Instead, the analysis can be conducted over a subperiod of time that will permit an evaluation of the likelihood function in terms of the unknown structural parameters. The reduced form thus calculated can be used in later periods for determining their rational forecasts.

If we assume that producers predict future prices on the basis of the observed current and past prices only, and no further information, then other, less costly procedures of generating rational predictions can be designed. Sargent (1973), McCallum (1976), and others have referred to the optimal prediction of time series on the basis of its own past history only as "partly rational expectations." The purely autoregressive assumption thus excludes the knowledge of present and future values of some time series, including the knowledge of certain policy variables. In the present context this assumption may mean that producers do not take into account the amount of grains in storage or the vacant storage capacity in forming their prediction about next year's price.

In general linear models the optimal solution of univariate autoregressive predictions is the ARIMA model of Box and Jenkins (1970). Nerlov's adaptive-expectations model is simply a special case of this model. Friedman (1979), shows, however, that even when the economic agents know the relevant current and past data plus the future values of selected time series, optimal least-squares learning yields short-run expectations that behave in a way for which the familiar adaptive expectations mechanism may be a usefully close approximation. In other words, by making efficient use of all the available information in forming least squares estimates that transform all this information into objectively unbiased conditional forecasts, people make predictions that have the form of adaptive expectations. The coefficient of adaptation β would vary over time, however, and not remain constant as in Nerlov's model. Friedman also shows that if people form their expectations according to a weighted estimation procedure that exponentially discounts older observations then the ordinary adaptive model with a fixed coefficient of adaptation may be a close approximation.

Taking either the autoregressive approach or the adaptive-expectations approximation, let us assume the expected price can be expressed as an exponentially weighted (moving) average of current and past prices:

$$P_{t+1}^{\exp} = E_t(P_{t+1}) = \sum_{j=0}^{n} \gamma^j P_{t-j}$$

where $P_{t+1}^{\exp}$ is the price prediction for period $(t + 1)$, one period earlier. This assumption allows the following procedure for generating a numerical solution for the partly rational expectations in a simulation analysis: For any given choice of the parameter γ and starting values $(P_0^*, \ldots, P_n^*)$, calculate successively the predicted prices $P_t^{\exp}, \ldots, P_T^{\exp}$ over the entire time horizon of the simulation analysis by dynamically solving the model from one year to the next.

Given these predictions, calculate each period the prediction error

$$e_t = P_t - P_t^{\text{exp}} \quad : \quad t = 1, \ldots, T$$

These errors are conditional on the choice of the starting values (P^*) and the adjustment parameter γ. This can be made explicit by writing: $e_t = e_t(P^*, \gamma) \quad : \quad t = 1, \ldots, T$. Given these errors, calculate the mean square error of prediction by

$$S(P^*,\gamma) = \frac{1}{T} \sum_{t=1}^{T} e_t^2(P^*,\gamma).$$

For the starting values (P^*) of the prices, their unconditional mean can be taken, which is usually an input parameter in the model. To minimize the effect of this arbitrary choice, calculate the $e_t(P^*,\gamma)$ from the $(n + 1)$th period onward. Solve in this way the mean square error of prediction $S(P^*,\gamma)$ for different values of γ. The partly rational solution is the one that minimizes the mean square error $S(P^*,\gamma)$. This numerical least-squares solution is, of course, model-specific in that it automatically takes into account the behavioral parameters and the policy rules examined in that experiment. In most situations this is also the Maximum Likelihood estimate.

Consider now the case in which the analyst has prior information about the parameter of the ARIMA model that generates the price series. If, for example, the price distribution can be assumed to be approximately Gaussian (Normal) before the implementation of the policy, then the Maximum Likelihood predictions are the simple averages of current and past prices (discussed later). Given this prior information, Box and Jenkins (1970, chap. 5) offer a procedure for updating the coefficients of the ARIMA model with the passage of time, and the implementation of policies, as new observations become available. Consider, as an illustration, an IMA (0,1,1) process, given by

$$P_{t+1} - P_t = -\Theta u_t + u_{t+1}$$

If expectations are rational, then predictions of future prices would differ from their eventual realization by the purely random term only:

$$P_t = E_{t-1}(P_t) + u_t$$

Under this assumption, the revised or updated forecast would be given by

$$E_t(P_{t+1}) = E_{t-1}(P_t) + (1 - \Theta)u_t$$

Having seen that the previous forecast $E_{t-1}(P_t)$ fell short of the realized value by u_t, producers update their forecast by an amount equal to $(1 - \Theta)u_t$. The coefficient $(1 - \Theta)$ thus measures the proportion of any given shock u_t that is permanently absorbed by the level of the process. The revised forecast can also be written as

$$E_t(P_{t+1}) = (1 - \Theta)P_t + \Theta \cdot E_{t-1}(P_t)$$

This implies that the revised forecast is a weighted average of the previous forecast and the new observation.

Consider now a price series generated by a stationary stochastic process. Fair and Taylor (1983) have shown that the rational-expectations solution can then be represented as *some* distributed lag on its own past, and the random term would then be orthogonal to all past information, provided the distributed lag can be arbitrarily long.

Let

$$P_{t,t+1}^{RE} = \sum_{i=0}^{n} w_i(P)P_{t-i}$$

denote the 'partly' rational expectations solution for P_{t+1} predicted at time t. The weights $w_i(P)$ are dynamically determined as a function of past prices, (P) being the vector $(P_{t-n}, \ldots, P_{t-1}, P_t)$. The weights may therefore change from year to year as more information is accumulated. $P_{t,t+1}^{RE}$ is an *efficient* predictor of P_{t+1} in the sense that the forecasting error $(P_{t,t+1}^{RE} - P_{t+1})$ is purely random with zero mean and no serial correlation.

Let the measure for evaluating the accuracy of forecasts be the mean square error (MSE), given by

$$\text{MSE}(P_{t+1}^{\text{exp}}) = E(P_{t+1}^{\text{exp}} - P_{t+1})^2$$

$$= \pi_p^2 + \sigma_p^2 - 2\rho_{pp} \cdot \rho_p \cdot \sigma_p$$

where P_{t+1}^{exp} is any possible predictor of P_{t+1}, σ_p^2 is its variance, σ_p^2 is the variance of the price, and ρ_{pp} is the correlation coefficient between P_{t+1} and P_{t+1}^{exp}.

From a statistical point of view, rational expectations involves the formulation of prediction on the basis of past data and an estimated relationship between the observed and the predicted variables. As prediction of a random event, expectations are subject to an error. The formation of rational expectations is therefore a question of selecting an accurate predictor. The variance of the prediction error, decomposed previously into the variance of the event itself, the variance of the predictor, and a covariance factor, has been decomposed by Theil (1966) into a bias component, an error-of-regression component, and a disturbance component. As the sample size rises to infinity, the bias and the error of the regression components of Maximum Likelihood predictors tend to zero, provided the time series of the variable under consideration satisfies the standard assumptions ordinarily made in a regression analysis. In that sense they are *efficient* predictors.

For Gaussian or Normal time series, the simple average of current and past prices is obviously the most efficient predictor of next year's price. For these series the correlation coefficient ρ_{pp} is equal to zero, so that

$$\text{MSE}\,(P_{t+1}^{exp}) = \sigma_{\bar{p}}^2 + \sigma_p^2$$

The moving average predictor of the form

$$\bar{P}_t = \frac{1}{n+1} \cdot \sum_{i=0}^{n} P_{t-i}$$

has a mean equal to the mean of the population of the price series and its variance is decreasing monotonically to zero as n rises to infinity. Hence,

$$\text{MSE}(\bar{P}_t) \rightarrow \sigma_p^2 \text{ as } n \rightarrow \infty$$

and therefore, for *any other* possible predictor $\hat{P}_{t+1}$ (including the rational one $P_{t,t+1}^e$)

$$\text{MSE}\,(\operatorname*{Lim}_{n \rightarrow \infty} \bar{P}_t) \leq \text{MSE}(P_{t+1}^{exp})$$

In the present study, the random weather events are assumed to be generated from a Normal distribution. Taking a Bayesian approach to the estimation of the parameters in an ARIMA model, the simple average can serve as a prior for generating efficient predictions. With the implementation of nonsymmetric and discontinuous price policies, however, the price series may no longer be Normal. A possible method of generating the posterior distribution—that is, updating the predictors in accordance with the new information as it accumulates—is to correct them if the prediction errors are systematically biased or serially correlated. This systematic bias can be estimated by the average prediction error of past periods as

$$B_t = \frac{1}{n+1} \sum_{i=0}^{n} [P_{t-i} - E_{t-i-1}(P_{t-i})]$$

If the prediction errors are purely random and n is large enough, then B_t should be equal to zero. If the predictions are systematically biased, then they will be corrected as part of the simulation analysis according to

$$E(P_{t+1}) = \sum_{i=0}^{n} w_i P_{t-i} + B_t$$

The bias is thus assumed to represent a permanent change in the *level* of the process, and $\sum_{i=0}^{n} w_i P_{t-i}$ is the *prior* estimate.

The latter is also the approach taken in this study. We have termed this type of predictors as adaptively rational, and the weights ws in the prior are assumed to be equal to each other. In actual work there is still a question, however, about how long the distributed lag should be. The answer is often model-specific and can be determined in the analysis by measuring the variance of the predictor for different number of lags. To illustrate possible outcomes of this experiment, figures 2–1(a) through 2–1(d) present the coefficient of variations of adaptively rational predictors for different numbers of lags that were obtained in simulation experiments with the econometric model used for this study. (The details of the model are given in chapter 2 and the parameter values in chapter 4.) The predictors were calculated as moving averages of the past specified number of years. The results show that the coefficient of variation of the predictors converges rather rapidly to zero as the number of lags rises. Rapid convergence is revealed even when serial correlation is present and even when farmers exhibit risk aversion (in the latter case the price distribution is no longer symmetric). In the simulation analysis for this book, the forecasted price was calculated as the average of the preceding nine prices.

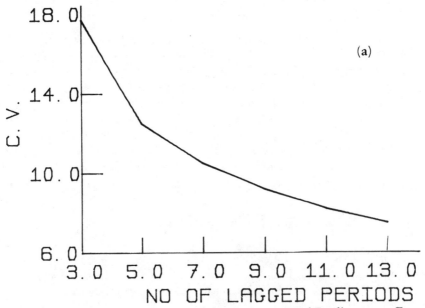

Figure 2–1. The Variability of the Adaptively Rational Predictor as a Function of the Number of Lags

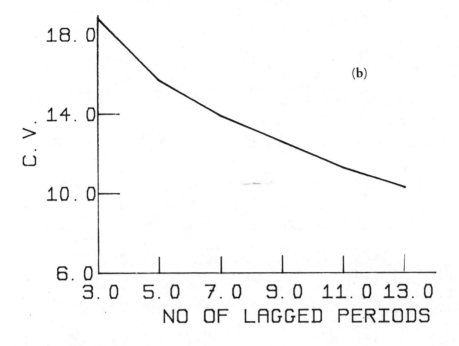

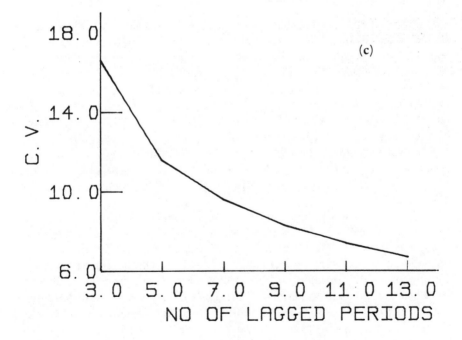

Figure 2–1 (continued)

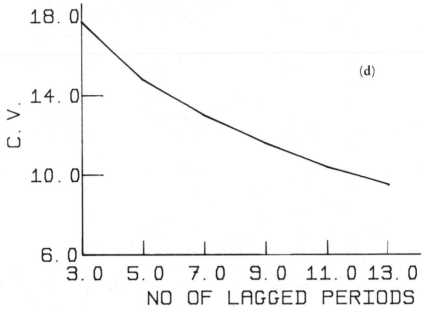

Figure 2–1 *(continued)*

Risk Response

The effects of risk on investment and production decisions have been discussed at length in the economic literature following the seminal work of
Sandmo (1971). Indeed, the main point of departure of the recent literature
on price stabilization from the simple Marshallian analysis of Waugh, Oi,
and Massell is its emphasis on the effects of the instability of prices and
incomes in agriculture on risk-averse producers, and on their response to the
reduction in risk as an effect of stabilization policies (see, for example, Newbery and Stiglitz 1979, 1981; Turnovsky, Shalit, and Schmitz 1980; Bigman
1982). Newbery and Stiglitz (1981, p. 3) demonstrated that "the standard
specification . . . (in the Waugh-Oi-Massell model) . . . strongly *biases* the
results which emerge from the analysis even before the empirical study is
undertaken."

In a previous study (Bigman 1982, chap. 4) where I estimated the gains
from buffer stocks in a prototype model of the food grains sector, I made a
distinction between *transfer* gains and *risk-response* gains. The former are
the gains captured by the ordinary Waugh-Oi-Massell model that result from
temporizing food consumption via stocks—that is, the transfer of supply
from periods of excess to periods of shortage. In essence, the transfer gains
are due to the decreasing marginal utility of consumption and the increasing
marginal costs of production. A transfer of food from a period of abundant
supply to one of low supply is likely to raise the welfare of an individual who

has decreasing marginal utility from food consumption, even after accounting for the time differences.[2] The risk-response gains are those resulting from the increase in production by risk-averse producers as they respond to the greater stability provided by the storage operation. According to my estimates, a storage operation with capacity equal to 6 percent of average annual production involves transfer losses (which include amortization costs of the storage facility) equal to 0.08 percent of total expenditures on the product, but risk-response gains equal to 2.31 percent. Hence the economic gains or losses from price-stabilization policies crucially depend on the risk-response gains and therefore on the degree to which producers are averse to risk.

Empirical estimates of risk-response in either the supply or the production functions, however, did not produce conclusive, statistically significant results. The main reason is that these estimates are ex post, and the response is already embodied in the other parameters of the functions. Direct behavioral studies have clearly demonstrated, however, that risk aversion is a highly significant determinant of farmers' investment and production decisions (see, for example, Binswanger 1980, 1981; Binswanger and Sillers 1983; Grisley and Kellog 1983).

The simulation analysis, however, does not raise any methodological problems in incorporating the risk-response factor because the function specification is ex ante. In other words, regardless of the form in which this factor can be estimated from *past* data, all theoretical and behavioral studies clearly indicate that the effects of risk can be represented as a negative shifter in the supply function, indicating that, ceteris paribus, the higher the risk in production of a certain product, the smaller the area allocated for its production.

Sandmo (1971) examined a firm facing uncertain prices for its products and selecting its output level so as to maximize its expected utility from profits. The firm is assumed to have a continuous, differentiable, and concave utility function $U(\pi)$, where $\pi = PX - C(X)$ is the firm's profit, and $C(X)$ its cost function. First-order conditions for profit maximization imply

$$E\{U'(\pi)[P - C'(X)]\} = 0$$

But

$$E\{U'(\pi)[P - C'(X)]\} = E[U'(\pi)][\bar{P} - C'(X)]$$

$$+ \text{Cov}\{U'(\pi)[P - C'(X)]\}$$

where $\bar{P} = E(P)$. Rearranging terms, we can therefore write the latter equation as

$$\bar{P} + \frac{\text{Cov}[U'(\pi)P]}{E[U'(\pi)]} = C'(X)$$

For the risk-averse firm, $\text{Cov}[U'(\pi)P] < 0$ (Ishii 1977), whereas $U'(\pi) > 0$. Hence $\text{Cov}[U'(\pi)P]/E[U'(\pi)] < 0$, and the firm therefore equates the marginal costs to a price lower than the mean price in order to determine its optimal level of output. The difference between that price and the mean price represents the risk premium that rises with a rise in the firm's degree of risk aversion. The optimal level of output of the risk-averse firm would therefore be smaller than that of the risk-neutral one, and the output would be smaller, the larger its aversion to risk. Using the concept of the mean-preserving spread, Sandmo has shown that the optimal level of output would decline as the price variability increases.

To provide a measure of economic surplus under risk, Just (1975, 1976) has considered a single risk-averse firm operating in a competitive market facing a random product price, and making short-term decisions by maximizing a mean-standard-deviation expected utility function:

$$E\{U[P,C(X),\sigma_p]\} = E(\pi) - \alpha \text{Var}(\pi)$$
$$= \bar{P}X - C(X) - \alpha X^2 \sigma_p^2$$

where α is the risk-aversion parameter and $X^2 \sigma_p^2$ is the variance of the firm's profits. The term $\alpha \cdot X^2 \cdot \sigma_p^2$ is therefore the firm's risk premium.

By differentiating the last equation with respect to X, we can determine the first-order conditions for maximizing the expected utility, given by

$$\bar{P} - 2\alpha X\sigma_p^2 = C'(X)$$

The marginal risk premium $2\alpha \cdot X\sigma_p^2$ measures the discounting of the expected price because of the uncertainty associated with it. This formulation implies that the risk-averse supply curve lies vertically parallel and to the left of the risk-neutral supply curve.

When both the firm's price and its output are subject to random (though possibly correlated) disturbances, the mean-standard-deviation utility function is given by

$$E[U(\pi)] = E(\pi) - \alpha \text{Var}(\pi) = E(PX) - C(\bar{X}) - \alpha \text{Var}(PX)$$

where $C(\bar{X})$ is the firm's cost function as a function of its *planned* output $\bar{X}$. Let σ_x^2 denote the output variance. The variance of the firm's revenues can be expressed as

$$\text{Var}(PX) = \bar{P}^2\sigma_x^2 + \bar{X}^2\sigma_p^2 + 2\bar{P}\bar{X}\text{Cov}(P,X) - \text{Cov}(P,X)^2$$

(see Bohrnsteadt and Goldberg 1969; Hazell 1982). Hence

$$V(P \cdot X) = (\bar{P}\sigma_x + \bar{X}\sigma_p)^2 - 2(1 - \rho)\bar{P}\bar{X}\sigma_p\sigma_x - \rho^2\sigma_x^2\sigma_p^2$$

where ρ is the correlation coefficient, and, by definition,

$$\text{Cov}(P,X) = \rho\sigma_x\sigma_p$$

P and X would, in general, be negatively correlated. Inserting the latter results to the expected utility equation yields

$$E[U(\pi)] = \bar{P}\bar{X} - C(\bar{X}) + \rho\sigma_x\sigma_P - [(\bar{P}\sigma_x + \bar{X}\sigma_P)^2 - 2(1 - \rho)\bar{P}\bar{X}\sigma_x\sigma_p$$

$$- \rho^2\sigma_x^2\sigma_p^2] \cdot \alpha$$

Differentiating the latter equation with respect to $\bar{X}$ yields the first-order conditions for utility maximization given by

$$\bar{P} - 2\alpha(\bar{X} \cdot \sigma_p^2 + \rho\sigma_x\sigma_p)$$

The marginal risk premium with deterministic supply and stochastic prices was found earlier to be equal to $2 \cdot \alpha \bar{X}\sigma_p^2$. From the latter equation we can therefore conclude that the risk premium with stochastic prices and yields is smaller than that with deterministic supply if and only if yields and output are negatively correlated.

If $\rho = 0$,

$$\text{Var}(PX) = \bar{P}^2\sigma_x^2 + \bar{X}^2\sigma_p^2$$

and the marginal risk premium with deterministic or stochastic supplies are equal.

In a simulation analysis there is no need to decompose the variability of revenues into its component, since this variability can be calculated directly from the simulation results. This is the approach taken in this study. The firm would be assumed to determine its optimal level of output by equating its (deterministic) marginal costs to a price lower than the expected price. The difference represents a risk premium, assumed to be proportional to the variability of the unit revenues.

The Model

The model consists of the following main components:

1. An econometric model specifying the demand and supply functions for the crop or crops under consideration.

2. The stochastic process describing the random fluctuations in the country's agricultural production, in the world price of these products, and in nonagricultural income.

3. A set of policy rules that define the government practices under different contingencies (in good and bad years, for high and low world prices, and so on).

The purpose of this section is to describe the details of the simulation model and of the solution method so that the analysis may be replicated or applied by other researchers to specific countries or cases.[4]

The General Structure of the Simulation Analysis

The simulation model applied in this study describes a discrete dynamic process of an economic system. The state of the system at the beginning of the tth period is described by the vector of state variables Y_{t-1} that has been determined in the previous period. In the present context the elements of Y_{t-1} may include the area allocated for cultivation, the level of stocks, the vacant storage capacity, and the different supply and demand parameters. During the tth period, random (weather) events, denoted by the vector Z_t, occur, the probability distributions of which are assumed to be known. Policy actions, denoted by the vector X_t, are then determined by the initial state of the system and the current random events, according to a set of decision rules D. That is:

$$X_t = D(Y_{t-1}, Z_t) \tag{2.11}$$

Examples of such decisions are the quantities put into or released from storage, as determined by the prespecified buying or selling prices and the realized weather event. In that case the decision rules—that is, the trigger prices—do not change over time, although the policy actions themselves—that is, the actual quantities stored or released from storage—do, of course, vary from year to year. Together, the initial state of the system, the random events, and the policy actions determine the state of the system at time t:

$$Y_t = F_t(Y_{t-1}, Z_t, X_t) = F_t[Y_{t-1}, Z_t, D(Y_{t-1}, Z_t)] \tag{2.12}$$

A deterministic and known relation F_t is assumed to exist between the state variables Y_t, on the one hand, and the state variable in the preceding period Y_{t-1}, the random events Z_t, and the policy decisions X_t on the other hand. The function F_t may also incorporate technological progress, population growth, and other time-dependent processes.

As a result of the recurrent nature of equation 2.12, the state variables Y_t may be written as a function of the initial condition Y_0, the set of decision rules D, and the random events $Z_1, \ldots, Z_T$. Given an objective function that depends on the entire sequence of state variables, the decision problem becomes one of finding a set of decision rules D that, for given initial conditions Y_0 and a sequence of random events $Z_1, \ldots, Z_T$, would yield the highest-ranking outcome attainable according to the order determined by the objective function.

The objective function itself is thus a function of all the state variables, and can be written as:

$$H = H(Y_0, Y_1, \ldots, Y_T) \tag{2.13}$$

H can also be a multiple objective function—that is, a vector $H = (h_1, \ldots, h_n)$ consisting of several objectives, each being a function of all the state variables. Possible objectives of the storage operation are the net economic gains from the policy, and its effect on the variability of the market price, on the stability of food supply, on the level and variability of farmer's income, and so forth. Since the state variables depend on the random events $(Z_1, \ldots, Z_T)$, they are also stochastic variables. The optimization problem is therefore one of maximizing the expected value of each of the decision criteria. If the n decision criteria conflict, maximizing $h_i(Y)$ may preclude attaining the maximum of $h_j(y)$ for $j \neq i$. In that case, the vector-valued function H defines only a partial ordering of the solution space. A possible solution of the vector optimization problem is the weighting method in which weights are given to each of the terms in the objective vector H. The problem thus becomes

$$\text{Max} E \quad \sum_{i=1}^{n} \lambda_i h_i$$

$$h_i = h_i(Y_0, Y_1, \ldots, Y_T)$$

$$\lambda_i = 0, \quad \sum_{i=1}^{n} \lambda_i = 1 \tag{2.14}$$

where the maximization is with respect to D—that is, the time-invariant set of decision rules, and given the recursive relationships specified in equation 2.12.

The numerical solution is as follows. A sequence of random numbers $(Z_1, \ldots, Z_T)$ is drawn from a prespecified probability distribution. These random numbers characterize the random (weather) events. Given these numbers, the initial conditions Y_0, and the decision rules D, the sequence of the state variables $(Y_1, \ldots, Y_T)$ can be calculated, via the mathematical model specified in equation 2.2. The model determines the behavioral relationships between the state and control variables such as demand and supply, the policy actions, and so on. The calculated state variables in turn determine the value of the objective function or functions via equation 2.3. The process is repeated many times for different sequences drawn from the same probability distribution. The frequency distributions of the outcomes yield the expected value of the objective function for that set of decision rules.

The Econometric Model

Consumers' Demand. Consumers in the country are disaggregated into several income groups and between urban and rural consumers. The level of aggregation is determined by the data available and by the specific subject matter under consideration. A separate demand function is specified for each group, its parameters being the price and income elasticities, the share of the group in total demand, and the rates of income and population growth of the group. Demands are assumed to be a deterministic function of the current price. They may, however, be affected by stochastic variations in income (see the following section).

The demand functions are assumed to be either log-linear or kinked-linear.[5] When all consumer groups are aggregated into a single group, the log-linear specification would be used. This would be the case when the discussion is focused on the production side of agricultural or trade policies.

When consumers are disaggregated into several income groups, the log-linear specifications may raise computational problems. The reason is that with a log-linear specification, total demand has the form

$$D = \sum_{i=1}^{m} D_i = \sum_{i=1}^{m} A_i P^{\alpha_i}$$

where $D_i = A_i P^{\alpha_i}$ is the demand function of the ith consumer group. The market price would then be solved as the root of that polynom. The solution, however, may be very costly in terms of computer time; additionally, it is not even certain that this polynom would have a single real positive root. To overcome the computational difficulties, the kinked-linear approximation has been used in these cases. Another possible solution is to express the system of demand functions in terms of growth rates rather than actual levels. In terms of growth rates, the system of demand functions can be written as

$$D_i^g = \alpha_i P_i^g + \alpha_i M_i^g + N_i^g \quad : \quad i = 1, \ldots, m$$

where $Q^g = (1/Q)(dQ/dt)$ is the rate of growth of the variable Q, N_i^g is the rate of population growth, and M_i is the rate of income growth of the corresponding income group. Aggregate demand would therefore be given, in terms of growth rates, by

$$D^g = \sum_{i=1}^{m} \lambda_i D_i^g$$

where λ_i is the share of the ith group in total demand for that commodity. This change in aggregate demand is equated to the *change* in aggregate supply. If the system was initially in equilibrium, then it would remain in equilibrium at each consecutive stage; that is, market-clearing conditions imply that if at $t = 0 : D_0 = S_0$, then at each consecutive *equilibrium* point, $t > 0$,

$$S_t^g = D_t^g = \sum_{i=1}^{m} \lambda_i D_i^g$$

where S^g registers the rate of change in supply. The latter is a linear system of demand and supply equations, expressed in terms of growth rates, from which the rates of change in prices can be solved. Given this solution and the initial price *level*, the actual levels of the prices can be found at each consecutive time period. The initial equilibrium state at time $t = 0$ will be generated by inserting the base year's prices and incomes into the original demand function in order to determine that level of demand D_0 at which the system is in equilibrium.

The division of consumers into several income groups is aimed at examining the distributional consequences of different policies in general and of target-group subsidy or income-transfer programs in particular. The model can also accommodate random shifts in demand—for instance those associated with changes in income. Of particular interest are the effects of shifts in demand of rural consumers associated with weather-induced variations in supply. These effects are discussed in detail in chapter 4.

Producers' Supply. The functional form of the supply function in a stochastic-dynamic model must clearly specify the formation of expectations and the response to price and production risks. The issues involved in this specification were examined in the previous section. On the basis of this discussion, the functional form of the supply function that has been assumed in the simulation analysis is log-linear-constant-elasticity, given by

$$\log \bar{S}_t = \alpha_0 + \alpha_1 \log P_t^e - \alpha_2 \log R_t$$

where S^t is planned output or the area allocated for cultivation, P_t^e is the price expected at time $(t - 1)$ or the beginning of the crop season—for time t—or the end of the season, and its formation is specified in the previous section. R_t is the risk factor, represented by the variability of income and measured as

$$R_t = \left(1 + \frac{\sigma_I}{I}\right)$$

where

$$\sigma_I^2 = \frac{1}{n} \sum_{i=1}^{n} (I_t - \bar{I}_t)^2$$

$$I_t = \frac{1}{n + 1} \sum_{j=0}^{n} I_{t-j}$$

where I_t is the farmers' income at time t.

Disturbances in supply are multiplicative and generated from a prespecified probability distribution. In the present simulation analysis the disturbances in supply are assumed to be generated from the normal distribution. The model can accommodate serial correlation in production as well as correlation between production in the country and world production.

The Solution Method in the Stochastic-Dynamic Model

The introduction of stochastic and dynamic elements into the model and its accommodation to a short-run analysis require the solution procedure to be different from that in ordinary comparative static analysis. In the comparative static analysis with partial or general equilibrium models, all the endogenous variables are solved *simultaneously* for the given exogenous and control variables. In a short-run dynamic analysis, production and resource-allocation decisions in any given year are made at the beginning of the year on the basis of expected prices, before the weather event and the actual prices for that year become known. Consequently, the solution method is *recursive* and *sequential* rather than simultaneous. In what follows, the series of steps in the solution method for each year is described.

1. In any given year the initial conditions are specified by (1) a set of exogenous, possibly time-dependent parameters such as demand and supply, elasticities, population and income (by income group), technology, the parameters specifying the stochastic process, and so on, and (2) a set of endogenous variables that have been derived in the previous years, such as past prices and carry-in stocks.

2. Given these initial conditions, the production decision—the area allocated for cultivation and the planned (derived) demand for other factor inputs for that year—is made at the beginning of the crop season. The supply function specifies planned production as a function of technology, *expected* output prices, and the price elasticity of supply. As noted in the previous section, the expected price itself is assumed to be a function of past prices, and this lag generates the recursive structure of the model.

3. Actual supply in that year is subsequently determined according to the actual weather conditions and the area allocated for cultivation in that year.

4. Given actual supply, the market price of the product and its distribution among consumers are determined by the corresponding demand functions. This set of prices and quantities can be termed the *reference solution*.

5. The reference prices are equated with the CIF import price and the FOB export price. The world price is also random and depends on the weather events and policy decisions in the foreign countries. The border price accounts for transportation and insurance costs. If the (closed economy) reference price is higher than the CIF import price, the product is imported. The market price is then determined by the import price, and the quantity imported by the difference between the quantity consumed at that price and the quantity produced in the country. Similarly, if the reference price is lower than the FOB export price, the product is exported. The market price and the quantities exported and domestically consumed are determined by the export price. The set of prices and quantities obtained at this stage can be termed the *free-market solution*.

6. The free-market prices and quantities are equated with trigger prices that determine the government intervention rules. These interventions can take many forms, manifesting the diversity of the government's objectives. The following are few examples:

If the free-market price exceeds the price at the upper band specifying the storage operation rule, the product is released from storage (to the extent available).

If the free market price falls below a certain floor price the government takes measures to secure the floor price to producers through restitution payments, procurement to government storage or exports, crop insurance, constraints on imports, etc.

If the import bill on that account exceeds a prespecified foreign-exchange constraint, actual imports would have to be curtailed.

If consumption of a target population falls below a certain minimum level, measures are taken to prevent (or moderate) that decline through subsidy programs, income transfers, transfers in kind, subsidized imports, food aid, and so forth.

The entire set of government intervention rules forms a complex decision tree even with a small number of policies, since it must include all combinations of these policies. Indeed, the system of decisions is the core of the model. The set of prices and quantities derived after all these interventions have taken place is the ultimate solution for that year. Various performance measures can then be calculated, including the economic gains or losses to the various sectors, the fiscal costs, and the foreign-exchange expenses.

The dynamic process will then proceed to the following year, after correcting the following year's expected price (taking into account this year's price) and after accounting for all time-dependent changes such as population and income growth, technical change, and the like. This in turn provides the initial conditions for the following year. A flow chart diagram describing this cycle is given in figure 2–2.

The process will continue until the (predetermined) end period, thus generating the entire dynamic path of the product's prices and quantities. This path depends on the set of initial conditions at the beginning of the process; on the set of the model's parameters (some of which may vary over time); on the set of decision rules (some of which may also change over time, though in a predetermined manner), and on the sequence of random weather events in both the country and the world.

By applying Monte Carlo simulations specified by the predetermined parameters of the stochastic process, the entire sequence is repeated numerous times for different sets of random weather events. The summary statistics of this entire process includes not only the expected outcomes of the various performance measures but also their frequency distribution. Varying the decision rules permits different scenarios to be described and the corrsponding performance measures to be calculated, on the basis of which a complete evaluation of the policies involved can be made.

Other Features of the Model

The World Model

When a country is engaged in trade with the rest of the world in the product under consideration, the volume of trade is determined by the world price of the product relative to the domestic price, and by the specific government objectives and policies relating to trade and internal stabilization. The world price is also a random variable dependent on stochastic variations in world production. The world-price model consists of log-linear demand and supply

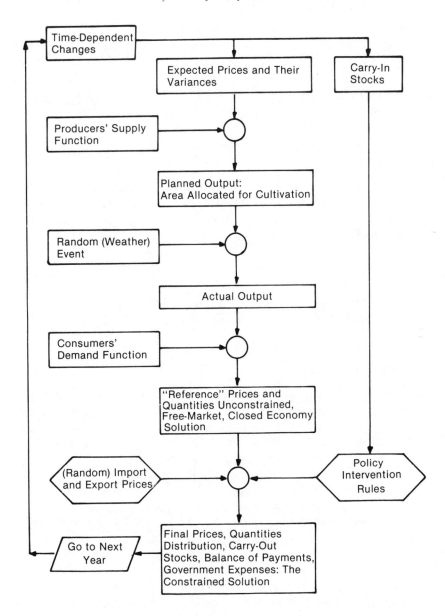

Figure 2–2. The Solution Procedure of the Simulation Model: A Flow Chart Diagram

curves. Multiplicative disturbances in world production determine the frequency distribution of the world price, subject to the policy measures implemented in the rest of the world. Of particular interest in the present context are the effects of world storage and price agreements as part of an international commodity agreement on the various sectors in the country considered.

Correlation

The model can accommodate serial correlation in production as well as correlation in production between the country and the world. If, for instance, serial correlation is present in the country's production, the disturbances u_t will have the form

$$u_t = \rho u_{t-1} + \sqrt{1 - \rho^2} \cdot e_t$$

where e_t is a normally distributed random disturbance and ρ is the coefficient of serial correlation.

Small and Large Countries

The model can accommodate both a small country, whose excess supply or demand has no effect on the world price, and a large country, whose trade does affect the world price. The latter country can therefore reap monopolistic gains and will take this into account in determining its trade policy.

The solution method for the large country requires one more stage for a consistency check. In this case the equilibrium price cannot be simply determined as the price that simultaneously clears both the world's and the country's markets, given the corresponding demand and supply functions. The level of the world price and the corresponding trade balance and level of domestic consumption may trigger government interventions either to constrain or to encourage trade. In the large country these interventions would in turn change the world price. A consistent solution is one in which the world price that triggers government interventions is equal (or sufficiently close) to the world price resulting from these interventions. To secure consistency, the model feeds the new world price—after it has been changed by the government interventions—back into the decision-making subroutine to determine the new levels of intervention. This process is repeated until adequate convergence is achieved.

Self-Sufficient, Importing, and Exporting Countries

Trade is conducted either by private traders or by government agencies. Private, profit-motivated traders would import whenever the import price, which includes transportation and insurance costs as well as government tariffs (or subsidies), is lower than the domestic price; they would export whenever the export price FOB (plus the net taxes levied on exports) is higher than the domestic price. Private trade may be regulated further by quota constraints. Direct government imports (or external food aid) are motivated by other objectives and can take place even when they are unjustified on the basis of the price differential.

The level of trade defines three types of countries:

A *self-sufficient* country is one in which, in a normal year—that is, when both the world's and country's production are at their mean—there is no price differential between the country and the world and thus no incentive for trade. Random fluctuations in the country's production and in the world price may, however, create price differentials wide enough to trigger imports in some years and exports in others.

A *generally importing* country is one that, in a normal year, supplies only part of its demand at the normal import price and therefore must import to supplement its normal supply. In some years, however, a glut in domestic production or a rise in the world price may preclude private imports. In other years the country's imports may rise above the normal level as a result of a shortfall in domestic production or a low world price.

Generally exporting describes a country that exports part of its production in a normal year. Its actual level of exports may change from year to year, however, according to the local harvest and the world price.

Dynamics

The model incorporates time-related changes in the relevant parameters, thus allowing an analysis of the long-run effects of alternative policy options. These parameters include population and income by income group, mean output and its variability, and so on.

Changes in Income and Their Effects on Demand

The model is partial equilibrium, and the level of income is determined exogenously. However, it accommodates the effects of *changes* in income on demand. Three types of income changes can be taken into account:

1. Policy-induced changes in income, by income groups—for example, changes due to income transfers to target consumer groups.
2. Variations in income due to variations in nonagricultural economic activities.
3. Variations in the income of the rural population caused by weather-induced changes in agricultural production or by government price policies that affect producers' revenues.

Initial Conditions and a Steady-State Solution

The set of initial conditions for the simulation analysis is typically arbitrary and may be very different from the stationary or steady-state condition. For instance, the simulation analysis of storage operations starts with no grains in storage; only over the years do grains accumulate (or decumulate) with the production tides. In addition, the initial value of endogenous variables such as market prices is likely to be quite different from their steady-state value, sometimes by wide margins. To minimize the effects of the (arbitrary) initial value of the endogenous variables and allow them to converge to their steady-state level, the following procedure has been applied. Starting with an arbitrary value of the endogenous variables along with the other initial conditions, the simulation analysis proceeds for a number of years without retrieving any results. Only after the system has reached its steady-state level do annual values of the performance criteria enter into the calculation of the objective function. This procedure also avoids (or minimizes) the pitfalls mentioned in the Lucas critique. The reason is that the steady state toward which the simulation model gravitates is one that by definition has been and continues to be governed by the same policy measures or modes of behavior. Risk-averse producers, for example, will respond to the increased stability provided by a given policy by raising their output, thus lowering the average market price. In the simulation analysis the calculation of the market price enter into the results only after several years, when the market price would have reached its new equilibrium which reflects this response of risk averse producers. In the simulation analysis for this study, the dynamic evolution of the system proceeds for ten years prior to starting calculation of the averages and the frequency distributions of the endogenous variables and of the other performance criteria. These calculations themselves were based on a dynamic process that was assumed to last twenty years.

Numerical Optimization in a Simulation Analysis

The main disadvantage of the simulation analysis is that the policy rules are arbitrarily prespecified by the analyst and therefore can be quite different from the optimal rules. Although sensitivity analysis allows a comparison of alternative policies, it provides an extremely inefficient method of searching for the best policy. For one thing, this search becomes prohibitively expensive when the number of control variables is larger than two or three. Furthermore, the search may end by finding a local optimum.

A particularly serious problem arises in comparing alternative policies when more than a single control variable exists. Consider, for example, a storage policy. Three control variables define the storage rule: the two trigger prices for storing and releasing from storage, and the storage capacity. Typically the comparison is made between different storage capacities, leaving the trigger prices unchanged. This comparison may lead to an erroneous conclusion, however, because if the trigger prices were *optimally* determined *together* with the capacity level, the conclusion might be entirely different. Suppose, for instance, that two storage capacities are being compared and that the larger of the two is found to perform better given the objective function specified. If the trigger prices were optimally adjusted, however, the smaller capacity might be found to perform better.

This deficiency of the simulation analysis is especially pronounced when packages of different types of policies are being compared. Consider, for example, a package consisting of storage and price-support policies. A bad performance of the storage policy may well be the result of an inadequate choice of support price. In order for the comparison of alternative policy packages to be *consistent,* all the control variables specifying the policy rules must be optimally selected. To overcome these difficulties, Bigman and Yitzhaki (1983) have developed an algorithm for incorporating numerical optimization methods into the simulation analysis. The algorithm permits an optimization with respect to several control variables, and can accommodate any simulation model, however complex.

The algorithm works as follows: The simulation analysis yields values for the objective function (which may be specified as a weighted sum of several performance criteria). The optimization algorithm is then applied to the search for a new set of decision rules that can improve the value of the objective function. The search is conducted along the hyperplane perpendicular to the gradient determined by the control variables. The optimization algorithm calculates the gradient and determines the size of the change to be made in the control variables along its perpendicular hyperplane. A new set of decision rules is thus generated, and another iteration of the simulation analysis is conducted for the new rules. The whole process is repeated several times until no further improvement of the objective function beyond a prespecified level can be achieved.

Heuristically, the integration of numerical optimization with simulation analysis can be regarded as a sophisticated procedure for conducting a sensitivity analysis, whereby the direction and the magnitude of the change in the control variables are optimally determined by the optimization algorithm, rather than being arbitrarily determined by the analyst.

The specific numerical optimization procedure applied by Bigman and Yitzhaki is a variant of the Variable Metric Method (see Yitzhaki 1982 for references and description), which proved to be highly efficient. The numerical optimization procedure and the simulation model are written as separate computer programs. The linkage between the two is a user-supplied subroutine that receives as inputs the numerical values of the control variables from the optimization procedure. These numerical values are then plugged into the simulation model and applied in the simulation analysis to generate a new set of values of the objective function. The results of the simulation are transferred through the connecting subroutine to the optimization procedure, which then searches by the gradient method for the best direction in which to change the control variables. The process continues for several cycles until the improvement in the objective function is smaller than the prespecified tolerance level. A flow chart diagram describing this process is given in figure 2-3.

This structure makes the operation of the model fairly simple. The user simply constructs the connecting subroutine and provides initial values for the parameters. Any parameter in the simulation model can be selected as a policy variable, and any outcome or combination of outcomes of the simulation can be selected as the target for optimization.

Development of the Model and Future Extensions

The simulation model used in this study originated with the work of Reutlinger (1976) on worldwide buffer stocks for wheat. Later, Reutlinger, Bigman, and Eaton (1976) and Bigman and Reutlinger (1979a, 1979b) extended the model to an open economy trading with the rest of the world and engaged in storage and stabilizing trade policies. Further extensions of the model have proceeded in three directions. The first was extensions of the functional specification of the model to accommodate log-linear supply and demand functions, multiplicative disturbances, risk-response in supply, variations in consumption due to variations in income, dynamics, and so on. The second direction involved extension of the scope of policies considered. Originally the model concentrated on buffer stocks. Later work (Bigman 1982) extended the analysis to include internal price policies such as subsidies to consumers, minimum price or guaranteed income to producers, tariffs or subsidies to trade, and the like. For the present study, the model has been further extended to examine nonmarket policies such as enforced procurement and direct government distribution. The third direction was application of the model in actual country analysis for an evaluation of price, trade, and stocks policies.

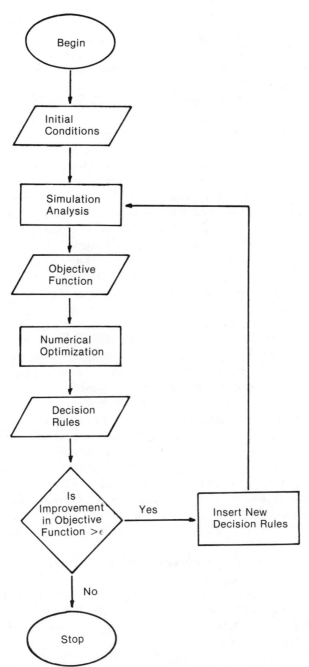

Figure 2–3. The Integration of Simulation Analysis with Numerical Optimization: A Flow Chart Diagram of the Solution Procedure

So far the model has been used to evaluate the existing policies and alternative policy options in Turkey, Israel, the Pacific Rim, Indonesia, India, and Nigeria. These applications and those presented in this study required further extensions of the scope of policies to accommodate the specific policies implemented in these countries.

So far, however, the model has been partial equilibrium, although variations in farmers' income associated with weather-induced variations in agricultural output or with government price policies have been endogenized into the model. The level of farmers' income, the employment of landless rural workers, the use of fertilizers, the choice of production technology, and other factors remain exogenous. The partial equilibrium model, therefore, cannot deal with important policy issues such as the effects of input subsidies on agricultural production and food security; the effects of government price and procurement policies on employment, income, and food consumption of small farmers and landless rural workers; or the effects of government policies in one crop on resource allocation to and production of other crops. To answer these questions, an extension of the model has been planned that would extend the stochastic-dynamic analysis to sectorial or general equilibrium models.

The power of sectorial or general equilibrium models lies in their ability to highlight possible inconsistencies between the direct effects of different policies and their total effects, since the indirect effects of intersectoral linkages are quite difficult to trace. These models have one important drawback, however. The structure of the model—and, therefore, also the conclusions drawn—are country-specific and cannot be extended to other countries. The partial equilibrium model, by contrast, requires a much smaller set of parameters and has a structure general enough that its conclusions are more widely applicable. Sensitivity analysis can determine the robustness of these conclusions. Another advantage of partial equilibrium models is that their data requirements are quite small; they can therefore be instrumental in a relatively rapid examination of policy issues, especially when the data available are limited. Sectorial and, even more so, general equilibrium models require extensive data set that is hard, if not impossible, to find in most developing countries.

Future extensions of the model to sectorial or general equilibrium models will offer a new dimension to the stochastic-dynamic analysis of the policy issues examined in this and related studies. The partial equilibrium model, though aggregating out important issues, will still be instrumental, however, in a preliminary evaluation of policy alternatives, or when the data (or the time) are too constrained.

Notes

1. Although risk and uncertainty are usually associated with instability, they are not synonymous. Uncertainty is related to the ex ante behavioral response to contingent events (which may or may not be stochastic); instability is an ex post record of the stochastic events.

2. Formally, a transfer of food from period t to any future period $(t + \tau)$ would benefit the individual if and only if

$$U_t'(C_t) < e^{-\gamma\tau} \cdot U_{t+\tau}'(C_{t+\tau})$$

where $u'(C)$ is the individual's marginal utility of food consumption and γ is the rate of time preference. Under the ordinary assumptions on the utility function U, a necessary condition for that is $C_t > C_{t+\tau}$.

3. A multicommodity extension of the model will also include the derived demand and supply functions for factor inputs.

4. The computer program itself can be made available to interested researchers on request from the author.

5. A simple linear specification, though very attractive for analytical purposes, is clearly undersirable in applied work since it would be in contradiction to the evidence that the larger the quantity already consumed of a product, the higher the price elasticity of demand. (A linear specification suggests, in contrast, that the price elasticity of demand *declines* with the rise in the quantity purchased).

References

Bigman, D. 1982. *Coping with hunger: Toward a theory of food security and price stabilization.* Cambridge, Mass.: Ballinger.

Bigman, D., and Reutlinger, S. 1979a. National and international policies toward food security and price stabilization. *American Economic Review* 69:159–163.

———. 1979b. Food price and supply stabilization: National buffer stocks and trade policies. *American Journal of Agricultural Economics* 61:657–667.

Bigman, D., and Yitzhaki, S. 1983. Optimizing storage operations: An integration of stochastic simulations and numerical optimization. Working Paper No. 8305, Center for Agricultural Economic Research, Hebrew University of Jerusalem.

Binswanger, H.P. 1980. Attitude toward risk: Experimental measurement in rural India. *American Journal of Agricultural Economics* 62:395–407.

———. 1981. Attitudes toward risk: Theoretical implications of an experiment in rural India. *Economic Journal* 91:867–890.

Binswanger, H.P. and Sillers, D.A. 1983. Risk aversion and credit constraints in farmers' decision making: A reinterpretation. *Journal of Development Studies* 20:5–21.

Bohrnstedt, G.W., and Goldberg, A.S. 1969. On the exact covariance of products of random variables. *Journal of American Statistical Association* 64:1439–1442.

Box, G.E.P., and Jenkins, G.M. 1970. *Time-Series Analysis*. San Francisco: Holden-Day.

Cochrane, W.W. 1980. Some nonconformist thoughts on welfare economics and commodity price stabilization. *American Journal of Agricultural Economics* 62:508–511.

Fair, R.C., and Taylor, J.B. 1983. Solution and maximum likelihood estimation of dynamic non-linear rational expectations models. *Econometrica* 51:1169–1185.

Friedman, B.M. 1979. Optimal expectations and the extreme information assumptions of "rational expectations macromodels." *Journal of Monetary Economics* 5:23–41.

Green, C. 1983. Insulating countries against fluctuations in domestic production and exports. *Journal of Development Economics* 12:303–325.

Grisley, W., and Kellog, E.D. 1983. Farmers' subjective probabilities in northern Thailand: An elicitation analysis. *American Journal of Agricultural Economics* 65:74–82.

Hazell, P.B.R. 1982. Instability in Indian foodgrain production. Research Report No. 30, International Food Policy Research Institute, Washington, D.C.

Hazell, P.B.R., and Scandizzo, P.L. 1975. Market intervention policies when production is risky. *American Journal of Agricultural Economics* 57:641–649.

———. 1977. Farmers' expectations, risk aversion and market equilibrium under risk. *American Journal of Agricultural Economics* 59:204–209.

Ishii, Y. 1977. On the theory of the competitive firm under price uncertainty: Note. *American Economic Review* 67:768–769.

Just, R.E. 1975. Risk response models and their use in agricultural policy evaluation. *American Journal of Agricultural Economics* 57:836–843.

———. 1976. The welfare economics of agricultural risk. In *Market risks in agriculture: Concepts, methods and policy issues*. Department Technical Report No. 78-1, Texas Agricultural Experiment Station, pp. 1–19.

Lucas, R.E. 1976. Econometric policy evaluation: Critique. In K. Brunner and A.H. Meltzer, eds., *Phillips curve and labor market*. Carnegie-Rochester Conference Series on Public Policy, vol. 1. Supplementary Series to the *Journal of Monetary Economics*.

MacCallum, B.T. 1976. Rational expectations and the natural rate hypothesis: Some consistent estimates. *Econometrica* 44:43–52.

Massell, B.F. 1969. Price stabilization and welfare. *Quarterly Journal of Economics* 83:284–298.

———. 1970. Some welfare implications of international price stabilization. *Journal of Political Economy* 78:404–417.

Muth, J.F. 1961. Rational expectations and the theory of price movements. *Econometrica* 29:315–335.

Nerlov, M. 1956. Estimates of supply of selected agricultural commodities. *Journal of Farm Economics* 38:496–509.

———. 1958. *The dynamics of supply:: Estimation of farmers' response to price*. Baltimore, Md.: Johns Hopkins University Press.

Newbery, D.M.G., and Stiglitz, J.E. 1979. The theory of commodity price stabilization rules: Welfare impacts and supply responses. *The Economic Journal 89:* 799–817.

———. 1981. *The theory of commodity price stabilization.* Oxford: Clarendon Press.

Oi, W.Y. 1961. The desirability of price instability under perfect competition. *Econometrica 29:*58–64.

Reutlinger, S. 1976. A simulation model for evaluating worldwide buffer stocks of wheat. *American Journal of Agricultural Economics 58:*1–12.

Reutlinger, S.; Bigman, D.; and Eaton, D. 1976. Should developing countries carry grain reserves? In Eaton and Steel, eds., pp. 12–38.

Sandmo, A. 1971. On the theory of the competitive firm under price uncertainty. *American Economic Review 61:*65–73.

Sargent, T.J. 1973. Rational expectations, the real rate of interest and the natural rate of unemployment. *Brookings Papers of Economic Activity 2:*429–472.

Scandizzo, P.L.; Hazell, P.B.R.; and Anderson, J.R. 1980. Risky agricultural markets. Unpublished ms.

———. 1981. Risky agricultural markets. Unpublished ms.

Theil, H. 1966. *Applied economic forecasting.* Chicago: Rand McNally.

Turnovsky, S.J. 1974. Price expectations and the welfare gains from price stabilization. *American Journal of Agricultural Economics 56:*706–716.

Turnovsky, S.J.; Shalit, H.; and Schmitz, A. 1980. Consumers surplus, price instability, and consumer welfare. *Econometrica 48:*135–152.

Waugh, F.V. 1944. Does the consumer benefit from price instability? *Quarterly Journal of Economics 58:*602–614.

Yitzhaki, S. 1982. A tax programming model. *Journal of Public Economy 19:* 107–120.

3
Trade and Trade Policies under Instability

In the decade since the crisis of 1972–1974, world trade in food grains has undergone massive and very rapid changes. During these years, the volume of world trade in cereals has almost doubled, and its share in total production has continued to rise. From 1970–1971 to 1981–1982, wheat trade grew from 55 million metric tons (MMT) to 100 MMT, and its share in total wheat production rose from 17 to 23 percent. Trade in coarse grain grew during that period from 46 MMT to 103 MMT, and its share in production rose from 9 to 16 percent. Total volume of trade in cereals more than doubled, from 112 MMT to 232 MMT.

Cereals exports have increasingly concentrated in the five major exporters—the United States, Canada, Australia, Argentina, and France—which now dominate more than 90 percent of the trade. Cereals imports have substantially changed its destination. In the two decades from 1960 through 1979 the share of Eastern Europe in total imports has increased from 13 to 25 percent, the share of Western Europe has dropped from 40 to 20 percent, and the share of the LDCs has increased from 38 to 43 percent.

In the LDCs total cereal imports grew during the 1970s at an average annual rate of 9.1 percent, from 41 MMT in 1970 to 99 MMT in 1980. Their wheat imports grew from 26 MMT to 45 MMT, and their share in world trade in wheat rose from 46 to 52 percent. The lion's share of the increase was in the imports of middle-income countries, whose net cereal imports more than doubled during the 1970s while the imports of the low-income countries increased by only 22 percent. Table 3–1 summarizes these trends over the last two decades.

Together with these changes in the volume and directions of trade—and to some degree because of them—there has been a considerable increase in its variability and a dramatic rise in the variability of world prices of all cereals. The coefficient of variation of world price of wheat rose from 3.6 percent in the 1960s to 30 percent in the 1970s, and that of rice from 17.5 percent to 39 percent. United Nations Conference on Trade and Development (UNCTAD) study of sixty-three countries showed that food imports of the LDCs was especially unstable. Table 3–2 summarizes these results.

Table 3–1
Cereal Production and Trade: Main Economic Indicators

	Average Annual Growth Rates, Total Cereals, 1970–1980	
	Developing Countries	*Developed Countries*
Imports	9.1	5.4
Imports per capita	6.9	4.6
Production per capita	0.5	1.8

	Average Annual Growth Rates, Total Cereals, 1961/63–1981	
	Total Imports	*Imports per Capita*
Low-income LDCs[a]	0.5	−1.7
Middle-income LDCs[b]	6.8	4.5
High-income LDCs[c]	8.0	5.4
Total LDCs	6.1	3.7

	Distribution of Wheat Production Consumption and Trade, Average, 1970–1980			
	Production	*Consumption*	*Exports*	*Imports*
Developed	35	24	87	23
Developing	22	29	6	51
Centrally planned	43	47	7	26

Sources: T.K. Morrison, "An Analysis of Recent Trends and Determinant of Cereal Imports by Developing Countries," *Food Policy,* 1983; FAO, *Food Outlook,* 1981; FAD *Production Yearbook;* B. Huddleston, "Closing the Cereals Gap with Trade and Food Aid," International Food Policy Research Institute Research Report No. 43, Washington, D.C., 1984.

Note: 1978–1979 compared with average 1969–1970 through 1973–1974.

[a]Countries with per capita income above $900 in 1976–1978.

[b]Countries with per capita income between $300 and $900 in 1976–1978.

[c]Countries with per capita income less than $300 in 1976–1978.

Trying to explain the mounting instability in world trade, Abbott (1979) estimated the extent to which production fluctuations influence trade flows. In his study of thirty-three countries, he found, however, only a modest influence. Blandford and Schwartz (1983) found that for four out of the five major wheat exporters, the principal determinant of annual deviations from export trends was fluctuation in production. Imports were also found to be responsive to short-term fluctuations in domestic production. Blandford (1983) also found an inverse relationship between fluctuations in domestic production and net imports.

These findings, however, cannot explain the full extent of the instability in world trade of grains, for several reasons. First, instability in grain production has increased only marginally over the past decade. The Green Revolu-

Table 3-2
Import Instability Indexes for Wheat, Maize, and Rice, 1970–1980
(percentages)

	Volume			Value			Unit Value		
	Wheat	Maize	Rice	Wheat	Maize	Rice	Wheat	Maize	Rice
Developed Countries	2.0	5.9	8.6	17.4	19.2	14.8	18.2	13.8	19.2
Less-developed countries	7.4	8.4	9.9	29.6	20.0	13.6	21.7	14.9	20.2
Least developed	15.9	50.7	22.2	36.2	72.3	18.0	22.4	17.8	23.2
USSR and other Eastern European countries	13.0	22.0	6.2	14.8	31.7	26.6	11.9	12.7	26.4

Source: UNCTAD, "Instability in Food Trade and Its Impact on Food Security for Developing Countries," Trade and Development Board Report No. TD/B/C.1/235.

tion and the transition to more productive crop varieties that are at the same time more susceptible to weather variations has sometimes been blamed for the growing instability. Hazell (1983) showed some evidence for an increase in instability in India and in the United States. The modest increase that was found, however, cannot explain the extent of the instability in the volume of trade, let alone the wild price gyrations.

Second, production variations can be transmitted into variations in trade only if trade between countries is relatively free. Only then can price gaps resulting from shortfalls or excesses in production in any one country trigger flows of imports and exports as products gravitate to the highest-paying markets. In practice, however, not only is trade restricted, but a shortfall in production is often accompanied by a rise in the import price—due to a rise in the import tax—that moderates or even prevents the rise in imports and a bumper crop harvest is often accompanied by a fall in the export price for domestic producers—either because of equally good harvests in the other countries or, more likely, because of a rise in protection in the importing countries—that inhibits exports.

Third, the increase that has taken place in variability in the volume of world trade, however large, still cannot explain the wide fluctuations in prices. Blanford (1983) could not find a statistically significant relationship between the increase in variability of the volume of world trade and the sharp rise by 35 percent in the variability of wheat prices and by 65 percent in the variability of the prices of coarse grains. Even the upheavals in the world grains market in 1972–1974 cannot be explained by the changes in production alone. One widely held view is that the largest single factor behind the shortages in the world markets in 1973–1974 was the cutback in acreage since 1968. Indeed, the area sown to wheat by the three leading exporters (the United States, Canada, and Australia) fell from 45 million hectares in 1968 to 29 million in 1970. To be sure, the reduction in stocks during the early 1970s through the use of production controls in the United States and stock disposal (Project LIFT) in Canada did make the world market much more vulnerable to demand shocks. Nevertheless, the wheat purchases of the Soviet Union in 1972–1973 and the poor harvest in many developing countries cannot themselves explain the full extent of the turbulence in the world market that has caused prices to tripple in less than eighteen months.

Grennes, Johnson, and Thursby (1977 and 1978) have estimated that an extra supply of only 6 to 7 MMT could have prevented most of the rise in price. In another study (Johnson, Grennes, and Thursby 1977b) they could not find support to the argument raised by Schuh (1974) that the devaluation of the U.S. dollar with the collapse of the Bretton Woods exchange rate system was a significant factor in the rise in wheat prices.

It appears that the major factor responsible for the growing instability in world price, including the turbulence in 1972–1974, is the mounting intervention of governments in both developed and developing countries in agricultural trade in general and cereals trade in particular. D. Gale Johnson (1975) and Josling (1977) have emphasized the effects of trade restrictions on the increased instability in world markets. Shei and Thompson (1977) have demonstrated that as more countries prevent world price signals from being reflected across their borders into the domestic market through trade controls, the variability of the world market price has risen. Zwart and Meilke (1979) have shown that the destabilizing effects of these policies mean that small shocks in world supply are magnified because domestic demand and supply are not allowed to respond to the changes in the world price. Sarris and Freebairn (1983) estimated that with free trade the variability of the world price would have declined by 35 percent. Blandford and Schwartz (1983, p. 309) concluded that "the tendency towards a high degree of domestic market *insulation* coupled with substantial domestic transmission of instability is a major determinant of potential price variability."

The analysis in this chapter of the protection measures implemented by most importing countries over the period 1962–1981 show that there has been a vast increase in the extent to which countries varied the levies (or the subsidies) imposed on wheat in order to shield their consumers or producers from disturbances in the world markets or to export their own instability to other countries. In this analysis, the nominal protection coefficients for wheat have been estimated in thirty-nine countries (twenty-two LDCs, thirteen European, and four other importers) during the period 1968–1980. It is shown that there has been a three to four times increase in the *variability* of the protection rates since the mid-1970s, and these variations were significantly correlated with variations in the variability of the world price. Table 3–3 summarizes the aggregate results of this analysis.

The growing instability in world grain markets is particularly detrimental to the least developed countries. Many of these countries, especially those in sub-Saharan Africa have to rely increasingly on food imports since their population growth outstrips production. Having severe foreign-exchange constraints and limited access to the foreign-exchange markets, these countries are restricted in their capacity to finance their highly volatile food import bill and prevent the fluctuations in the world price from being transmitted into their own economy. When most cereal-importing and -exporting countries are making efforts to insulate their own economies in order to secure a stable flow of supply to their consumers and a stable price to their producers, any supply or demand shocks would have to be absorbed by those countries that are least capable of protecting their consumers and producers. Worse still, consumers in these countries are the most vulnerable to price hikes or supply shortages.

The ability of the poorest LDCs to finance their cereal imports is a significant constraint on the role of trade in reducing their food insecurity.

Table 3–3
Nominal Protection Coefficients for Main Groups of Countries, 1968–1980

	Importing Countries[a]			Exporting Countries[b]	World Price ($ per MT)
	LDCs	European Countries	All Countries		
Average NPC 1968–1980	1.09	1.28	1.24	0.81	125.3
(CV%)	(19.1)	(20.2)	(21.9)	(9.9)	(43.5)
Adjusted average NPC 1968–1980[c]	1.17	1.33	1.36	0.80	115.7
(CV%)	(12.1)	(15.2)	(14.8)	(7.6)	(45.0)
Average NPC 1968–1972	1.24	1.41	1.35	0.80	65.8
(CV%)	(4.5)	(7.4)	(4.4)	(8.5)	(5.2)
Average NPC 1975–1980	1.10	1.32	1.30	0.79	143.0
(CV%)	(13.8)	(16.2)	(15.9)	(7.6)	(16.7)

[a] A sample of the thirty-nine major importing countries.
[b] A weighted average of the NPCs on the United States, Canada, and Australia.
[c] Excluding 1973 and 1974.

Huddleston (1984) found that in a group of ninety-nine LDCs, in 1976–1978 one-third of the countries had food imports higher than 25 percent of their total food consumption. In thirty-two out of eighty-two countries the *maximum* ratio of cereal imports to total export earnings in the period 1961–1978 exceeded 10 percent; in ten countries it exceeded 25 percent. Their difficulties have worsened as a result of the stagnation of their export earnings in the late 1970s through the mid-1980s. Their import capacity has been further eroded by the simultaneous rise in the price of their other imports, notably energy prices. (For the group of LDCs as a whole, the energy import costs rose from $4.6 billion in 1970 to $56.3 billion in 1979.) Faced with shrinking revenues on the one hand and increasing food bills on the other, these countries may be forced to economize further on their food import bills and restrict consumption.

Recognizing the importance of trade and trade policies to internal stability and food security, attention in the recent literature has shifted from "traditional" stabilization schemes such as buffer stocks to the stabilizing effects of free trade and to the design of trade policies under instability. These issues are also the subject of this chapter. The first section sets the scene by determining the various effects of free trade under instability in a conventional two-country model. The emphasis in the section is on the lasting effects of purely random disturbances in the production of the two countries on the volume of trade, their balance of payments, their welfare and income distribution. The second section extends the analysis to a more complex log-linear-multiplicative-disturbances model and presents the results of some characteristic simulation experiments. So far, however, the model assumes risk-neutral producers and consumers. The third section allows for the response of risk-averse producers. The point of departure for the analysis in this section is the argument made by Newbery and Stiglitz (1981) that in a stochastic environment free trade can be Pareto-inferior to no trade. The section examines the range of parameters (the price elasticity of demand and supply and the degree of risk aversion) within which the argument is valid and examines the implications on the country's balance-of-payments position.

The fourth section carries the analysis to the design of trade policies. The point of departure is, again, the two countries conventional (linear-additive-disturbances) model, and the discussion is focused on the policy of variable levies. It examines the welfare, income distribution, trade, and budgetary effects of variable levies on both the country that imposes them and on its trading partner. The fifth section further extends the analysis to the more general model. The two sections show that even when free trade is Pareto-inferior to no trade, an appropriately designed trade policy can still be superior to no trade.

Finally, the sixth section presents the empirical analysis of the trade policies with respect to wheat in thirty-nine major importing countries, which together account for 95 percent of world wheat imports excluding those of the USSR and the four major exporting countries, which together account for 90 percent of world wheat exports. The section analyzes the levels and the variability of the nominal protection coefficients (NPCs) in these countries over the period 1968–1980. It clearly indicates that much of the increase in instability in the world wheat market should be attributed to the growing tendencies of most if not all importing countries to insulate their own economies from external shocks by varying their level of production. The end result of these trade and domestic policies would have to be much larger instability worldwide, from which all countries would eventually suffer.

Trade Creation under Instability: The Theory

Traditional trade theory has emphasized different factor abundance in countries, different factor intensities in production, different technologies, and different tastes in explaining the patterns of production and trade between countries. In a world marked by wide fluctuations in supply and demand, these fluctuations themselves trigger considerable trade flows, sometimes larger than those explained by the countries' permanent comparative advantage. In particular, a large portion of the world trade in agricultural commodities results from temporary shortfalls or excesses in production as an effect of unstable weather conditions. Countries that are normally self-sufficient in certain agricultural products may become net importers in some years and net exporters in others as an effect of variations in climatic conditions.

This section deals with the ex post effects of temporary aberrations in demand and supply. To focus on these effects, we assume at present that the economic agents are risk-neutral (or, alternatively, that a complete set of risk markets exists). Subsequently the discussion will be extended to include also the ex ante response of risk-averse producers and consumers to the attendant uncertainties (a subject that has been at the center of recent writings on international trade and payments). The present analysis is carried out in a simple partial equilibrium model, which will suffice, however, to illustrate some important consequences of trade under instability. (When appropriate, I will comment on the general equilibrium implications of these results). It is assumed, for simplicity, that the aberrations in supply and demand are purely random; that is, over the long run they cancel each other out.

Even under these simplifying assumptions, it is evident that the attendant instability is likely to have *lasting real* effects on the country's balance of payments and its internal income distribution. The reason is that even though a shortfall and an excess of the same magnitude would affect consumption and trade in opposing directions, the size of these effects would not be the same; thus they would not cancel each other out over the long run.

The basic argument that ties the lasting effects of purely random fluctuations to different supply and demand elasticities can be illustrated heuristically in a general equilibrium framework, via the familiar offer curves: In figure 3–1, country 1 is an exporter of product X and an importer of product Y; country 2 is an exporter of Y and an importer of X. R_0 denotes the offer curve of country 1 under stable production; R_1 and R_2 denote the offer curves of that country in years of excess and shortfall in production, respectively. R^* and R^{**} denote two possible offer curves of country 2, which differ only in their leftmost segment after their intersection with R_0. Excess production in country 1 worsens the country's terms of trade, whereas a shortage improves them. If these two events occur at the same frequency, their long-term effects would depend crucially on the demand elasticity for imports in country 2. Under the more elastic curve R^{**}, both imports and exports would rise in a year of excess production, though at a rate that may differ substantially from that at which they fall in a year of production shortfall. Under the less elastic curve R^*, the deterioration in the country's terms of trade in a year of excess production may actually *lower* its imports (and, in extreme cases, even its exports). When the trade flows created are summarized over a long

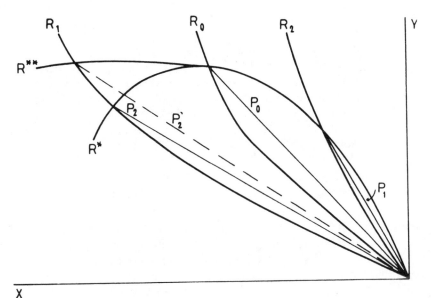

Figure 3–1. Determination of Exports and Imports under Instability

sequence of shortfalls and excesses, the result would thus depend on the demand elasticity for imports in country 2.

Consider now a partial-equilibrium model of a given sector consisting of the following linear demand and supply equations for the home country:

$$D(P) = c - dP + v \tag{3.1}$$

$$S(P) = a + bP + u \tag{3.2}$$

and, for the foreign country:

$$D^*(P^*) = c^* - d^*P^* + v^* \tag{3.2}$$

$$S^*(P^*) = a^* + b^*P^* + u^* \tag{3.4}$$

The disturbances in supply and demand are purely random, uncorrelated across countries or time with $E(u^2) = \sigma_u^2$, $E(v^2) = \sigma_v^2$, $E(u,v) = 0$, $E(u) = 0$, $E(v) = 0$ for the home and the foreign countries.[1]

In the absence of trade, the market clearing price in the home country is given by

$$P = \bar{P} + \frac{v - u}{e} \tag{3.5}$$

where $\bar{P}$ is the expected price and $e = b + d$. The two countries under consideration are assumed to be self-sufficient in the product, in the sense that in a normal year—that is, one with no random disturbances—there is no price differential between the two countries and thus no trade. Disregarding transportation costs for the time being, self-sufficiency thus implies $\bar{P} = \bar{P}^*$. When the countries are opened to trade, the world market clearing price, denoted by P^T, is given by

$$P^T = \bar{P} + \frac{V - U}{E} \tag{3.6}$$

where $V = v + v^*$, $U = u + u^*$, and $E = e + e^*$.

As an effect of trade, both countries may (though not in all cases) enjoy a greater stability. To see this, calculate the variance of the price in the closed economy, yielding

$$\text{Var}(P) = \frac{\sigma_u^2 + \sigma_v^2}{e^2} \tag{3.7}$$

and the variance of the world price under free trade, yielding

$$\text{Var}(P^T) = \frac{\Sigma^2}{E^2} \tag{3.8}$$

where $\Sigma^2 = \sigma_u^2 + \sigma_v^2 + \sigma_u^{*2} + \sigma_v^{*2}$, and $E = e + e^*$.

It can be verified that in the case of n trading countries, the variance of the world price is given by

$$\text{Var}(P^T) = \sum_{i=1}^{n} (\sigma_{u_i}^2 + \sigma_{v_i}^2) / \left(\sum_{i=1}^{n} e_i\right)^2$$

where subscript i denotes the country. The latter can also be written as

$$\text{Var}(P^T) = \sum_{i=1}^{n} e_i^2 \cdot \text{Var}(P_i) / \left(\sum_{i=1}^{n} e_i\right)^2$$

Hence the variance of the world price is a weighted *sum* of the variances of the closed countries' prices, which add up to *less* than the weighted averages of these variances. In that sense, international trade can be regarded as a risk-pooling arrangement that works to stabilize the price. As the number of trading countries increases, the variance of the world price decreases; as n approaches infinity, $\text{Var}(P_T)$ decreases to zero. Nevertheless, for a finite number of trading countries, it is possible that one of the countries will experience *larger* rather than smaller price instability under free trade than under no trade.

We now turn to the balance-of-payments implications of random aberrations in supply and demand. In a normal year we assume that there is no price differential between the two countries, and thus no trade. Uncorrelated random fluctuations in supply or in demand, however, may create price gaps in certain years that would provide an incentive for trade, allowing commodities to gravitate to the highest-paying market and thereby equalizing the price across all markets. In the present model, where all demand and supply equations are linear and the random disturbances are symmetrically distributed with zero mean and no correlation across countries or time, the *physical* volume of the trade flows would even out. Nonetheless, there would still be lasting effects on the balance of payments. In the home country, the trade balance of the product under consideration is given by

$$B = P^T[D(P^T) - S(P^T)] \tag{3.9}$$

and, therefore, on average (assuming that the country is normally self-sufficient, so that $D(\bar{P}) = S(\bar{P})$,

$$E(B) = \frac{e^*}{E^2}(\sigma_u^2 + \sigma_v^2) - \frac{e}{E^2}(\sigma_u^{*2} + \sigma_v^{*2})$$

$$= \frac{e \cdot e^*}{E^2}[e \cdot \mathrm{Var}(P) - e^* \cdot \mathrm{Var}(P^*)] \qquad (3.10)$$

Hence, even under purely random disturbances, one of the countries is likely to become a net importer and the other a net exporter of that product. In other words, these random disturbances are likely to generate trade and financial flows that will have real and lasting effects, turning a normally self-sufficient country into a net borrower or lender on this account. Whether the country becomes a net borrower or a net lender as an effect of instability depends on the degree of instability, on the corresponding supply and demand elasticities, and on its share in total demand for the product. Specifically,

$$E(B) > 0 \quad \Leftrightarrow \quad \frac{\Theta^* \cdot (\epsilon^* + \eta^*)}{\Theta(e + \eta)} > \frac{\sigma_u^{*2} + \sigma_v^{*2}}{\sigma_u^2 + \sigma_v^2}$$

where ϵ and η denote the price elasticities of supply and demand, respectively, at the mean price; Θ denotes the share of the country's demand in total world demand at the mean price; and asterisks denote the foreign country. With n trading countries, the balance of trade of the jth country is given by

$$E(B_j) = \sum_{i=1}^{n} \frac{e_i \cdot e_j}{\left(\sum_{i=1}^{n} e_i\right)^2} [e_j \cdot \mathrm{Var}(P_j) - e_i \cdot \mathrm{Var}(P_i)]$$

and

$$E(B_j) > 0 \quad \Leftrightarrow \quad \sum_{i=1}^{n} \frac{\Theta_i(\eta_i + \epsilon_i)}{\Theta_j(\eta_j + \epsilon_i)} > \sum_{i=1}^{n} \frac{(\sigma_{ui}^2 + \sigma_{vi}^2)}{(\sigma_{uj}^2 + \sigma_{vj}^2)}$$

In more general cases, our earlier analysis via the offer curves and our simulation analysis in the following sections with more general, nonlinear, multiplicative-disturbances models, suggest that the random fluctuations are likely to change the *physical* volume of trade as well.

To examine the general equilibrium implications of these results, we assume that the home country has traditional exports—say, ores—and traditional imports—say, machinery—and that in a normal year the country is self-sufficient in the product under consideration—say, food grains. Temporary shortfalls in the domestic production of food grains need not force the country to adjust its traditional imports and exports in order to afford the additional imports of food grains. If the international financial markets are sufficiently developed, the country can mobilize the foreign exchange needed from financial intermediaries and have the debt repaid in the years in which food grain is exported.[2] Furthermore, if food grains are neither substitutes nor complements to the country's traditional exports and imports, no adjustments would be made in the demand for these two products as an effect of the temporary fluctuations in the price of food grains.[3] Also, if producers are risk-neutral, as we assume at this stage, no adjustments would be made in production as a result of the instability.

Suppose the country becomes a net borrower on its food grains foreign-exchange account. The emerging deficit would force the country to forego some of its traditional imports and/or increase its traditional exports in order to finance its long-term food deficit. This in turn would worsen the country's terms of trade, and thus be detrimental to the economy as a whole. The opposite would happen if the country became a net lender on its food grains account.

Now let us relax the assumption that the local demand for the country's traditional export or import goods is invariant to changes in the price of food grains. Specifically, let us assume the country's traditional imports include products that can substitute for food grains (wheat and rice, where wheat is imported, can be one example). A temporary rise in the price of food grains would thus increase the demand for the country's traditional imports and, therefore also change their price and worsen the country's terms of trade. The opposite would happen in the event of a temporary drop in the price of food grains. The instability existing in the demand for and supply of food grains would therefore also destabilize the price of the country's traditional imports (or exports) and its terms of trade. Whether these variations in the price would even out over time, and to what extent they are likely to have lasting effects on the country's balance of payments, would depend largely on the corresponding parameters.

The instability introduced to the price of substitutes and complements of food grains through the response of consumers is likely to affect producers of these other products also. These indirect effects need to be reckoned with in evaluating trade policies and stabilization schemes in food grains.

Finally, we calculate the net welfare gains of the various sectors from trade. Note that these gains or losses are not the ordinary gains discussed in trade theory, which result from specialization according to the country's lasting relative advantage. Instead, these gains result from the option open to the country to buffer supply shortages or price fluctuations via trade. The analysis of the welfare gains or losses to the different sectors in the partial-equilibrium framework is carried out via the ordinary consumer's and producer's surplus. Producers' gains are given by

$$G_P^T = \frac{1}{2}[S(P^T) + S(P)](P^T - P) \tag{3.11}$$

where G_P^T denotes the gains of producers from trade. By inserting equations 3.5 and 3.6 into the supply function 3.2, together with the assumption that $P = P^°$, we can thus calculate the expected gains of producers from trade, given by

$$E\left(G_P^T\right) = \frac{1}{2}\left[\frac{b}{E^2}\Sigma^2 - \frac{b}{e^2}(\sigma_v^2 + \sigma_u^2)\right] + \frac{e^°}{eE}\cdot\sigma_u^2$$

$$= \frac{b}{2}[\text{Var}(P^T) - \text{Var}(P)] + \frac{e^°}{e\cdot E}\cdot\sigma_u^2 \qquad (3.12)$$

Hence producers in the home country may *lose* from trade if the variability of the domestic price under trade is smaller than that in the closed economy— that is, if trade indeed stabilizes the domestic market. This, however, is only a necessary but not a sufficient condition. Consumers' gains from trade, denoted by G_C^T, are given by

$$G_C^T = -\frac{1}{2}[D(P^T) + D(P)](P^T - P) \qquad (3.13)$$

Their expected gains from trade are therefore given by

$$E\ G_C^T = \frac{1}{2}\left[\frac{d}{E^2}\Sigma^2 - \frac{d}{e^2}(\sigma_v^2 + \sigma_u^2)\right] + \frac{e^°}{e\cdot E}\cdot\sigma_v^2$$

$$= \frac{d}{2}[\text{Var}(P^T) - \text{Var}(P)] + \frac{e^°}{e\cdot E}\cdot\sigma_v^2 \qquad (3.14)$$

Again, consumers may (but will not necessarily) *lose* from trade if it stabilizes the domestic market. In other words, the larger the price instability prior to trade, the more likely it is that either producers or consumers (but not both, as we shall see) would lose from trade. If, for instance, the domestic price variability is due only to instability in supply, then consumers would lose but producers gain from trade. Total welfare gains from trade denoted G_E^T are given by

$$G_E^T = G_P^T + G_C^T$$

and therefore

$$E \quad G_P^T = \frac{1}{2}\left[\frac{e}{E^2}\Sigma^2 - \frac{1}{e^2}(\sigma_v^2 + \sigma_u^2)\right] + \frac{e^*}{eE}(\sigma_v^2 + \sigma_u^2)$$

$$= \frac{e \cdot e^{*2}}{2E}[\text{Var}(P^*) + \text{Var}(P)] > 0$$

Hence the economy at large always gains from trade, and these gains are larger the larger the degree of instability in the two trading countries prior to free trade.

The gains to the country at large from ex post opportunities for trade are, however, well in line with traditional trade theory, since trade occurs in this model whenever autarkic prices differ in the home country from those in the rest of the world. In other words, in a stochastic environment as well as in a static one, international trade generates gains by coordinating prices where, under instability, the coordination is redetermined at each and every period in time. Under risk neutrality, trade generates gains by allowing the country to maximize its ex post real income, even when it in fact destabilizes its price. This conclusion may, however, change under more realistic assumptions that producers and consumers are risk-averse and respond to the increase in instability by reducing their output. This issue will be discussed further in subsequent sections.

Trade Creation and the Effects of Trade under Instability: Some Simulation Illustrations

The simulation analysis in this section illustrates the main results of the previous section in a more complex and thus perhaps a more realistic model. The details of the model are given in chapter 2. It is still a partial-equilibrium model. Supply and demand are assumed now to be log-linear-constant-elasticity with multiplicative disturbances. Consumers and producers are still assumed to be risk-neutral. It should be noted, however, that any change in the price *distribution* and, in particular, in the mean price as a result of the policy under consideration is taken into account with the assumption of rational expectations (see Newbery-Stiglitz 1981, section 5.1). To keep the discussion as general as possible and avoid reference to any specific crop or country, all prices and quantities are normalized to be 100 at their mean, and financial magnitudes are expressed as percentages of total expenditures on the product in a normal (stable) year. Following are some further details on the structure and the specific parameters of the model in the present analysis.

1. The analysis is carried for three different demand elasticities in the country: 0.25, 0.75, and 1.5.

2. Supply elasticity is assumed to be 0.25.
3. The sources of instability are multiplicative random disturbances in supply in both the country and the world. The coefficient of variation of the country's production is assumed to be 9 percent and of the world's production 7 percent.
4. Price elasticity of demand in the world is assumed to be 0.5.
5. Trade between the country and the world is triggered by price differentials between the FOB export price or the CIF import price and the internal price. Initially, however, no transport costs will be assumed.
6. We consider both a small country, whose excess demand or supply does not affect the world price, and a large country, which would have such an effect.
7. We consider both a *self-sufficient* country, which in a normal year would have no trade; an *exporting* country, which is 150 percent self-sufficient; and an *importing* country, which is 50 percent self-sufficient.
8. In the sensitivity analysis we examine also other values of some of the key parameters and consider also the possibility of correlation between disturbances in the country and in the world.

Table 3–4 presents the direct extensions of the linear model of the previous section to a log-linear (constant-elasticity) multiplicative-disturbances model of a self-sufficient country for different demand elasticities, ignoring for the time being the transport costs. The results show that a substantial *volume* of trade is generated by the instability in production, and this volume is larger, the higher the price elasticity of demand in the country. For a price elasticity of 1.5, the combined volume of imports and exports would be on average almost 20 percent of the country's total annual production. The income-distribution effects are also quite sensitive to the magnitude of the price elasticity of demand. Consumers would, on average, gain from trade that stabilizes domestic supply. Their gains would, however, be significant only when demand is very inelastic, but would be almost negligible even for an elasticity of 0.75. Producers, on the other hand, would *lose* from trade when demand is highly inelastic but increasingly *gain* when demand becomes more elastic. As anticipated, the economy as a whole would always gain from trade. Similar gains would be recorded for importing and exporting countries.

Simulation results for a country that is, on average, 50 percent self-sufficient (not reported in table 3–4) show that when the demand elasticity is 0.25, its overall gains from trade under instability would be 7 percent higher than the welfare gains registered in a comparative static analysis. Its gains under instability would be 22 percent higher than the static gains when the demand elasticity is 1.5. For an exporting country that is 150 percent self-sufficient, the overall gains from trade would be 15 percent higher under

Table 3–4
Trade Creation and the Gains under Instability in a Self-Sufficient Small Country

	Demand Elasticity		
	0.25	*0.75*	*1.5*
Trade Creation			
Exports[a]	3.5	5.3	8.8
Imports[a]	3.6	5.7	10.7
Balance of Trade[b]	0.3	1.5	1.7
Gains from Trade			
Consumers[b]	+ 5.6	+ 0.1	+ 0.2
Producers[b]	– 3.4	+ 1.2	+ 1.9
Economy[b]	+ 2.2	+ 1.3	+ 2.1

[a]Expressed as percentage of total production in a normal year.
[b]Expressed as percentage of annual expenditures on the product in a normal year.

instability than it gains under stable productions when the demand elasticity is 0.25, and 37 percent higher when the demand elasticity is 1.5.

To add an extra dose of reality to the analysis, we add transportation costs and examine the trade flows for different country cases. The transport costs are assumed to be 15 percent of the normal world price, thus creating a wedge of 30 percent between the FOB and the CIF prices. These results are summarized in table 3–5.

The presence of correlation in price fluctuations between the country and the world would markedly reduce the volume of trade. Such correlation can be related to correlated weather conditions or to the effects of a large country whose internal price fluctuations spill over to the rest of the world.

Table 3–6 summarizes the expected economic gains from trade and their distribution among consumers and producers for the different countries under consideration.

It shows that the distribution of these country's gains from trade is highly sensitive to the specific parameters. Thus, for example, the more stable the country without trade, the larger the gains of producers and the losses of consumers.

Finally, table 3–7 examines some stability effects of trade under different price elasticities. Two conclusions are noteworthy. First, the higher the price elasticity of demand in the country, the smaller the domestic instability without trade and the smaller, therefore, the stabilizing effects of international trade. When the price elasticity is 1.5, free trade actually *destabilizes* domestic price and supply. Second, more stable prices may actually increase the instability of farmers' income, and that may have adverse effects on production if they are risk-averse. We shall return to this issue in the next section.

Table 3–5
Trade Creation under Instability for Different Self-Sufficient Country Cases

	Trade Creation[a]		
	Exports	Imports	Balance of Trade
Free trade[b]	2.3	2.0	+ 0.2
Trade with correlation in production[c]	1.3	1.3	− 0.4
Large country[d]	1.3	1.3	− 0.5
More stable world[e]	1.9	1.9	− 0.4
More stable country[f]	0.8	1.2	+ 0.4
More elastic demand[g]	2.7	1.3	+ 2.0

[a]Volume of trade as percentage of total annual expenditures on food grains.
[b]Price elasticity of demand in the country is 0.3.
[c]A correlation coefficient (R^2) of 30 percent between the country's and the world's productions.
[d]Trade takes place between two equal trading countries.
[e]Coefficient of variation of world production is 4 percent against 7 percent in the base case.
[f]Coefficient of variation of country production is 5 percent against 9 percent in the base case.
[g]Price elasticity of demand in the country is 1.5 against 0.3 in the base case.

Table 3–6
Expected Economic Gains From Trade
(expressed as percentage of annual expenditures in a normal year)

	Consumers	Producers	Economy
Free trade[a]	+ 0.6	+ 0.3	+ 0.9
Trade with correlation in production[b]	+ 1.2	− 0.6	+ 0.6
Large country[c]	+ 1.1	− 0.7	+ 0.4
More stable world[d]	+ 1.4	− 0.6	+ 0.8
More stable country[e]	− 0.5	+ 0.7	+ 0.2
More elastic demand[f]	− 0.9	+ 1.2	+ 0.3

[a]Price elasticity of demand in the country is 0.3.
[b]A correlation coefficient (R^2) of 30 percent between the country's and the world's productions.
[c]Trade takes place between two equal trading countries.
[d]Coefficient of variation of world production is 4 percent against 7 percent in the base case.
[e]Coefficient of variation of country production is 5 percent against 9 percent in the base case.
[f]Price elasticity of demand in the country is 1.5 against 0.3 in the base case.

Table 3–7
The Stabilizing Effects of Trade under Different Demand Elasticities
(percent)

	Elasticity					
	0.25		*0.75*		*1.5*	
	No Trade	*Free Trade*	*No Trade*	*Free Trade*	*No Trade*	*Free Trade*
Price variability (CV%)	39	16	12	11	6	8
Supply variability (CV%)	9	4	9	8	9	11
Supply risk[a]	11	—	12	9	12	16
Variability of farmers income (CV%)	29	13	3	9	3	9

[a]Probability that supply falls by more than 10 percent below the normal supply.

Trade Instability and Uncertainty

So far we have assumed that both producers and consumers are risk-neutral. Even for risk-averse producers and consumers, the risks associated with production and price instability can be avoided if there are adequate insurance markets. Newbery and Stiglitz (1979, p. 6) have pointed out, however, that

> the absence of complete set of risk markets which are required for the optimality of the market equilibrium is a sufficiently important market failure to cast serious doubt on the usefulness of the perfect market hypothesis for policy purposes, at least where the central policy concern is with the allocation of risk bearing.

In the developing countries, financial and insurance markets are mostly absent. In the agricultural sector in particular, costly and asymmetric information, disincentives resulting from an insurance arrangement (moral hazard) for the use of fertilizers and pest prevention, and the immanent covariance of risks all lead to the failure of insurance markets (see Binswanger and Rosenzweig 1983).

With risk aversion and incomplete risk markets, Newbery and Stiglitz have shown (chapter 23) that *free trade may be Pareto-inferior to no trade*. This result is so intriguing and important, especially in the present context, that I would like to present the main thrust of their argument in some detail.

In their specific illustration Newbery and Stiglitz consider farmers producing two crops. The production of one is unstable, that of the other completely stable. They also assume that the demand functions have *unitary* price elasticity. In a closed economy that would mean that farmers' income is always stable, as any rise or fall in output is exactly compensated by a movement of the price in the opposite direction. With the opening of trade, prices are stabilized—partly or entirely—and price variations no longer offset the output variations. As a result, the income derived from the unstable crop becomes stochastic under free trade, but mean income remains unchanged, so that farmers are motivated to shift production away from the risky crop. This shift would not raise, however, the average price of that crop because the excess demand can be met by imports. Farmers, therefore, become worse off with trade. The question ramains, however, how general this conclusion is and to what extent it depends on the specific values of the elasticities. We will examine this question later.

Figure 3–2 shows the variability of farmers' income calculated in the simulation experiments with log-linear (constant-elasticity) demand and supply functions in closed and open economies, and for different price elasticities of demand. (Instability in the open economy is partly a result of the instability in world production, which is assumed here to be equal to that in the country. (See the preceding section for the other parameters of the model.)) It shows that under a fairly wide range of price elasticities—approximately above 0.6—income fluctuations with trade are larger than those with no trade. The partial-equilibrium model ignores, however, the possibility of substituting the unstable for the stable crop. At lower demand elasticities—below 0.6— farmers would tend to shift to the stable crop more rapidly in the closed than in the open economy. In the closed economy, however, the shift would

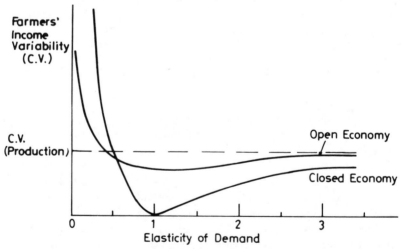

Figure 3–2. **Variability of Farmers' Income under Different Demand Elasticities in Closed and Open Economies**

prompt, at this elasticity range, a more than equiproportional rise in price, thus *raising* farmers' mean income and consequently moderating the pace of the shift to the stable crop. In the open economy, the price in the small country would not be affected by this shift, and the substitution of the risky for the stable crop would reflect the farmers' degree of risk aversion.

For low price elasticities of demand for the unstable crop and a unitary elasticity for the stable one, farmers' income would therefore be *less* stable but, on average, *higher* in the closed than in the open economy. It is not certain, therefore, that farmers would indeed be better off with trade, and the answer depends on their subjective preferences (but also on the other parameters of the model). The share of the unstable crop in total production would be higher in the closed than in the open economy. These shifts in production will affect also the balance of payments. At higher price elasticities for the unstable crop—above 0.6 but less than unity—farmers' income is likely to be both higher (as an effect of the substitution) and more stable in the closed economy. For demand elasticity larger than 1, the shift away from the risky crop in the closed economy would be smaller than that in the open economy because the income variability would be smaller. The shift would, however, lower farmers' average income in the closed economy despite the compensating rise in the average price. Nevertheless, the fall in farmers' mean income would still be smaller in the closed than in the open economy.

Figure 3–3 shows that variability of the price in closed and open economies. As mentioned earlier in this chapter, the stabilizing effects of free trade

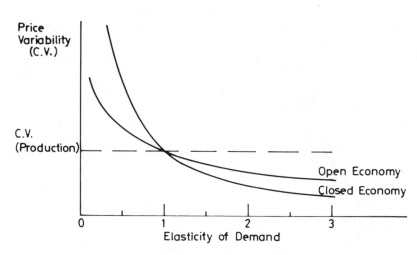

Figure 3–3. Price Variability under Different Demand Elasticities in Closed and Open Economies

depend not only on the supply variability in the country but also on the demand and supply elasticities and on the variability of the world price. In the model under consideration, trade increases price stability in the country only for demand elasticities less than 1. For higher elasticities the *closed* economy proved to be the more stable one. Thus not only is the price less stable in the open economy for higher price elasticity, but so is farmers' income. In the open economy the price fluctuations do not contribute to stabilizing farmers' income, since they may no longer be inversely related to domestic supply fluctuations as they are in the closed economy. Price movements in the open economy therefore need not compensate for the movements in output, as they always do in a closed economy.

The results in the two figures lead to the following conclusions:

1. For price elasticties of demand greater than or equal to 1, both consumers and producers are better off without trade than with free trade.
2. For price elasticities less than 1 and greater than (approximately) 0.6, producers are better off with free trade but consumers are worse off.
3. For price elasticities less than 0.6, consumers are better off with free trade. Producers are also likely to be worse off, given the very special assumptions on the stable and the unstable products.

This, however, may not be the case if the resulting increase in producers' income more than compensates them—given their subjective preferences—for the increase in income instability with free trade. For demand elasticity equal to 1, Newbery and Stiglitz proved (proposition 3, p. 345) that farmers are always worse off with free trade, and (proposition 1, p. 343) that they would shift resources from the risky to the riskfree crop. Our simulation analysis, with a model quite similar to that of Newbery and Stiglitz but for different levels of demand elasticities, shows that their conclusion that trade can be Pareto-inferior to autarky applies only to higher demand elasticities (above 0.6). At lower demand elasticities, free trade is still likely to be Pareto-superior to autarky. If, in addition the price elasticity of demand for the stable crop (say, cash crop) is more than 1, then the shift away from the risky crop to the stable one may actually raise their total mean income, and producers as well as the economy at large are more likely to gain from free trade at this elasticity range. (If, in contrast, the price elasticity of demand for the stable crop is *less* than 1, a shift into this crop may actually lower their total mean income, despite the rise in their income from the risky crop, and producers would then be more likely to lose from free trade even at low elasticities.)

The bottom line of all this analysis is that the question whether or not free trade is indeed Pareto-inferior to autarky is essentially an empirical one, and the answer is quite sensitive to the specific parameters of the crops under consideration.

Let us now examine the output, welfare, and balance-of-payments consequences of opening the economy to free trade in a partial equilibrium model when risk-averse producers respond to the change in risk by changing their output. The analysis is carried out via simulation analysis with the model detailed in chapter 2, and the parameter values given in the second section of this chapter, except that the supply function in the country now includes a shift parameter proportional to the variability of farmers' income that reflects producers' risk aversion. The supply function thus has the following form:

$$\log S_t = \alpha + \beta \log P_t^{exp} - \gamma \log R_t + v_t$$

where P_t^{exp} is the expected price at time t, calculated as detailed in chapter 2 and R is a risk factor, measured by the coefficient of variation of farmers' *incomes* over the past nine years. The risk-response elasticity γ is assumed to have the value 0.5 (see chapter 2 for the details of this functional form).

Figure 3–4 describes the quantity produced under risk-response for different demand elasticities and in closed and open economies (expressed as percentages of the stable production). The results reflect both the price and the risk effects. Thus, for instance, when demand elasticity is 0.5, the domestic price is 107.5 in the closed economy (that is, 7.5 percent above the stable price), and 103.9 in the open economy. As a result, production in the closed economy is slightly higher than that in the open economy even though income variability is still 15 percent higher in the closed economy. Obviously this result is sensitive to the assumed price elasticity of supply and the degree of risk aversion.

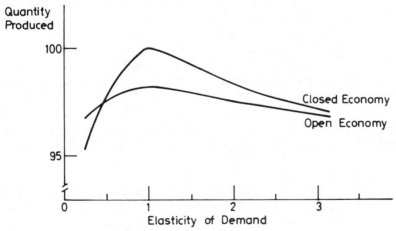

Figure 3–4. Quantity Produced under Risk Response in Closed and Open Economies

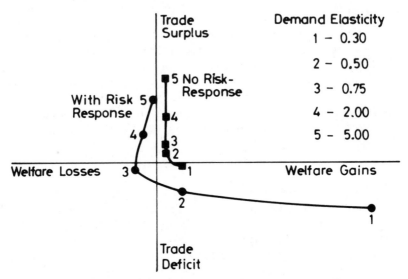

Figure 3–5. Gains from Trade and Trade Deficit under Different Demand Elasticities

Finally, figure 3–5 describes the gains from trade and the trade deficit for different demand elasticities. It shows that although at high price elasticities of demand the economy would suffer welfare losses from free trade, it would have, however, on average, a large trade surplus on this account that would be larger the larger the demand elasticity. Hence, despite the welfare losses from trade, there may still be an incentive, related to the countries' foreign-exchange position, that makes trade desirable.

We conclude this section by examining the trade and welfare effects of free trade in the different self-sufficient countries that were considered in the preceding section, taking into account the response of risk-averse producers to the income risks. The price elasticity of demand in the country is assumed to be 0.3, and the risk-response elasticity is assumed to be 0.5. Earlier we saw that with this value of the demand elasticity, the variability of farmers' income would be higher under autarky than under free trade, and producers would lose from free trade although the price becomes more stable. Consumers, however, gain from the reduction in both the average price and its variability. These gains and the resulting trade flows are presented in table 3–8.

Several results stand out. First, as planned production of the risky crops declines, imports would rise and exports fall because of the risk response. Thus, for instance, with free trade there is a trade *surplus* equal to 0.2 of the annual expenditures under risk neutrality (or complete insurance markets), but a trade *deficit* equal to 2.7 percent under risk aversion. Second, the risk-

Table 3–8
Trade Creation and the Gains from Trade under Instability and Risk-Response in Different Self-Sufficient Countries

	Free Trade[b]	Trade with Correlation in Production[c]	Large Country[d]
Trade Creation[a]			
Exports	1.2	0.5	0.8
Imports	3.6	2.7	2.2
Balance of trade	− 2.7	− 2.8	− 2.1
Economic Gains			
Consumers	+ 6.3	+ 5.5	+ 4.3
Producers	− 5.1	− 3.7	− 3.7
Economy	+ 1.2	+ 1.8	+ 0.6

[a]See footnotes in table 3.5.

response gains or losses, associated with the reduction in planned output, outweigh by far the transfer gains due to the price adjustment and income transfers resulting from opening the economy to free trade. Although the *total* net welfare gains from free trade are only 0.3 to 1.2 percentage points higher under risk aversion than under risk neutrality, the changes in income distribution are quite substantial. Under free trade, producers lose from both the fall in price and the reduction in planned output, despite the decrease in risk, an amount equal to 5.1 percent of total annual expenditures on the crop, compared with net gains of 0.3 percent under risk neutrality. Consumers' gains are 6.3 percent under risk aversion and 0.6 percent only under risk neutrality.

Although the analysis in the section strengthens the result of Newbery and Stiglitz—that free trade can be, in certain cases, Pareto-inferior to autarky—countries should be careful in choosing a policy of self-sufficiency and autarky. In their subsequent analysis, Newbery and Stiglitz prove that *some* trade, albeit restricted, will be a Pareto improvement over both autarky and free trade. The question that confronts the analyst and the policymaker is, therefore: What *should* be the country's trade policy? What restrictions, if any, should be imposed? These questions are examined in the remainder of this chapter.

The Theory of Variable Levies and Stabilizing Trade Policies

Our starting point for the analysis of variable levies is the simple, partial-equilibrium linear model presented in the first section. The main distinction between the present analysis and the one put forward by Waugh, Oi, and Massell is that in their model stabilization is achieved by buffer stocks, whereas here it is achieved by trade. As a consequence, in the Waugh-Oi-Massell model the costs of stabilization are ignored, whereas in the present model these costs, which equal the government's net subsidy payments on imports or exports, are taken into account.[4]

The model is still a two-country model, although extensions to any number of countries are straightforward. The international market clearing price is determined in a Cournot oligopoly fashion in the sense that an individual country does not take into account the possible reaction of its trading partners to any policy action the country may decide to take.

We examine first the extreme but analytically more tractable case of complete stabilization and conclude the section by examining the more general case of partial stabilization.

Complete Stabilization

The principle of the policy are straightforward: If the free market price (which, in the absence of transportation costs, is simply the world price) falls below the target stable price, imports are taxed or exports subsidized in order to raise the price to the target level. If, on the other hand, the free-market price rises above the stable price, imports are subsidized or exports taxed in order to lower the domestic price to the target level. The detailed policy rules are listed in table 3–9, in reference to the random events illustrated in figure 3–6.

Suppose now that the foreign country is the one that stabilizes its price at the mean. The international market clearing equation becomes

$$D(P^{ST}) - S(P^{ST}) = S^*(\bar{P}) - D^*(\bar{P}) \qquad (3.15)$$

where superscript ST denotes the stabilizing trade policy and starred variables denote the foreign country. For the model described in equations 3.1–3.4, we can solve the international market price, given by

$$P^{ST} = \bar{P} + \frac{V - U}{e} \qquad (3.16)$$

where, as before, $V = v + v^*$, $U = u + u^*$, v and u being the random disturbances in demand and supply, respectively; and $e = b + d$, b and d being the slopes of the supply and demand schedules, respectively.

The tax-cum-subsidy rate in the foreign country is thus given by

$$t = \bar{P} - P^{ST} = -\frac{V - U}{e}$$

Table 3–9
Policy Rules of National Stabilization Schemes with Trade by Reference to Events Shown in Figure 3–6

Random Event		
Country's Production	World Price	Policy Rules
Q1	P1	Subsidy of $(P1 - \bar{P})$ to imports
Q1	P2	Tax of $(\bar{P} - P2)$ on imports
Q2	P1	Tax of $(P1 - \bar{P})$ on exports
Q2	P2	Subsidy of $(\bar{P} - P2)$ to exports

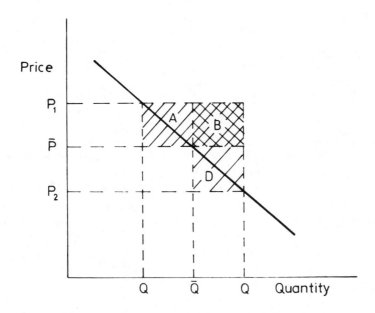

Figure 3–6. Completely Stabilizing Trade Policy: Tariff and Subsidy Rules

This policy has the form of "leaning against the wind," whereby the government does not attempt to affect the long-run average price but prevents any random fluctuations in the current year's price. The policy is therefore of the feedback type in the sense that the tax-cum-subsidy rates in each year depend on the realization of the current year's values of the stochastic disturbances u_t, v_t, u_t^*, and v_t^*. The variability in world demands and supplies is thus shifted in its entirety to the home country, and the variance of its market price becomes

$$\text{Var}(P^{ST}) = \Sigma^2 / e^2 \tag{3.17}$$

where, as before, $\Sigma^2 = (\sigma_u^2 + \sigma_v^2 + \sigma_u^{*2} + \sigma_v^{*2})$. This variance is larger than that both under free trade and in a closed economy. Variable levies thus enable the foreign country to export its own instability to its trading partners, and on these grounds this policy can appropriately be termed one of "destabilize thy neighbor" (see Bigman 1982, chap. 6). Nevertheless, if producers and consumers in the home country are risk-neutral, the home country is not necessarily worse off as a result of this policy of the foreign country, as we shall see.

The balance of trade between the two countries can be summarized by

$$B^* = [D^*(\bar{P}) - S^*(\bar{P})] \cdot P^{ST}$$

where B^* denotes a trade deficit for the foreign country and a trade surplus for the home country. Thus, on average,

$$E(B^*) = \bar{B}^* + \frac{\sigma_v^{*2} + \sigma_u^{*2}}{e} \tag{3.18}$$

where $\bar{B}^*$ denotes the value of the trade balance under the stable price $\bar{P}$. Hence, over the long run the foreign country would incur a trade deficit as a result of its policy, whereas the home country would accumulate a surplus. By comparing the latter result with that in equation 3.10 it can be verified that the deficit in the foreign country will always be larger than the deficit incurred under free trade. Obviously, in a general equilibrium model, this trade imbalance would require further adjustments in the patterns of production and consumption in the two countries until a new equilibrium is restored.

The fiscal costs or revenues of implementing this policy in the foreign country are given by

$$TX^* = [D^*(\bar{P}) - S^*(\bar{P})](\bar{P} - P^{ST})$$

where TX^* denotes the foreign country's net revenues from the export or import tariffs. Hence, on average

$$E(TX^*) = -\frac{\sigma_v^{*2} + \sigma_u^{*2}}{e} = -[E(B^*) - \bar{B}^*]. \tag{3.19}$$

Thus the foreign government would, on average, have to subsidize its trade in order to stabilize its price and afford the emerging trade surplus. Thus accumulating balance of payment surplus and budget deficit as a result of this policy (over and above the normal surplus or deficit) would necessarily have widespread effects across the other sectors in the economy that would be reflected in a general equilibrium framework. Over the long run the government would have to accommodate its revenues and expenses in order to be able to finance this policy.

We can now calculate the welfare gains or losses of the various economic sectors in the foreign country as a result of this policy. At this stage, both consumers and producers are assumed to be risk-neutral. The welfare gains to consumers are therefore measured by the change in the consumers' surplus as an effect of the policy compared with that under free trade. These gains are given by

$$G_c^{*ST} = -1/2[D^*(\bar{P}) + D^*(P^T)][\bar{P} - P^T]$$

where, as before, superscript T denotes free trade. Hence, on average,

$$E(G_c^{*ST}) = -1/2\left[\frac{d^*}{E^2} \cdot \Sigma^2 - \frac{2}{E} \cdot \sigma_v^{*2}\right] \qquad (3.20)$$

Similarly, producers' welfare gains are measured by the change in their economic surplus and are given by

$$G_P^{*ST} = 1/2[S^*(P) + S^*(P^T)][\bar{P} - P^T]$$

and, on average,

$$E(G_P^{*ST}) = -1/2\left[\frac{b^{*2}}{E^2} \cdot \Sigma^2 - \frac{2}{E} \cdot \sigma_u^{*2}\right] \qquad (3.21)$$

The total expected welfare gains from stabilization via trade and variable levies are the combined gains of consumers, producers, and the government and are given via equation 3.19, 3.20, and 3.21, by

$$E(G_E^{*ST}) = E(G_c^{*ST}) + E(G_P^{*ST}) + E(TX^*)$$

$$= -1/2\frac{e^*}{E^2} \cdot \Sigma^2 - \frac{e^*}{eE}(\sigma_v^{*2} + \sigma_u^{*2}) < 0 \qquad (3.22)$$

Hence the economy as a whole would lose, over the long run, from price stabilization via trade restrictions through variable levies. These losses are largely due to the government expenses on trade subsidies. (This conclusion cannot be directly related to the one emerging from the Waugh-Oi-Massell model, where the costs of stabilization are not taken into account.) From equations 3.20 and 3.21 we can readily conclude, however, that the private sector—consumers and producers combined—would always gain from price stabilization via trade restrictions if the instability originates in their own country, and lose if the price instability originates in the other country.

The home country faces two types of questions. First, what are the internal consequences of the stabilizing trade policy that the foreign country is implementing. Second, given this policy that its trading partner has unilaterally implemented, would it still be beneficial for the home country to allow free and unconstrained trade activities in its own economy? To examine the first question, we evaluate the welfare changes as an effect of the policy compared with free trade. Consumers' gains or losses in the home country are given by

$$G_c^{ST} = -1/2[D(P^{ST}) + D(P^T)](P^{ST} - P^T)$$

Hence, over the long run,

$$E(G_c^{ST}) = \frac{d \cdot e^* \cdot (e + E)}{2 \cdot e^2 \cdot E^2} \cdot \Sigma^2 - \frac{e^*}{e \cdot E} \cdot \sigma_v^2 \qquad (3.23)$$

Producers' gains or losses are given by

$$G_P^{ST} = 1/2[S(P^{ST}) + S(P^T)](P^{ST} - P^T)$$

Hence,

$$E(G_P^{ST}) = \frac{b \cdot e^* \cdot (e + E)}{2 \cdot e^2 \cdot E^2} \cdot \Sigma^2 - \frac{e^*}{e \cdot E} \cdot \sigma_u^2 \qquad (3.24)$$

Thus both consumers and producers can either gain or lose from the foreign country's trade policy, depending on the specific parameters. The combined expected change in welfare is therefore given by

$$E(G_E^{ST}) = E(G_c^{ST}) + E(G_P^{ST})$$

$$= \frac{e^*(e + E)}{2 \cdot e \cdot E^2} \Sigma^2 - \frac{e^*}{e \cdot E}(\sigma_v^2 + \sigma_u^2)$$

$$= \frac{e^*}{2 \cdot e \cdot E^2}\left[\frac{(e + E)}{e}(\sigma_v^{*2} + \sigma_u^{*2}) - e^*(\sigma_v^2 + \sigma_u^2)\right] \qquad (3.25)$$

From equation 3.15 we can conclude that it is possible for the home country actually to *gain* from the foreign country's stabilizing policy. This would be the case if and only if

$$\frac{(e + E)}{e \cdot e^*} > \frac{\sigma_v^2 + \sigma_u^2}{\sigma_v^{*2} + \sigma_u^{*2}}$$

The home country would always *lose* from its trading partner's policy if the source of the disturbances is in its own market, but *gain* if the source of the disturbances is in the foreign market. These gains, it should be reemphasized, would be incurred only if domestic producers and consumers are neutral to the increased risk as a result of this policy. If, however, risk-averse producers respond to the increased risk by lowering their output, the resulting losses in welfare may outweigh the gains registered in equation 3.25, which we have termed the *transfer gains*. We will return to this issue later.

To examine the second question facing the home country—namely, whether *some* trade, restricted as it is by its trading partner, is still better than *no* trade—we compare the welfare of the various groups under that policy implemented by its trading partner with their welfare under autarky. Let superscript *SN* denote the transition from autarky to a state of restricted trade where the foreign country stabilizes its trade via variable levies. Consumers' gains are given by

$$G_c^{SN} = -1/2[D(P^C) + D(P^{ST})](P^{ST} - P^C)$$

where P^C is the price in the closed economy. Hence,

$$E(G_c^{SN}) = \frac{d}{2 \cdot e^2}(\sigma_v^* + \sigma_u^*) > 0 \qquad (3.26)$$

Similarly, producers' gains are given by

$$G_P^{SN} = 1/2[S(P^C) + S(P^{ST})][(P^{ST} - P^C)$$

and therefore, on average,

$$E(G_c^{SN}) = \frac{b}{2e^2}(\sigma_v^{*2} + \sigma_u^{*2}) > 0 \qquad (3.27)$$

for the economy as a whole. Therefore,

$$E(G_E^{SN}) = E(G_c^{CN}) + E(G_P^{CN})$$

$$= \frac{1}{2e}(\sigma_v^{*2} + \sigma_u^{*2}) > 0 \qquad (3.28)$$

Each sector of the economy will therefore gain even from the controlled trade, and the economy at large will still be better off with some trade than without it.

This conclusion is, again, well in line with the traditional trade theory since even restricted trade allows the home country to gain from the price coordination still permitted by trade, however restricted it becomes. These welfare gains, however, must be traded off against the larger instability enforced on the country by its trading partner. Moreover, if producers and consumers are risk-averse, their response may create losses that must be weighed against the transfer gains registered by equations 3.26 through 3.28.

A complete analysis must also recognize the option open to the home country to retaliate by unilaterally imposing its own restrictions on trade. The end result of such a process may well be shrinking international trade and welfare losses to all countries. Put differently, free trade is a positive-sum game from which all countries may gain. If any individual country chooses not to go along with the cooperative structure required by free trade, then, as all "free riders", it will enjoy some extra gains, at least temporarily. All too often, however, these unilateral actions lead to the collapse of the entire cooperative structure, and ultimately all will lose. The collapse of the international monetary system following the "Beggar-Thy-Neighbor" policies of the 1930s is a vivid illustration of such a process. The various rounds of multilateral trade negotiations in the past two decades manifest the determination of the international community to prevent this process from ever happening again. In all these rounds, however, much too little attention has been given to the instability aspects of international trade and to the mounting efforts of countries or groups of countries to insulate themselves and stabilize their own economies via variable levies and other unilateral policy measures. Nevertheless, the more countries resort to these types of policies the more likely it is that ultimately all will lose, as demonstrated in the empirical study that concludes this chapter.

Partial Stabilization and Optimal Tax Rates

This policy offsets only part of the fluctuations in the world price via variable levies and therefore provides only partial insulation for the country. Assume, as before, that the foreign country is the one implementing this policy. In the specific illustration in this section we consider a linear partial-stabilization scheme whereby the price in the foreign country would then be given by

$$P^* = \tau \bar{P} + (1 - \tau)P^w \qquad (3.29)$$

where P^w is the world price under the policy and $0 < \tau \le 1$. The scheme amounts to a specification of a target demand curve for the country, its elasticity being $(1 - \tau)$ times the original elasticity of the country's demand curve. An illustration of the tax decision rules for the scheme under consideration is given in figure 3–7, where the source of the instability is assumed to be

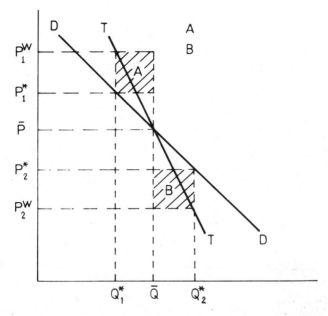

Figure 3–7. Partially Stabilizing Trade Policy: Tariff Rules

random fluctuations in the world price. Suppose, therefore, that the (foreign) country's production is $\bar{Q}$ and the world price is P_1^w. The stabilizing trade policy allows the export price to rise only to P_1^* by imposing an export tax of $t_1 = (P_1^w - P_1^*) = \tau(P_1^w - \bar{P})$. If, however, at that same year the country's production should have been *less* than Q_1^*, an *import subsidy* would have to be paid in order to permit the consumption of Q_1^* and the price P_1^*. Suppose now that the world price drops to P_2^w. In this case the policy prevents the price from falling too steeply by imposing an import tax equal to $t_2 = (P_2^* - P_2^w) = \tau(\bar{P} - P_2^w)$. If, however, at that year the country's production would have been *more* than Q_2^w, an export subsidy of that amount would have to be paid in order to raise the market price to P_2^*.

Equilibrium conditions in the world market are given by

$$D(P^w) - S(P^w) = S(P^*) - D(P^*) \qquad (3.30)$$

Inserting equation 3.29 into 3.30 together with the basic equations of the model 3.1 through 3.4 yields the equilibrium world price

$$P^w = \bar{P} + \frac{V - U}{\tilde{E}} \qquad (3.31)$$

where $\tilde{E} = e + (1 - \tau) \cdot e^*$, and the equilibrium price in the foreign country,

$$P^* = \bar{P} + (1 - \tau)\frac{V - U}{\tilde{E}} \tag{3.32}$$

The variable tax in the foreign country is given by

$$t = P^* - P^w = -\tau \cdot \frac{V - U}{\tilde{E}} \tag{3.33}$$

and hence $\partial t / \partial \tau > 0 <=> (V - U) < 0$

The variability of the world price, the foreign country's price, and the tax rate are given by

$$\text{Var}(P^w) = \frac{1}{\tilde{E}^2}\Sigma^2$$

$$\text{Var}(P^*) = \frac{(1 - \tau)^2}{\tilde{E}^2}\Sigma^2 = (1 - \tau)^2 \cdot \text{Var}(P^w)$$

$$\text{Var}(t) = \frac{\tau^2}{\tilde{E}^2}\Sigma^2 = \tau^2 \cdot \text{Var}(P^w)$$

The balance of trade of the foreign country is given by

$$B^* = [D(P^*) - S(P^*)] \cdot P^w$$

Hence, on average,

$$E(B^*) = \bar{B}^* - \frac{(1 - \tau)e^*(\sigma_v^2 + \sigma_u^2) - e(\sigma_v^{*2} + \sigma_u^{*2})}{\tilde{E}^2} \tag{3.34}$$

and, therefore,

$$E(B^*) > \bar{B}^* <=> \tau > 1 - \frac{e(\sigma_v^2 + \sigma_u^2)}{e^*(\sigma_v^{*2} + \sigma_u^{*2})}$$

The trade balance may either increase or decrease with τ, depending on the market parameters in the two countries. After some algebra it can be shown that if all disturbances originate in the foreign country—that is, if $\sigma_u^2 = \sigma_v^2 = 0$—then $E(B^*) > \bar{B}^*$ and $\partial E(B^*)/\partial \tau > 0$. If, however, all disturbances originate in the home country—that is, if $\sigma_v^{*2} = \sigma_u^{*2} = 0$, then $E(B^*) = \bar{B}^*$ and

$$\frac{\partial E(B^*)}{\partial \tau} > 0 <=> \tau > 1 - \frac{e^*}{e}$$

The net revenues on the import and export taxes would then be

$$TX^* = [D^*(P^*) - S^*(P^*)] \cdot t$$

Hence, on average,

$$E(TX^*) = \tau \cdot \left[\frac{(-\tau)e^* (\sigma_v^2 + \sigma_u^2) - e(\sigma_v^{*2} + \sigma_u^{*2})}{\bar{E}^2} \right] \qquad (3.35)$$

$$= \tau \cdot [\bar{B}^* - E(B^*)]$$

Following our earlier conclusions, we can therefore observe that

$$E(TX^*) > 0 <=> \tau < - \frac{e(\sigma_v^2 + \sigma_u^2)}{e^*(\sigma_v^{*2} + \sigma_u^{*2})}$$

We can also derive the *optimal* τ at which the tax revenues are maximized (or the trade subsidies minimized), given by

$$\tau = 1 - \frac{e}{e^*} \cdot \left[\frac{(\sigma_v^2 + \sigma_u^2) - 2(\sigma_v^{*2} + \sigma_u^{*2})}{(\sigma_v^2 + \sigma_u^2)} \right]$$

Thus, if $[(e - e^*)/2e] < [(\sigma_v^2 + \sigma_u^2)/(\sigma_v^{*2} + \sigma_u^{*2})]$, the optimal tax rate τ, from a fiscal point of view—namely, the tax rate that maximizes the government net revenues—would be greater than 1. If

$$e^*/e < \left[1 - 2 \frac{\sigma_v^* + \sigma_u^*}{\sigma_v + \sigma_u} \right]$$

then the optimal τ would be negative. In these two cases the optimal fiscal policy for the foreign country would therefore be to *destabilize* the domestic market via variable levies.

The expected change in the consumers' and producers' surplus as an effect of partial stabilization is given by

$$E(G_c^{*PS}) = -1/2 \left[\frac{d^* \tau e}{(E \bar{E})^2} [(1 - \tau) E + \bar{E}] \cdot \Sigma^2 - \frac{2\tau e}{E \bar{E}} \sigma_v^{*2} \right]$$

$$(3.36)$$

$$E(G_P^{*PS}) = -1/2 \left[\frac{b^* \tau e}{(E \bar{E})^2} [(1 - \tau) E + \bar{E}] \cdot \Sigma^2 - \frac{2\tau e}{E \bar{E}} \sigma_u^{*2} \right]$$

$$(3.37)$$

where superscript *PS* denotes the policy of partial stabilization. (The detailed calculations are omitted for brevity.) Hence for the economy as a whole,

$$E(G_E^{*PS}) = E(G_c^{*PS}) + E(G_P^{*PC}) - E(TX^*)$$

$$= \frac{\tau \cdot e^* [2(1 - \tau)e^* E - \tau e^2]}{2(E \tilde{E})^2} \Sigma^2 - \frac{\tau \cdot e^*}{E \tilde{E}} (\sigma_u^{*2} + \sigma_v^{*2}) \quad (3.38)$$

Hence, if the tax rate is such that

$$\tau < \frac{E[2e^* \cdot (\sigma_v^2 + \sigma_u^2) - 2e (\sigma_v^{*2} + \sigma_u^{*2})]}{2e^* \cdot E(\sigma_v^2 + \sigma_u^2) + e^2 \cdot \Sigma^2} \quad (3.39)$$

the economy may actually *gain* from partial stabilization via variable levies *both* by enhancing its stability *and* by obtaining net welfare gains. Now there is an obvious temptation to derive the first-order conditions for maximization in equation 3.38 and find the welfare maximizing rate τ. This temptation should be overcome, for two reasons. First, the results (not presented here) provide an extremely complex combination of all the model's parameters and thus lose any intuitive meaning. Second, this analysis still neglects the more important economic gains (or losses) from the policy—namely, the risk-response gains associated with the change in income variability. In the following section the optimal stabilizing trade policy is further examined via the more complex log-linear-multiplicative-disturbances econometric model, which explicitly recognizes the risk response. Two conclusions emerging from the present analysis, however, should be highlighted.

1. The results in equations 3.38 and 3.39 give yet another reason for what has become known as the *optimal tariff* argument—namely, if the country is large enough to affect the level of the world price and thus also its variability, it can *gain* from trade restrictions via variable levies that would not only increase its domestic stability but might also render welfare gains. These gains, it should be emphasized, are obtained even under risk neutrality. If greater price stability increases also the stability of producers' income (as may or may not be the case), then the likely response of risk-averse producers would further increase the economy's welfare gains.

2. From equation 3.39 we can conclude that if the parameters of the model are such that

$$(e^*/e) < (\sigma_v^{*2} + \sigma_u^{*2})/(\sigma_v^2 + \sigma_u^2)$$

so that $\tau < 0$, then the economy may be better off, in terms of welfare, by *destabilizing* its trade. The latter conclusions may, however, change once the risk response is taken into account.

Simulation Analysis

The simulation analysis in this section extends the theoretical analysis of variable levies to the more general log-linear-constant-elasticity model with multiplicative disturbances. In addition, the model also incorporates the risk response in supply as described in the third section. The stabilizing trade policy has the basic structure of the partial-stabilization program discussed in the previous section, but the policy is now assumed to be implemented by the home country. The market price in the country is thus given by

$$P = \tau \cdot \bar{P} + (1 - \tau)P^w \quad : \quad 0 \leq \tau \leq 1$$

where P^w is the (random) world price. In the simulation analysis, several values of the target elasticity parameter τ have been experimented with, ranging from

$$\tau = 0 \quad : \quad \text{free trade}$$

to

$$\tau = 1 \quad : \quad \text{complete stabilization}$$

The experiments were conducted for two values of price elasticity of demand in the country, denoted by η: $\eta = 0.3$ and $\eta = 1.25$. In the basic case, the risk-response elasticity (denoted by $R \cdot \epsilon$) is, conservatively, assumed to be 0.25. Other values of this elasticity have also been experimented with.

Figure 3–8 presents the simulation results describing the stabilizing effects of this trade policy on the market price and on farmers' income. The results suggest that under the two demand elasticities, some level of variable levies-cum-subsidies are likely to be a Pareto improvement over free trade. The decrease in the variability of the market price *and* the decrease in the price level (not reported here) will improve the state of consumers. As for producers, the policy would initially stabilize their income. Beyond a certain level of the tax-cum-subsidy rates, however, the larger price stability resulting from the policy would only increase the variability of their income as the stochastic, weather-induced variations in supply become increasingly dominant. Furthermore, at the range where the income variability declines, there may also be a slight decline (by 1 to 2.5 percent, depending on the demand and the risk elasticities) in the mean level of farmers' income. Hence, whether or not the policy would indeed improve the condition of the farmers would depend on their subjective preferences.

Figure 3–9 presents the simulation results summarizing the economic gains for different levels of the policy parameter τ, and under different assumptions on the level of the demand and risk elasticities. The results clearly show that, from the welfare point of view, some government intervention to

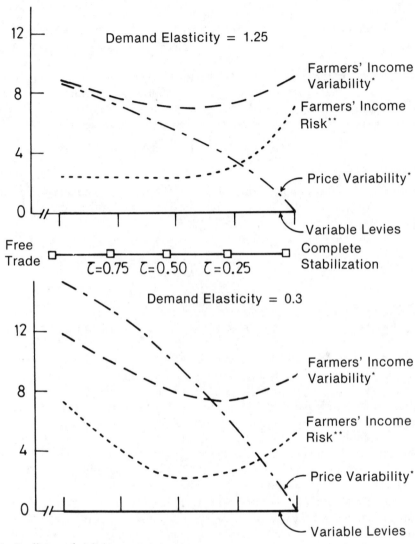

* Coefficient of variation.
** Probability that farmers' income falls by more than 15 percent below their normal income.

Figure 3–8. Stability Effects of Stabilizing Trade Policies under Different Demand Elasticities

stabilize trade is superior to free trade. The only exception is the case of both high demand elasticity and risk neutrality. In this case the greater stability would affect neither consumption nor production decisions, and the departure from free trade would then involve welfare losses as an effect of the income redistribution that would result from the policy. At lower price elas-

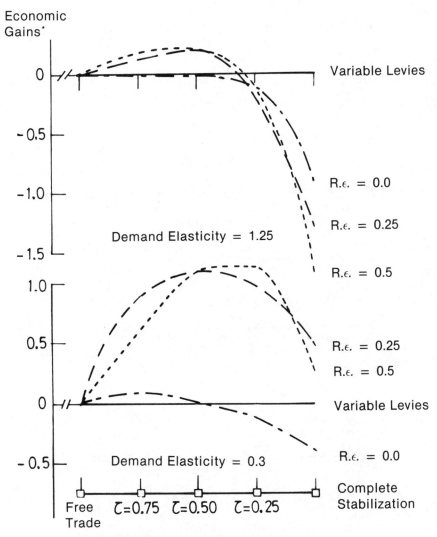

Note: Gains expressed as percentage of annual expenditures on food in a normal year.

Figure 3-9. Economic Gains from Stabilizing Trade Policies under Different Demand and Risk Elasticities

ticities, however, some intervention would still be a Pareto improvement over tree trade, even under risk neutrality.

Figure 3-10 presents the simulation results of the distribution of the gains and losses among the different sectors in the economy. Consumers always gain from the policy—the more so the higher is the policy parameter τ—that is, the higher the degree of stability secured by the policy. These gains, it should be emphasized, result from the decrease in the mean price as

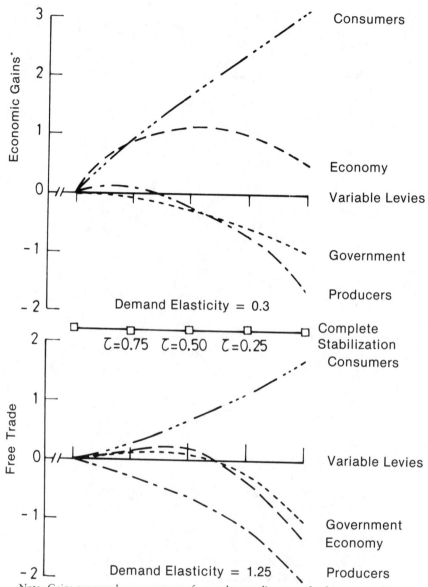

Note: Gains expressed as percentage of annual expenditures on food in a normal year.

Figure 3–10. Gains from Stabilizing Trade Policies by Economic Sector under Different Demand Elasticities

an effect of the policy, not counting the additional gains associated with the greater stability of the market price. Their gains would be higher the lower the price elasticity of demand and the higher the risk elasticity.

Producers always lose from this policy, which not only reduces the mean price but also reduces the variability originating from the foreign sector. This conclusion is, therefore, well in line with the conventional Waugh-Oi-Massell analysis and further accentuated by the risk response in supply. Producers' losses are higher, the higher the price elasticity of demand. The latter result is especially noteworthy since the reduction in the *mean* price is *smaller,* the higher the price elasticity of demand. Thus, for example, in the transition from free trade to complete stabilization via variable levies, the mean price declines by 3.5 percent when the demand elasticity is 0.3, but by only 2 percent when the demand elasticity is 1.25. Nonetheless, producers' losses from this policy would amount to 1.6 percent of their annual revenues when the demand elasticity is 0.3, and 2.0 percent when the demand elasticity is 1.25. The reason is the redistribution or the income-transfer losses of producers resulting from this policy, which, under a log-linear demand curve, are higher the more elastic is consumers' demand.

The stabilizing trade policy would increase the volume of trade and the frequency of trade activities into and out of the country. The country under consideration is assumed to be self-sufficient in a normal year. Nevertheless, under the policy of complete internal stabilization, the volume of imports rises by 70 to 300 percent, depending on the demand elasticity, and the volume of exports rises by 20 to 60 percent. This policy, it should be emphasized, not only insulates the country from external instability but also exports the existing domestic instability. To achieve this, the country would have to increase its trade activities significantly. Figure 3–11 summarizes the simulation results measuring the changes in the volume of imports and exports and in the value of the trade account as an effect of changes in the policy parameter. It shows that with complete stabilization the trade deficit (expressed as percentage of total annual expenditures on food) would rise by 4.1 percentage points, when the demand elasticity is 1.25, as the volume of imports rises by 206 percent, but the volume of exports rises by only 23 percent. The trade deficit would rise by 1.8 percentage points only when the demand elasticity is 0.3, as the volume of imports then rises by 70 percent and the volume of exports by 60 percent. The rise in the trade deficit would be higher, the larger the risk response. Even under risk neutrality, however, the trade deficit would rise by 2.6 percentage points when the demand elasticity is 1.25 and by 1.2 percentage points when the demand elasticity is 0.3.

The stabilizing trade policy, therefore, works by effectively transforming the domestic price instability into foreign-exchange instability. The latter is revealed not only by the rise in the average trade deficit but also by the rise in the probability of having unusually large foreign-exchange expenditures on that account. To measure the instability introduced by the policy into its external trade account, we have measured the *foreign-exchange risk,* defined as the probability that the trade deficit in any given year would exceed a

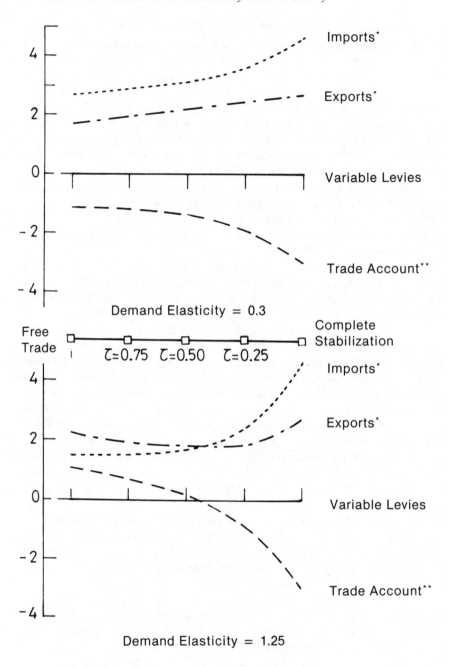

* As percentage of annual food production in a normal year.
** As percentage of annual expenditures on food in a normal year.

Figure 3–11. Trade Flows Generated by the Stabilizing Trade Policies under Different Demand Elasticities

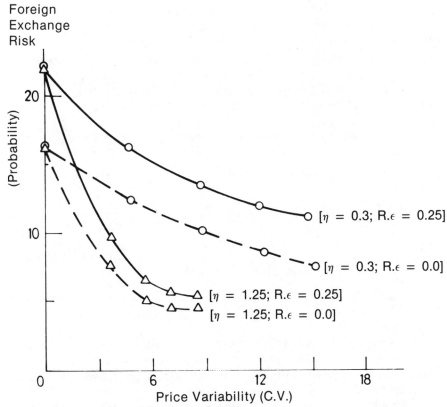

Figure 3–12. **Trade-off between Domestic Price Instability and the Foreign-Exchange Risk as an Effect of Stabilizing Trade Policies**

certain critical level. In the simulation analysis the critical level was assumed to be 10 percent of the total annual expenditures on food. For a country like India, that would mean a trade deficit larger than $1.25 billion. Figure 3–12 illustrates the trade-off revealed by the simulation analysis between domestic price instability and the foreign-exchange risk as an effect of the stabilizing trade policy. It shows that the trade-off becomes more acute, the higher the price elasticity of demand. Other simulation results show that the trade-off rises, though not very significantly, with a rise in the degree of risk aversion.

Trade Policies and Price Distortions in Wheat, 1968–1980

The most common measure of the extent to which governments intervene in the commodity markets is the divergence between the world price of these commodities (after accounting for transport costs) and their domestic price. Traditionally, any such divergence is regarded as a distortion. Despite some limitations, border prices are frequently used as reference points against which the effects of market interventions can be assessed, both because for most products they represent the true opportunity costs of the country's tradables and because in most countries there is no other observable or computable system of values on accounting (shadow) prices with which the domestic prices can be compared.[5]

A direct measure of the divergence between the border and the domestic prices in any given commodity is the nominal protection coefficients (NPC), calculated as

$$\text{NPC}_i = \frac{P_i^d}{P_i^b}$$

where

P_i^d = the domestic price of the ith commodity.

P_i^b = the border price of the ith commodity, calculated as the foreign price CIF times the official exchange rate.

In theory, the border price should be worked back to the producer's point—that is, adjusted for internal transport costs. In practice this is seldom done, either because the differences are not very large or because the data on internal transport costs are deficient and inaccurate.

The NPC represents the tariff rate equivalent (calculated as a percentage of the CIF price) of the government internal (for example, support price) and external (for example, import levies) policies *combined*. A coefficient larger than 1 indicates that government interventions protect the domestic producers against foreign competition, thus providing an incentive to produce the commodity. A coefficient smaller than 1 indicates that the government subsidizes the imports of the commodity for the benefit of consumers but against the local producers.

A theoretically more relevant measure of protection is the effective protection coefficient (EPC), which indicates the effects of the protective measures on the value added, taking into account taxes or subsidies on traded inputs. For agricultural commodities, especially in LDCs, however, purchased imports make up only a small proportion of the costs of production, so that the difference between the value and the value added is generally not very large. Furthermore, in many countries subsidies on purchased inputs (such as fertilizers) are varied together with variations in taxes or subsidies on outputs. Normally, therefore, the EPC and the NPC follow the same trend and are sufficiently close to each other. A discrepancy does exist when the official exchange rate is significantly different from the accounting exchange rate. In these cases part of, say, the disincentive embodied in an overvalued exchange rate will not be manifested by the NPC (see chapter 7 for an example).

The NPCs are widely used by agricultural economists at the World Bank, at research institutes, and at planning bureaus of government ministries. The reasoning underlying their use has been explained by Gotsch and Brown (1980, p. 2) as follows: "Once divergence from relative world market prices is accepted, there is only limited theoretical support for setting the 'right' price." Scandizzo and Bruce (1980, p. vi) further emphasize that "at the very least, the use of border price reference points provides an estimation of the net welfare losses and transfers resulting from departures from free trade."

These arguments are valid and relevant in a static world; and, indeed, the NPCs are usually used in a comparative static analysis.[6] In a stochastic world the reasons for government interventions are far more complex, and a simple use of the NPCs to measure their effects may lead to misleading conclusions. For one thing, in a stochastic world some interventions may be superior, on welfare grounds, to free trade, as noted in the third section. Second, explicit stability considerations may make some measures of intervention desirable from the policymaker's point of view even if they entail some welfare losses. Obvious examples are measures to insulate domestic producers and consumers from external price variations, and measures to secure a stable flow of supply to domestic consumers through import subsidies or export levies. An evaluation of government interventions on the basis of the NPC (or the EPC or the other performance criteria), without taking into account the specific circumstances existing in that year and the explicit stability considerations, may provide an incorrect indication about the desirability of government interventions and their incentive/disincentive effects.

The purpose of this section is to estimate and analyze the NPCs for the thirty-nine major importing countries and four main exporting countries. Together the importing countries included account for 90–95 percent of total world imports outside the imports of the USSR. Twenty-two of these countries are developing; thirteen are European countries, seven of which are in the European Economic Community (EEC). The other four countries are Japan, Israel, Saudi Arabia, and Singapore. The exporting countries, the United States, Canada, Australia, and Argentina, account for 90 percent of world exports. The NPCs for all these countries were estimated over the period 1968–1980.

Data sources are as follows: Domestic producers' prices are FAO estimates. The world price is the FOB average price of wheat in the United States estimated by the FAO. It is thus assumed that *at the margins* the U.S. price is the appropriate opportunity price of imported wheat whether or not its source is actually in the United States or in one of the other exporting countries.

Transport costs from the United States to the ports of destination are U.S. Department of Agriculture (USDA) estimates for all ports of destination during the period 1975–1977 and extrapolations based on the transport costs to the five main points during all other years. Transport costs were calculated from the nearest port in the United States.

Table 3–10 presents the estimates of the NPCs for the thirty-nine importing countries and for the four groups of countries. The lowest raw figure in each group provides the average NPC for the group in each year and its coefficient of variations across countries. The last two columns provide the average NPC for each country over the entire time period of the study, and the adjusted average, which excludes the years 1973 and 1974. The most noteworthy observation is the sharp decline—on average by more than 45 percent—in the NPCs of *all* countries, developed as well as developing, during the two crisis years 1973 and 1974. The decline was especially pronounced in the developing countries, whose NPCs were lowered by an average of 55 percent. These changes marked the efforts of all countries to insulate their own economies from the abrupt and massive rise in the world price. Ironically, it was this simultaneous though obviously uncoordinated effort to insulate the domestic market that actually magnified the rise in the world price and ultimately frustrated the efforts of many countries to prevent the higher external prices from affecting their domestic price and to secure a stable flow of supply to their own consumers.

Another important observation is the marked and sometimes massive differences between the period's averages and their values in any given year. In the developing countries, as a group, the NPCs varied from 0.66 in 1973—an import *subsidy* of 34 percent—to 1.38 in 1977—an import *tax* of 38 percent. The period's average for the group was 1.08. In the EEC countries as a group the NPCs varied from 1.60 in 1972, to 0.74 in 1974, to 1.64 in 1977. The period's average was 1.35. This result further accentuates an earlier statement that evaluating the incentive/disincentive effects of government interventions on the basis of the NPC in any single year may lead to erroneous conclusions.

The variations in the NPCs are largely a reflection of the importing countries' effort to counter the external variations in the world price. Table 3–11 shows the deviations of the NPCs from their *adjusted* average. The last two columns calculate the coefficient of variation (CV) and the adjusted CV—which exclude 1973 and 1974—of the NPCs. The table shows that the range of change of the NPCs from the adjusted average was 10 to 25 percent and more above and below the adjusted average, even after excluding 1973 and 1974. In Brazil the NPC was 70 percent above the adjusted average in 1977 and 5 percent below in 1979. In India the NPC was 27 to 44 percent above the adjusted average in the subperiod 1968–1972, but up to 27 percent below the adjusted average in the subperiod 1975–1980. In the EEC countries as

Table 3–10
Nominal Protection Coefficients, 1968–1980

Country	1968	1969	1970	1971	1972	1973	1974	1975	1976	1977	1978	1979	1980	AVR.	ADJU.[a]
Developing Countries															
Algeria	0.74	0.72	0.63	0.69	0.58	0.26	0.22	0.28	0.37	0.48	0.51	N.A.	N.A.	0.50	0.56
Bangladesh	N.A.	N.A.	N.A.	0.80	1.36	0.54	0.92	1.31	0.51	0.90	0.83	0.59	N.A.	0.86	0.90
Brazil	1.39	1.38	1.21	1.36	1.16	0.63	0.71	1.34	1.18	1.70	1.42	0.95	N.A.	1.20	1.31
Chile	0.86	0.82	0.82	1.08	0.76	0.12	0.40	0.74	0.89	1.35	0.97	0.89	N.A.	0.81	0.92
Colombia	1.61	1.61	1.32	1.35	1.42	0.66	0.74	1.09	1.14	1.61	1.27	1.13	1.17	1.24	1.34
Egypt	0.99	1.01	1.10	1.12	0.98	0.53	0.51	0.68	0.74	1.03	1.01	N.A.	N.A.	0.88	0.96
India	1.33	1.44	1.38	1.37	1.27	0.63	0.69	0.76	0.80	1.00	0.94	0.73	0.74	1.01	1.07
Iran	1.22	0.97	1.02	1.42	1.36	0.74	0.57	0.68	0.85	1.29	1.28	1.05	N.A.	1.04	1.11
Iraq	0.88	0.82	1.05	1.26	0.96	0.65	0.42	0.48	0.60	0.87	0.77	N.A.	N.A.	0.80	0.86
Korea	1.21	1.17	1.02	1.10	1.16	0.63	0.68	0.83	1.14	1.71	1.72	1.35	1.18	1.15	1.24
Malaysia	1.60	1.66	1.59	1.79	2.01	1.37	1.40	1.69	1.83	2.19	2.04	1.64	N.A.	1.74	1.81
Mexico	0.95	0.96	0.90	0.99	0.87	0.42	0.47	0.73	0.71	0.76	0.78	0.68	0.71	0.76	0.82
Morocco	1.03	1.15	1.07	1.31	1.29	0.83	0.82	1.12	1.16	1.95	1.75	1.59	1.75	1.29	1.38
Nigeria	1.17	1.51	1.47	2.61	2.33	0.97	1.01	1.33	1.57	1.86	1.64	1.50	1.70	1.59	1.70
Pakistan	1.27	1.22	1.23	1.39	0.77	0.34	0.28	0.47	0.62	0.81	0.82	N.A.	N.A.	0.84	0.96
Peru	1.39	1.58	1.35	1.55	1.59	0.79	0.74	1.35	1.17	1.87	1.30	1.11	N.A.	1.31	1.42
Philippines	0.98	1.04	0.69	0.95	0.99	0.52	0.52	0.58	0.71	0.90	0.78	0.64	N.A.	0.77	0.83
Sri Lanka	1.35	1.35	1.22	1.31	1.21	0.86	1.03	1.11	1.05	1.15	0.67	0.54	0.56	1.03	1.05
Tunisia	1.09	1.08	0.92	1.11	1.09	0.56	0.55	0.80	0.87	1.20	1.15	N.A.	N.A.	0.95	1.03
Turkey	1.53	1.68	1.40	1.10	1.09	0.64	0.81	1.04	1.11	1.41	1.04	0.97	N.A.	1.15	1.24
Venezuela	1.37	1.39	1.32	1.43	1.32	0.66	0.72	1.02	1.44	1.88	1.55	N.A.	N.A.	1.28	1.41
Yemen	1.43	2.23	1.73	1.63	1.72	1.16	1.17	1.42	1.90	2.36	N.A.	N.A.	N.A.	1.67	1.80
C.V.	0.21	0.28	0.24	0.30	0.33	0.42	0.40	0.38	0.40	0.37	0.36	0.36	0.43	0.28	0.28
Average	1.21	1.28	1.16	1.30	1.24	0.66	0.70	0.95	1.02	1.38	1.15	1.02	1.11	1.08	1.17

a Adjusted average, excluding the years 1973 and 1974.

Table 3–10 (continued)

Country	1968	1969	1970	1971	1972	1973	1974	1975	1976	1977	1978	1979	1980	AVR.	ADJU.
EEC Countries															
France	1.33	1.31	1.34	1.38	1.39	0.80	0.59	0.82	1.00	1.31	1.31	1.12	1.09	1.14	1.22
Germany	1.47	1.56	1.68	1.73	1.72	1.04	0.79	1.00	1.27	1.69	1.67	1.43	1.35	1.42	1.51
Italy	1.47	1.51	1.47	1.65	1.54	0.91	0.81	1.04	1.18	1.64	1.61	1.37	N.A.	1.35	1.45
Netherlands	1.44	1.52	1.65	1.63	1.66	0.97	0.71	0.92	1.16	1.57	1.54	1.30	1.23	1.33	1.42
Ireland	1.09	1.07	1.01	1.09	1.07	0.85	0.50	0.78	0.88	1.22	1.14	0.95	N.A.	0.97	1.03
United Kingdom	0.96	1.06	1.17	1.20	1.23	0.97	0.65	0.68	0.87	1.25	1.22	1.18	1.21	1.05	1.09
Benelux	1.43	1.46	1.60	1.57	1.58	0.92	0.67	0.93	1.17	1.64	1.11	1.34	1.25	1.32	1.42
C.V.	0.22	0.20	0.16	0.20	0.18	0.10	0.18	0.22	0.21	0.23	0.19	0.13	0.20	0.98	0.99
Average	1.45	1.50	1.55	1.63	1.60	0.96	0.74	0.96	1.19	1.64	1.59	1.35	1.33	1.35	1.44
Other European Countries															
Finland	1.93	1.98	1.76	1.95	1.73	0.86	0.75	1.09	1.35	1.69	1.46	1.39	1.68	1.51	1.64
Hungary	0.77	0.78	0.77	0.79	0.75	0.42	0.31	0.37	0.49	0.64	0.59	0.50	0.51	0.59	0.63
Norway	2.05	2.05	1.93	2.23	2.11	1.09	0.97	1.35	1.68	2.39	2.16	1.72	1.84	1.81	1.95
Portugal	1.57	1.59	1.52	1.80	1.68	0.85	0.74	1.02	1.03	1.27	1.22	N.A.	N.A.	1.30	1.41
Switzerland	2.29	2.34	2.29	2.58	2.49	1.49	1.37	1.90	2.34	3.24	3.69	3.16	2.77	2.46	2.64
Yugoslavia	1.06	1.10	1.12	1.25	1.06	0.54	0.59	0.65	0.83	1.24	1.00	1.15	N.A.	0.96	1.05
C.V.	0.40	0.40	0.40	0.42	0.43	0.45	0.51	0.55	0.56	0.57	0.73	0.71	0.68	0.50	0.50
Average	1.45	1.48	1.41	1.58	1.46	0.83	0.71	0.97	1.15	1.55	1.51	1.43	1.65	1.30	1.40
Other Importers															
Israel	0.87	0.85	0.68	0.95	0.77	0.41	0.57	0.85	1.01	1.16	1.05	0.73	1.00	0.84	0.90
Japan	2.06	2.21	2.26	2.60	2.82	1.67	1.46	1.87	2.51	4.93	5.62	4.26	4.03	2.94	3.20
Saudi Arabia	1.95	2.18	2.31	2.42	2.17	1.34	1.18	1.63	2.48	3.82	3.39	N.A.	N.A.	2.26	2.48
Singapore	1.65	1.71	1.66	1.85	2.07	1.41	1.42	1.77	1.93	2.23	2.05	1.63	1.63	1.77	1.83
C.V.	0.33	0.36	0.44	0.38	0.44	0.46	0.35	0.30	0.35	0.55	0.65	0.83	0.72	0.45	0.47
Average	1.63	1.74	1.72	1.95	1.96	1.20	1.16	1.53	1.98	3.03	3.03	2.20	2.22	1.95	2.10

Table 3–11
Deviations of the Nominal Protection Coefficients from the Adjusted Averages

Country	1968	1969	1970	1971	1972	1973	1974	1975	1976	1977	1978	1979	1980	CV.	AD.CV.
Developing Countries															
Algeria	1.34	1.29	1.14	1.24	1.05	0.46	0.40	0.50	0.67	0.87	0.92	N.A.	N.A.	0.38	0.28
Bangladesh	N.A.	N.A.	N.A.	0.89	1.51	0.60	1.02	1.46	0.57	1.01	0.92	0.65	N.A.	0.36	0.36
Brazil	1.06	1.06	0.93	1.04	0.89	0.48	0.54	1.03	0.90	1.30	1.09	0.73	N.A.	0.25	0.15
Chile	0.94	0.90	0.90	1.18	0.82	0.13	0.44	0.81	0.97	1.48	1.05	0.97	N.A.	0.38	0.19
Colombia	1.21	1.20	0.98	1.01	1.06	0.49	0.55	0.82	0.85	1.21	0.95	0.85	0.88	0.24	0.15
Egypt	1.02	1.05	1.14	1.17	1.02	0.55	0.53	0.71	0.77	1.07	1.05	N.A.	N.A.	0.25	0.16
India	1.25	1.35	1.29	1.29	1.19	0.59	0.65	0.71	0.75	0.94	0.88	0.68	0.69	0.30	0.27
Iran	1.10	0.87	0.92	1.28	1.22	0.66	0.51	0.61	0.76	1.16	1.15	0.95	N.A.	0.27	0.21
Iraq	1.03	0.96	1.22	1.48	1.12	0.76	0.49	0.57	0.70	1.02	0.90	N.A.	N.A.	0.31	0.27
Korea	0.98	0.94	0.83	0.89	0.94	0.51	0.55	0.67	0.92	1.38	1.40	1.09	0.96	0.28	0.22
Malaysia	0.89	0.92	0.88	0.99	1.11	0.76	0.77	0.94	1.02	1.21	1.13	0.91	N.A.	0.14	0.12
Mexico	1.16	1.16	1.10	1.20	1.06	0.51	0.58	0.89	0.87	0.93	0.95	0.83	0.86	0.23	0.14
Morocco	0.75	0.83	0.78	0.95	0.93	0.61	0.59	0.81	0.84	1.41	1.27	1.16	1.27	0.28	0.23
Nigeria	0.69	0.89	0.86	1.54	1.37	0.57	0.59	0.78	0.93	1.10	0.97	0.88	1.00	0.29	0.25
Pakistan	1.33	1.28	1.29	1.45	0.80	0.36	0.30	0.50	0.65	0.85	0.86	N.A.	N.A.	0.47	0.34
Peru	0.98	1.11	0.95	1.09	1.11	0.55	0.52	0.94	0.82	1.31	0.91	0.78	N.A.	0.25	0.16
Philippines	1.19	1.26	0.84	1.15	1.19	0.63	0.63	0.70	0.86	1.09	0.95	0.78	N.A.	0.25	0.20
Sri Lanka	1.29	1.29	1.17	1.25	1.16	0.82	0.98	1.06	1.00	1.10	0.64	0.51	0.54	0.28	0.30
Tunisia	1.06	1.04	0.89	1.08	1.05	0.54	0.53	0.78	0.84	1.16	1.12	N.A.	N.A.	0.24	0.13
Turkey	1.24	1.36	1.13	0.89	0.88	0.52	0.65	0.84	0.90	1.14	0.84	0.78	N.A.	0.26	0.20
Venezuela	0.97	0.99	0.93	1.01	0.94	0.47	0.51	0.72	1.02	1.33	1.10	N.A.	N.A.	0.28	0.16
Yemen	0.80	1.24	0.96	0.91	0.95	0.64	0.65	0.79	1.05	1.31	N.A.	N.A.	N.A.	0.24	0.19
C.V.	0.17	0.16	0.15	0.17	0.16	0.25	0.27	0.26	0.15	0.15	0.16	0.19	0.26	—	—
Average	1.06	1.09	1.01	1.13	1.06	0.55	0.59	0.80	0.85	1.15	1.00	0.84	0.88	0.19	0.12

Note: Adjusted average and adjusted CV, excluding the years 1973 and 1974.

Table 3–11 (continued)

Country	1968	1969	1970	1971	1972	1973	1974	1975	1976	1977	1978	1979	1980	CV.	AD.CV.
EEC Countries															
France	1.09	1.08	1.10	1.14	1.14	0.65	0.48	0.67	0.82	1.07	1.07	0.92	0.90	0.23	0.15
Germany	0.97	1.04	1.12	1.15	1.14	0.69	0.52	0.66	0.84	1.12	1.11	0.95	0.90	0.22	0.15
Italy	1.02	1.04	1.02	1.14	1.06	0.63	0.56	0.72	0.82	1.13	1.11	0.94	N.A.	0.21	0.14
Netherlands	1.01	1.07	1.16	1.15	1.17	0.68	0.50	0.65	0.82	1.11	1.09	0.92	0.86	0.23	0.16
Ireland	1.06	1.04	0.98	1.06	1.04	0.83	0.49	0.76	0.86	1.18	1.10	0.92	N.A.	0.20	0.12
United Kingdom	0.88	0.97	1.07	1.10	1.12	0.89	0.59	0.62	0.80	1.15	1.11	1.07	1.11	0.20	0.17
Benelux	1.01	1.03	1.13	1.11	1.12	0.65	0.47	0.66	0.83	1.16	1.14	1.94	0.88	0.24	1.16
C.V.	0.07	0.04	0.06	0.02	0.04	0.15	0.08	0.04	0.02	0.04	0.02	0.06	0.10	—	—
Average	1.01	1.04	1.08	1.13	1.12	0.68	0.52	0.67	0.83	1.14	1.10	0.95	0.93	0.20	0.15
Other European Countries															
Finland	1.18	1.21	1.07	1.19	1.05	0.53	0.46	0.67	0.83	1.03	0.89	0.85	1.02	0.27	0.18
Hungary	1.22	1.23	1.22	1.24	1.19	0.66	0.49	0.59	0.78	1.01	0.93	0.79	0.81	0.29	0.23
Norway	1.05	1.05	0.99	1.14	1.08	0.56	0.50	0.69	0.86	1.22	1.11	0.88	0.94	0.24	0.15
Portugal	1.11	1.13	1.07	1.28	1.19	0.60	0.53	0.73	0.73	0.90	0.86	N.A.	N.A.	0.27	0.20
Switzerland	0.87	0.89	0.87	0.97	0.94	0.56	0.52	0.72	0.88	1.22	1.40	1.20	1.05	0.26	0.20
Yugoslavia	1.02	1.06	1.07	1.19	1.02	0.51	0.56	0.62	0.79	1.19	0.95	1.10	N.A.	0.26	0.18
C.V.	0.11	0.11	0.10	0.09	0.08	0.17	0.00	0.08	0.05	0.11	0.19	0.18	0.14	—	—
Average	1.08	1.09	1.05	1.16	1.07	0.62	0.51	0.68	0.81	1.09	1.02	0.97	0.96	0.21	0.14
Other Importers															
Israel	0.96	0.95	0.75	1.05	0.86	0.45	0.64	0.94	1.12	1.28	1.17	0.81	1.11	0.25	0.16
Japan	0.64	0.69	0.71	0.82	0.88	0.52	0.46	0.58	0.78	1.54	1.76	1.33	1.26	0.45	0.40
Saudi Arabia	0.79	0.88	0.93	0.98	0.88	0.54	0.47	0.66	1.00	1.54	1.36	N.A.	N.A.	0.35	0.28
Singapore	0.90	0.93	0.90	1.01	1.13	0.77	0.77	0.96	1.05	1.22	1.12	0.89	0.89	0.14	0.12
C.V.	0.17	0.13	0.13	0.10	0.14	0.23	0.24	0.24	0.14	0.12	0.21	0.28	0.17	—	—
Average	0.82	0.86	0.82	0.96	0.94	0.57	0.58	0.79	0.99	1.39	1.35	1.01	1.09	0.25	0.20

a group the NPC was 22 percent below the adjusted average in 1975 and 9 percent above in 1977. The coefficients of variation provide another measure of these variations.

In the remainder of this section we examine two questions. First, was there a significant difference in the wheat trade policies and other intervention practices of the importing countries since the mid-1970s—that is, in the 1975–1980 subperiod—compared with the 1968–1972 subperiod, and if so, in what direction? Second, is there a common pattern that can be traced in the trade policies of all countries or of groups of countries, and what effect may this have on the world wheat market?

Table 3–12 summarizes the main statistics for aggregate groups of countries over the two subperiods. Two observations stand out. First, the average NPC in the 1975–1980 subperiod was *lower* than that in 1968–1972. This suggests that in the second half of the 1970s emphasis has shifted from providing incentives to domestic wheat production to securing a stable flow of supply to domestic consumers in the aftermath of the 1973–1974 crisis. One notable exception is the group of "other importers," for which the average NPC has risen in the 1975–1980 subperiod. This, however, is largely a reflection of the increase in the NPCs of Japan and Saudi Arabia due to the appreciation of their currencies against the U.S. dollar.

Second, there has been a very large increase in the *variability* of the NPCs between these two subperiods. Two measures have been calculated to estimate this change in variability. One is the coefficient of variation (CV), and the other is the range between the largest and the smallest NPC in each subperiod, expressed as a percentage of the subperiod's average. For the group of all countries, both the CV and the range of change have increased nearly four times in the 1975–1980 subperiod, and increases of the same order of magnitude characterize both the developed and the developing countries.

Table 3–12
Nominal Protection Coefficients: Subperiod Averages and Variabilities

	1968–1972			1975–1980		
	AVE.NPC	*C.V.(%)*	*Range*[a]	*AVE.NPC*	*C.V.(%)*	*Range*[a]
LDCs	1.24	4.5	11	1.10	13.8	39
European countries	1.41	7.4	20	1.32	16.2	64
of which EEC	1.42	4.2	10	1.26	15.1	40
Other importers	1.80	8.2	18	2.33	26.2	64
All countries	1.35	4.4	10	1.30	15.9	45

[a]Range of change is calculated as the percentage difference between the largest and the smallest NPCs relative to the subperiod's average.

Table 3–13 presents these changes in individual countries. (Countries for which data are missing for more than three years have not been included in this table.) In many of them the changes are far more extreme. With the exception of three countries (Nigeria, Pakistan, and Turkey), the range of change of the NPCs has risen in the second subperiod, sometimes by as much as seven, eight, and even nine times. In the three exceptions, the main reason was large changes in the official exchange rate during the first subperiod (see chapters 6 and 7 for an analysis of trade policies in Turkey and Pakistan).

The large increase in the variability of the NPCs is mostly a reflection of a more active trade policy and a much larger effort to insulate the domestic economies against the growing instability of world wheat prices. For an individual country these measures may have been inevitable. As all countries were leaning against the external wind, however, preventing the world market signals from affecting their own economies, fluctuations in the world price and ultimately also in the internal prices of some countries were only enhanced. The multilateral trade negotiations have given little attention to these variations in the levels of protection and put all the emphasis on the average protection rates. Yet the experience of the decade since the crisis of 1973–1974 suggests that negotiations to achieve some form of a multilateral agreement that would at least moderate the tendency of countries to implement "Destabilize-Thy-Neighbor" policies are equally if not more important for the future development of world trade in agricultural commodities.

Table 3–14 provides another comparison between the NPCs during the two subperiods. The results show that in both the developing and the European countries there has been a considerable decrease, by more than 10 percent, in the average NPC from 1968–1972 to 1975–1980. In fifteen out of the twenty-two LDCs and in twelve out of the thirteen European countries sampled, the average NPC in the first subperiod was larger than that for the second subperiod. A comparison of the average NPCs for the two subperiods may not be adequate, however, because of the increase in the variability of the NPCs in the second subperiod. To overcome this difficulty, we have measured the percentage of cases—that is, the number of years in each country (summed up over all countries) in which the country's NPC in any year during the 1975–1980 subperiod was either larger or smaller than the *average* NPC for that country during the 1968–1972 subperiod. The results show that, with the exception of the four "other importers," in 70 percent or more of the cases the NPC in the second subperiod was smaller than the average NPC in the first subperiod.

The decrease in the level of protection was mostly due to the large increase in the world price, and the purpose of these measures was to moderate the rise in the price for consumers. Figure 3–13 manifests the inverse relationship between the NPCs of the main country groups and the world price. It also shows that the increase in the variability of the NPCs was associated with an increase in the variability of the world price. The important question

Table 3–13
Nominal Protection Coefficients: Subperiod Averages and Range of Change

Country	1968–1972		1975–1980	
	AVE.NPC	Range[a]	AVE.NPC	Range[a]
LDCs				
Algeria	0.67	24	0.4	56
Brazil	1.30	18	1.32	30
Chile	0.87	37	0.97	63
Colombia	1.46	20	1.24	42
Egypt	1.04	12	0.86	40
India	1.36	13	0.83	33
Iran	1.20	37	1.03	59
Korea	1.13	17	1.32	67
Malaysia	1.73	24	1.88	29
Mexico	0.93	13	0.73	14
Morocco	1.17	24	1.55	54
Nigeria	1.82	79	1.60	35
Pakistan	1.17	53	0.68	51
Peru	1.49	16	1.36	56
Sri Lanka	1.29	8	0.85	72
Tunisia	1.06	18	1.01	40
Turkey	1.36	43	1.11	40
Venezuela	1.37	8	1.47	58
EEC				
France	1.35	6	1.11	44
Germany	1.63	16	1.40	49
Italy	1.53	12	1.37	44
Netherlands	1.58	14	1.28	51
Ireland	1.07	8	0.99	44
United Kingdom	1.13	24	1.07	53
Benelux	1.53	11	1.32	54
Other Europe				
Finland	1.87	13	1.44	42
Hungary	0.77	5	0.51	52
Norway	2.07	15	1.85	56
Portugal	1.63	17	1.13	18
Switzerland	2.40	12	2.85	63
Yugoslavia	1.12	17	0.97	61
Other Importers				
Israel	0.82	33	0.96	45
Japan	2.39	32	3.87	97
Saudi Arabia	2.21	22	2.83	77
Singapore	1.79	23	1.87	32

[a]Range of change is calculated as the percentage difference between the largest and the smallest NPC relative to the subperiod's average.

Table 3–14
Nominal Protection Coefficients, 1968–1972, Compared with 1975–1980

	Developing Countries	European Countries		Other Importers	All Countries
		EEC	All Europe		
Average NPC 1968–1980	1.09	1.27	1.28	1.95	1.24
(C.V.)	(0.19)	(0.20)	(0.20)	(0.25)	(0.22)
Adjusted Average NPC (1968–1980)[a]	1.17	1.33	1.36	2.09	1.33
(C.V.)	(0.12)	(0.15)	(0.15)	(0.20)	(0.15)
Average NPC 1968–1972	1.24	1.54	1.51	1.80	1.39
Average NPC 1975–1980	1.11	1.34	1.33	2.38	1.31
Number of countries in which the average NPC in 1975–1980 was					
Larger	7	0	1	4	12
Smaller	15	7	12	0	27
than the average NPC in 1968–1972					
Percentage of cases in which the NPC in 1975–1980 was					
Larger	30	29	27	72	34
Smaller	70	71	73	28	66
than the average NPC in 1968–1972					

[a]Adjusted average, excluding the years 1973 and 1974.

raised by these results is whether the policy changes as manifested by the changes in the NPCs were the cause or the effect of the changes in the world price. Even without a formal causality test, however, the answer is obvious. If all major importing countries take similar policy measures, their cumulative response is bound to affect the world price. If, for example, in a given year all these countries lower their protection rate in order to prevent the high world price from raising the domestic price—as they all did in 1973 and 1974—the end result must be a much larger rise in the world price. Even a small decline in world supply would then cause a large rise in price as all countries attempt to prevent their own supply from falling. For an individual country, however, the direction of causality is the exact opposite. The country is forced to react to variations in the world price and to prevent them, at least in part, from being transmitted to the domestic market, or else it would have to absorb all the instability the other trading countries have exported.

To gain a further insight into these issues, we have conducted a regression analysis aimed at explaining the *variations* in the NPCs by the *variations*

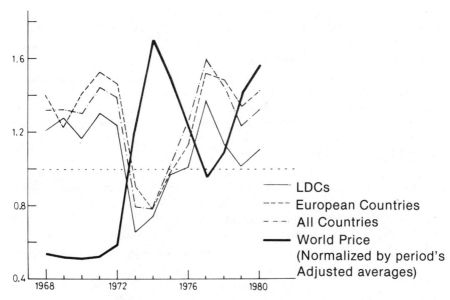

Figure 3–13. Nominal Protection Coefficients in Main Groups of Importing Countries

in the world price. The dependent variable in this analysis was the percentage deviation of the current NPCs in a country either from their period's adjusted average or from their level in the previous year. The explanatory variables were (1) the percentage deviation of the world price from its (adjusted) average over 1968–1980, or (2) the percentage deviation of the world price in the current year from the price in the previous year. The choice between the explanatory variables was made so as to minimize the degree of serial correlation.

Specifically, the following models have been examined

Model	Dependent Variable	Explanatory Variable
a	$n_t = N_t/\bar{N}$	$w_t = P_t^w/\bar{P}^w$
b	n_t	$d_t = w_t - w_{t-1}$
c	$b_t = n_t - n_{t-1}$	$d_t = w_t - w_{t-1}$
d	b_t	d_{t-1}
e	b_t	$f_t = d_t - d_{t-1}$

where

N_t = NPC in year t.

$\bar{N}$ = adjusted average NPC (excluding 1973 and 1974).

P_t^w = world price in year t.

$\bar{P}^w$ = adjusted average world price.

The regression results are presented in table 3–15. They show that in *all* countries the explanatory variable had the correct negative sign; that is, a decline in the NPC in any given year was associated with and possibly caused by a rise in the world price. In all countries except Morocco, Nigeria, Yugoslavia, and Bangladesh, the coefficients were significantly different from 0 at the 5 percent level. In thirty-two of the thirty-nine countries the coefficients were significant at the 1 percent level. The *F* values for all these countries were also significant at the 1 percent level. There is, however, a marked difference between the regression results for the LDCs and those for the other countries. In the group of LDCs, model *a* was the most suitable (in terms of having the least serial correlation and the highest explanatory power) for five countries; model *b* for three countries; model *c* for six countries; and model *e* for eight countries. In the seventeen developed countries, model *c* was the most suitable for fourteen of them, including all the EEC countries.

For the exporting countries other than the United States, the values of the NPCs as calculated in this study—namely, the ratio between the country's

Table 3–15
Explaining the Variations in the Nominal Protection Coefficients: Regression Analysis

Country	Model	R^2	F	Coefficient	t Value	D.W.
Developing Countries						
Algeria	a	0.89	73.6[b]	−0.75	−8.6[b]	1.61
Bangladesh	b	0.29	2.4	−0.85	−1.6	2.44
Brazil	b	0.71	24.2[b]	−0.70	−4.9[b]	1.65
Chile	e	0.57	11.8[a]	−0.86	−3.4[b]	2.43
Colombia	e	0.60	14.9[b]	−0.60	−3.9[b]	2.14
Egypt	c	0.66	15.5[b]	−0.55	−3.9[b]	2.32
India	a	0.89	92.8[b]	−0.61	−9.6[b]	2.20
Iran	c	0.62	14.7[b]	−0.72	−3.8[b]	2.05
Iraq	a	0.79	34.0[b]	−0.60	−5.8[b]	1.56[c]
Korea	c	0.60	15.0[b]	−0.64	−3.9[b]	2.04
Malaysia	c	0.64	16.0[b]	−0.45	−4.0[b]	2.34
Mexico	e	0.63	17.1[b]	−0.51	−4.1[b]	1.90
Morocco	e	0.34	5.1	−0.41	−2.2	2.01
Nigeria	e	0.33	5.0	−0.63	−2.2	2.00
Pakistan	a	0.81	37.7[b]	−0.85	−6.1[b]	1.73
Peru	b	0.58	14.3[b]	−0.62	−3.8[b]	1.63
Philippines	a	0.69	21.8[b]	−0.43	−4.7[b]	2.41
Sri Lanka	e	0.57	13.3[b]	−0.44	−3.6[b]	2.99[d]
Tunisia	c	0.59	11.7[a]	−0.59	−3.4[a]	2.64[c]
Turkey	e	0.52	9.6[a]	−0.46	−3.1[b]	2.19
Venezuela	c	0.65	14.7[b]	−0.64	−3.8[b]	2.17
Yemen	b	0.49	7.6[a]	−0.5	−2.8[a]	1.96

Table 3–15 (continued)

Country	Model	R^2	F	Coefficient	t Value	D.W.
EEC						
France	c	0.89	83.4[b]	− 0.64	− 9.1[b]	2.43
Germany	c	0.92	118.6[b]	− 0.65	− 10.9[b]	2.78[c]
Italy	c	0.76	29.2[b]	− 0.57	− 5.4[b]	2.66[c]
Netherlands	c	0.90	94.1[b]	− 0.68	− 9.8[b]	3.01[d]
Ireland	c	0.80	36.7[b]	− 0.60	− 6.1[b]	3.05[d]
United Kingdom	c	0.79	37.6[b]	− 0.54	− 6.1[b]	1.66
Benelux	c	0.91	97.2[b]	− 0.70	− 9.9[b]	2.83[d]
Other Europe						
Finland	c	0.58	14.0[b]	− 0.57	− 3.7[b]	1.90
Hungary	c	0.86	61.1[b]	− 0.64	− 7.8[b]	2.51[c]
Norway	c	0.74	28.0[b]	− 0.69	− 5.3[b]	2.65[c]
Portugal	a	0.88	65.2[b]	− 0.57	− 8.1[b]	2.45[c]
Switzerland	c	0.67	20.5[b]	− 0.27	− 4.5[b]	1.86
Yugoslavia	e	0.30	3.9	− 0.40	− 2.0	1.82
Other importers						
Israel	b	0.56	14.2[b]	− 0.63	− 3.8[b]	1.40[c]
Japan	c	0.55	12.3[b]	− 0.78	− 3.5	2.01
Saudi Arabia	c	0.72	21.0[b]	− 0.72	− 4.6[b]	2.23
Singapore	c	0.65	18.9[b]	− 0.48	− 4.4[b]	2.38

Note: D.W. is the Durbin-Watson statistic to test for first-order serial correlation in the residual term.

[a]Significant at the 5 percent level.

[b]Significant at 1 percent level.

[c]Indicates that the D.W. statistic suggest the presence of serial correlation.

[d]Indicates that the D.W. statistic is in the indeterminate range.

producers' price and the U.S. export price plus transport costs—may not be the relevant indicator since their reference price is likely to be quite different. Given the importance of the U.S. export price, however, even for these countries, the levels—and, even more, the variations in the NPCs thus calculated can provide first-order estimates for changes in the taxes or subsidies implicit in their trade policy. A rise in NPC above the period's average indicates that the wheat producers' subsidy equivalent in the country's trade policy have risen. In the absence of any consumer's subsidy program, this would also mean that the wheat consumers' subsidy equivalent has declined.

Table 3–16 presents these deviations of the exporting countries' NPCs from their period's averages, and figure 3–14 compares these deviations with those in the main groups of importing countries. In some years the NPCs of

Table 3–16
Deviations of the Nominal Protection Coefficients from the Adjusted Averages[a]

Country	1968	1969	1970	1971	1972	1973	1974	1975	1976	1977	1978	1979	1980	CV.	AD.CV.[a]
Argentina	0.99	1.15	1.02	0.97	0.70	0.64	0.63	0.38	0.77	1.22	1.47	1.11	1.22	0.32	0.30
Australia	0.92	0.97	1.01	1.06	1.03	1.18	0.84	0.84	0.81	1.06	1.19	1.10	1.02	0.12	0.11
Canada	0.87	0.86	1.03	0.98	1.24	1.43	0.97	0.76	0.92	1.08	1.15	1.12	N.A.	0.18	0.15
United States	0.90	0.94	1.02	1.01	1.19	1.29	0.94	1.00	0.88	0.97	1.06	1.06	1.00	0.11	0.08
Weighted average[b]	0.90	0.93	1.02	1.01	1.17	1.31	0.93	0.91	0.88	1.01	1.10	1.08	1.00	0.12	0.09

[a]Excluding 1973 and 1974.
[b]Weighted average of Australia, Canada, and the United States (excluding Argentina) according to their weights in world profits.

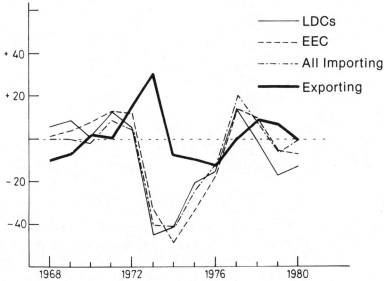

Figure 3–14. Deviations of the NPCs of the Main Country Groups from Their Period's Average

the exporting and the importing countries moved in opposite directions; in other years they moved in the same direction. The differences are most noticeable in the crisis period of the early 1970s. In the United States and Canada the rise in the NPCs had started by 1972 with the large decline in supply as an effect of early Soviet purchases, cutbacks in supply, and the depletion of stocks (see table 3–17). Consumer prices of wheat rose in 1972 by 60 percent in Canada and by 35 percent in the United States, and more than doubled in both countries in 1973. In contrast, consumer prices of wheat in the EEC countries rose by 25 percent in 1972 and by only 10 percent in 1973. It appears that much of the decline in world supply in these two years was absorbed by the exporting countries that initially refrained from any intervention. The large decline in the wheat consumers' subsidy equivalent and the economywide inflationary effects of the large rise in grain prices prompted the governments in these countries to check the rise in the export price through various restrictions, and their NPCs dropped from 31 percent above the period's average in 1973 to 7 percent below the average in 1974. Their consumer price for wheat consequently declined in 1974 by 2 percent in nominal terms and by 17 percent in real terms. The importing countries continued to insulate their economies, and in the EEC the consumer price of wheat was allowed to rise by only 8.5 percent. As a result, world price continued to escalate despite the increase in production in the three main ex-

Table 3–17

Wheat Production, Consumption, Exports, and Stocks Changes in the United States, Canada, and Australia

(in million metric tons)

	1970– 1971	1971– 1972	1972– 1973	1973– 1974	1974– 1975	1975– 1976	1976– 1977
Production	54.2	66.9	62.9	74.6	73.6	87.0	93.6
Consumption	28.2	30.9	29.3	28.5	26.7	27.4	28.6
Exports	41.8	37.8	51.1	51.6	46.7	52.1	48.3
Stock accumulation	− 15.8	− 1.8	− 17.5	− 5.5	+ 0.2	+ 7.5	+ 16.7

Source: T. Josling, "Developed-Country Agricultural Policies and Developing-Country Supplies: The Case of Wheat," International Food Policy Research Institute Research Report No. 43, Washington, D.C., 1980, based on USDA data. Data on stocks changes were calculated as residuals.

porters by 19 percent and the continued depletion of their stocks. In 1975 and 1976 world production continued to expand because of the high price, the abolition of all production restrictions, and the good weather conditions. The importing countries lowered their import subsidies, thus raising their NPCs, in order to prevent a decline in their producer's price. In the United States and Canada producer's prices consequently fell by 15–20 percent in 1975 and by another 18–22 percent in 1976 (the fall in real terms was much deeper because of the exceptionally high rates in inflation in these years). Again, the exporting countries appeared to have absorbed the effects of the glut in world supply. In 1977 both the exporting and the importing countries raised their protection rates, (and their stocks), reflecting their efforts to defend the price to their producers. The end result was a much sharper decline in world price to half its 1974 level and, in real terms, even below the 1968 price. Table 3–18 indicates that as a result the variability of producer's prices in the United States and Canada was two times higher than that in the EEC countries, and the variability of consumers' prices in the two exporting countries was four times higher than in the EEC countries.

The results of this study confirm the claim of T. Josling (1980, p. 11) that "domestic policies inadvertently exacerbated the problems that arose from production variablity." D. Gale Johnson (1975), Shei and Thompson (1977), Zwart and Meilke (1979), Sarris and Freebairn (1983), and others have made essentially the same claim on the basis of the revealed effects of these policies on production, consumption, trade, and stocks. The present study further strengthens this claim on the basis of the direct policy parameters that summarize the overall effects of the country's interventions on the product prices and estimate the taxes or subsidies embodied in them. These parameters show that during the 1970s all the importing countries took

Table 3–18
Variability of Consumers' and Producers' Prices, 1970–1976

	Producers' Prices	*Consumers' Prices*
United States	44.9	39.2
Canada	42.7	46.1
Australia	41.9	25.0
United Kingdom	27.2	36.4
EEC[a]	21.6	10.0

Source: T. Josling, "Developed-Country Agricultural Policies and Developing-Country Supplies: The Case of Wheat," International Food Policy Research Institute Research Report No. 43, Washington, D.C., 1980, based on FAO data.
[a]1970–1975.

measures to insulate their economies from external variations in the world price. As a consequence, even small variations in world supply were magnified to large variations in world price. For an additional country there appeared to be no alternative other than taking the same insulating measures as the other importing (and exporting) countries in order at least to moderate the adverse effects of these variations in the world price on consumers and producers. As all countries have taken the same measures, however, the end result has been growing instability, from which all were doomed to suffer.

Notes

1. The limitations of a linear model with additive disturbances are well known and need no further elaboration here (see, for example, Samuelson 1972, Bigman and Reutlinger 1979b, Newbery and Stiglitz 1981). Indeed, in the subsequent sections some of the more restrictive assumptions of the model will be relaxed. Nevertheless, this simple model, which is based on the model put forward by Waugh (1944); Oi (1961); and Massell (1969, 1970) and subsequently extended by Hueth and Schmitz (1972), Bieri and Schmitz (1974) and Turnovsky (1974, 1976, 1978b) can still be highly instrumental in demonstrating some of the effects of trade and trade policies in an unstable environment.

2. The Compensatory Finance Facility (CFF) of the International Monetary Fund (IMF) and, in particular, the Cereal Import Facility, which was added to the CFF in mid-1981, is one example for this type of insurance arrangement.

3. There could, however, be income effects, since the temporary slumps and hikes in food grains prices would change the real income of consumers. But if the capital market in the country is developed enough, individuals could protect themselves against these temporary aberrations with appropriate insurance arrangements.

4. Stabilization via buffer stocks involves increasing operating and amortization costs, which approach infinity if complete stabilization is sought. Stabilization via

trade, in contrast, permits any degree of stability if the government has access to the foreign-exchange market.

5. See Scandizzo and Bruce (1980) for a discussion of the merits of various methodologies for measuring agricultural price interventions.

6. See, for example, Josling (1980), Bale and Lutz (1979), and Duncan and Lutz (1983) for a cross-country comparison.

References

Abbott, P.C. 1979. Model in international grain trade with government controlled markets. *American Journal of Agricultural Economics* 61:22–31.

Bale, M.D., and Lutz, E. 1979. The effects of trade intervention on international price instability. *American Journal of Agricultural Economics* 61:512–516.

Bieri, J., and Schmitz, A. 1974. Export instability, monopoly power and welfare. *Journal of International Economics* 3:389–396.

Bigman, D. 1982. *Coping with hunger: Toward a system of food security and price stabilization.* Cambridge, Mass.: Ballinger.

Bigman, D., and Reutlinger, S. 1979a. Food price and supply stabilization: National buffer stocks and trade policy. *American Journal of Agricultural Economics* 61: 657–667.

———. 1979b. National and international policies toward food security and price stabilization. *American Economic Review* 69:159–163.

Binswanger, H.P., and Rosenzweig, M. 1983. Behavior and material determinants of production relations in agriculture. Report No. ARU5, Agriculture and Rural Development Department, World Bank.

Blandford, D. 1983. Instability in world grain markets. *Journal of Agricultural Economics* 34:379–395.

Blandford, D., and Schwartz, N.E. 1983. Is the variability of world wheat prices increasing? *Food Policy* 8:305–312.

Blom, J.C. 1982. *Stabilization of the international grain market.* Rotterdam: Brinkman.

Duncan, R., and Lutz, E. 1983. Penetration of industrial country markets by agricultural products from developing countries. *World Development* 11:771–786.

Gotsch, C., and Brown, G. 1980. Prices, taxes, and subsidies in Pakistan agriculture, 1960–1976. Staff Working Paper No. 387, World Bank, Washington, D.C.

Grennes, T.; Johnson, P.R.; and Thursby, M. 1977. *The economics of world grain trade.* New York: Praeger.

———. 1978. Insulating trade policies, inventories, and wheat price stability. *American Journal of Agricultural Economics* 60:132–134.

Hazell, P.B.R. 1982. Instability in Indian foodgrain production. Research report No. 30, International Food Policy Research Institute, Washington, D.C.

———. 1983. Sources of increased instability in Indian and U.S. cereal production. Unpublished manuscript.

Huddleston, B. 1984. Closing the cereals gap with trade and food aid. Research Report No. 43, International Food Policy Research Institute, Washington, D.C.

Hueth, D., and Schmitz, A. 1972. International trade in intermediate and final goods:

Some welfare implications of destabilized prices. *Quarterly Journal of Economics* 86:351–365.

Johnson, D.G. 1975. World agriculture, commodity policy, and price variability. *American Journal of Agricultural Economics* 57:823–828.

Johnson, P.R.; Grennes, T.,; and Thursby, M. 1977. Devaluation, foreign trade controls and domestic wheat prices. *American Journal of Agricultural Economics:* 59:619–627.

Josling, T.E. 1977. Government price policies and the structure of international agricultural trade. *Journal of Agricultural Economics* 28:261–278.

———. 1980. Developed-country agricultural policies and developing-country supplies: The case of wheat. Research Report No. 43, International food Policy Research Institute, Washington, D.C.

Massel, B.F. 1969. Price stabilization and welfare. *Quarterly Journal of Economics* 83:284–298.

———. 1970. Some welfare implications of international price stabilization. *Journal of Political Economy* 78:404–417.

Morrison, T.K. 1983. An analysis of recent trends and determinant of cereal imports by developing countries. *Food Policy.*

Newbery, D.M.G., and Stiglitz, J.E. 1979. The theory of commodity price stabilization rules: Welfare impacts and supply responses. *The Economic Journal 89:* 799–817.

———. 1981. *The theory of commodity price stabilization.* Oxford: Clarendon Press.

Oi, W.Y. 1961. The desirability of price instability under perfect competition. *Econometrica 29:58–64.*

Sampson, G.P., and Snape, R.H. 1980. Effects of the EEC's variable import levies. *Journal of Political Economy 88:1026–1040.*

Samuelson, P.A. 1972. The consumer does benefit from feasible price stability. *Quarterly Journal of Economics 86:476–493.*

Sarris, A.H., and Freebairn, J. 1983. Endogenous price policies and international wheat prices, *American Journal of Agricultural Economics 65:214–224.*

Scandizzo, P.L., and Bruce, C. 1980. Methodologies for measuring agricultural price intervention effects. Staff Working Paper No. 394, World Bank, Washington, D.C.

Schuh, G.E. 1974. The exchange rate and U.S. agriculture. *American Journal of Agricultural Economics 56:1–13.*

Shei, S.Y., and Thompson, R.L. 1977. The impact of trade restrictions on price stability in the world wheat market. *American Journal of Agricultural Economics 59:629–638.*

Turnovsky, S.J. 1974. Price expectations and the welfare gains from price stabilization. *American Journal of Agricultural Economics 56:706–716.*

———. 1976. The distribution of welfare gains from price stabilization: The case of multiplicative disturbances. *International Economic Review 17:133–148.*

———. 1978a. Stabilization rules and the benefits from price stabilization. *Journal of Public Economics 9:37–57.*

———. 1978b. The distribution of welfare gains from price stabilization: A survey of some theoretical issues. In F. Gerard Adams and Sonia A. Klein, eds., *Stabiliz-*

ing world commodity markets. Lexington, Mass.: Lexington Books, D.C. Heath and Company.

UNCTAD. 1983. Instability in food trade and its impact on food security for developing countries. Trade and Development Board Report No. TD/B/C.1/235.

Waugh, F.V. 1944. Does the consumer benefit from price instability? *Quarterly Journal of Economics* 58:602–614.

Young, L., and Kemp, M.C. 1982. On the optimal stabilization of internal producers' prices in international trade. *International Economic Review* 23:123–141.

Zwart, A.C., and Meilke, K.D. 1979. The influence of domestic pricing policies and buffer stocks on price stability in the world wheat industry. *American Journal of Agricultural Economics* 61:434–447.

4
A Comparative Analysis of Alternative Producers' Support and Stabilization Programs

Government interventions in support of the agricultural sector are widely practiced in both the developed and the developing countries. An important aspect of these interventions is the protection they provide to farmers against the effects of crop failures or price falls on their income and consumption. In the developing countries the need for interventions such as government insurance is especially strong, since these countries lack adequate insurance or credit markets that can offer at least some protection against these risks on a commercial basis. The losses farmers may suffer in bad years may not only endanger the long-run prospects of the agricultural sector but also jeopardize the very livelihood of small subsistence farmers. The reduction in farmers' income may also have so-called spread effects on the entire rural community in bad years, since local trade and employment may also decline with the drop in consumption and investment.

The protection that government stabilization programs can provide against wide fluctuations in income and the purchasing power of rural consumers will not only save farmers from default in bad years but also have long-term effects on the economy at large by inducing risk-averse farmers to make production decisions involving both higher average returns and higher risks. This response is likely to be reflected in a more extensive use of fertilizers, a shift to higher yield and riskier crop varieties, greater specialization in production, and larger investments in fixed capital.

This chapter analyzes the economywide effects of several producers' support policies commonly practiced in both developed and developing countries with the objective of promoting agricultural production and protecting farmers against instability. The policies analyzed are minimum price support, government procurement, guaranteed income, buffer stocks, and several trade policies.

Typically, each of these policies has both short- and long-term objectives and effects. The price-support program, for instance, is often designed to raise the *average* price for the product and hence to promote its production. At the same time, however, the program is also designed to protect farmers against sharp drops in price and income and hence to lower the risks involved in its production.

When government policies have explicit stabilization objectives, the policy decisions in any given year depend on the actual weather (or any other stochastic) event at that year. Thus, for instance, governments often decide to step up their interventions by increasing public procurement, raising the floor price, or raising the tariff rate in order to prevent a catastrophic fall in farmers' income when there is an extreme shortfall in production, a glut of cheap imports, or a drop in foreign demand for the country's farm exports. An analysis of short-term government policies therefore also requires an explicit analysis of the year-to-year variations of government policies as they respond to the actual realization of the stochastic event.

A theoretical analysis of policies of this type is often complex and requires many simplifying assumptions (see chapter 1). To allow a more complete evaluation of alternative policies, much of the analysis in this chapter is conducted through simulation experiments with a prototype model of the food grains sector. The simulation results are, obviously, model-specific; although sensitivity analysis may offer some guidelines as to how robust the conclusions are, they may not be valid for other crops or other parameter values. The simulation results highlight, however, the indirect effects of different programs, the degree to which policies can substitute for each other, and the possibility of ranking alternative policies according to their relative efficiency once their objectives have been determined. The chapter develops a behavioral model of farmers' production, consumption marketing and in-farm stocks decisions in order to explore their response to government price and stabilization policies.

The Model, Data, Parameters, and Policy Rules

The sectorial, partial-equilibrium model was constructed as a prototype model of the food grains sector in a developing country. However, to maintain the generality of the analysis at this stage and to avoid reference to any specific country or crop, all prices and quantities are expressed as index numbers rather than actual levels. A brief description of the main components of the model follows (see chapter 2 for a detailed description).

1. Supply is a log-linear-constant-elasticity function of the *expected* price. Weather-induced fluctuations in supply are caused by normally distributed multiplicative disturbances. In the base case, the price elasticity of supply is assumed to be 0.25 and its coefficient of variation 9 percent. The expected price itself is a function of past prices (see the first section of chapter 2 for further details on the formulation of expectations).

2. Initially, producers are assumed to be risk-neutral (or, alternatively, it

is assumed that a complete set of insurance markets exists in the country). Subsequently, however, an explicit risk response is introduced—assumed to be represented as a shift parameter in the supply function—which is inversely related to the variability of farmers' income (see chapter 2 for a discussion of this specification). The supply function thus has the form

$$\log s_t = \alpha + \beta \log P_t^e - \delta \log R_t + v_t$$

where P_t^e is the expected price calculated as an average of the prices in the preceding nine years, and R_t is the risk factor calculated as the coefficient of variation of farmers' income in the preceding nine years.

In the base case the risk-response elasticity δ is assumed to be 0.25, implying that a 1 percent rise in the coefficient of variation of farmers' income would cause producers to reduce their output by 0.25 percent.

3. Demand is a log-linear-constant-elasticity function of the actual market price. In the base case, the demand elasticity is assumed to be 0.3.

The decision rules in each of the producers' stabilization programs are as follows.

Price Support

The program takes the form of deficiency payments; that is, the government makes up the difference between the market price and the prespecified floor price whenever the market price falls below the floor level. The program considered in the next section assumes a fixed support price, determined at a level of 85 percent of the normal price. Later in the chapter, other forms of this program are considered. The government does not constrain production, nor does it remove any excess from the market. This program, therefore, has no direct effect on the market price and hence no immediate effect on consumers. In the long run, however, producers would respond to the resulting increase in the average price and possibly also to the reduction in their income variability by expanding production, thus eventually lowering the market price also.

Government Procurement

Under this program, the government procures the excess supply and removes it from the market whenever the market price falls below the floor price (assumed, as before, to be 85 percent of the normal price). The support (or procurement) price thus becomes the effective market price and all sectors in the economy are directly affected by the policy. The government stores the surplus and releases it in later periods when the market price rises above a prespecified ceiling (assumed to be 10 percent above the normal price). In this policy, the stocks operations are, therefore, by-products or even residuals of the procurement program, although their stabilizing effects on the market price and on food supply are potentially significant. It is further assumed that there is no capacity constraint on the amount extracted from the market and stored. If the existing storage facility is filled, the remaining surplus is stored in temporary facilities or even under cover in open areas. It is assumed, however, that this remaining surplus suffers from a greater decay, at a rate of 10 percent annually.[1] Operating costs are also taken into account, and each loading and unloading activity per unit (metric ton) costs an amount equal to 5 percent of the product's normal price.

Buffer Stocks

This program is operated primarily to stabilize domestic consumption and the market price. Nevertheless, the purchases into storage in years of good harvest and low prices may help prevent severe income losses to producers attributable to price drops. At the same time, the release of grains from storage in years of poor harvest would lower the market price and thus hurt producers even further. The final effect depends largely on the price elasticity of demand, on the frequency distribution of grain production, and on the storage rules. In the present analysis, the storage operations are assumed to be triggered by a price band. The upper and lower threshold prices are assumed to be 10 percent above and below the normal price, respectively, creating a price band of 20 percent within which the price is allowed to float freely. The costs of operating the storage facility include amortization costs (investment in the facility, assumed to be $150 per MT of storage facility, to be amortized over a period of twenty years at a 5 percent real interest rate),[2] and handling costs (assumed to be 5 percent of the normal price).

Guaranteed Income

This program has the form of a crop-insurance program, although in the present analysis no insurance premiums are assumed to be collected. The program is activated whenever farmers' income falls below a prespecified critical level—assumed to be 85 percent of their normal income—because of either a poor harvest or a fall in price. The program supplements farmers' income up to the critical level.

Two types of instability measures have been used to evaluate the different policies. One is the standard coefficient of variation. The other, which has been termed *risk,* measures the probability of events occurring in one tail of the distribution only. Thus, for instance, *farmers' income risk* measures the probability that farmers' income falls below a certain critical level.

Main Results

In evaluating the performance of different producers' support and stabilization programs, their effect on the average level and the variability of farmers' income and price should be weighed against the claim they place on the government financial resources. The main performance criteria are the average level and the variability of farmers' price (or, when relevant, farmers' unit value); the average and the variability of farmers' income; and their *income risk*—defined here as the probability that their income falls by more than 15 percent below their normal income. Government expenditures on the program is the main performance measure against which the above measures are weighted.

Table 4–1 summarizes the effects of the policies under consideration on these performance criteria in a closed economy and when there is no risk response in production (that is, when farmers are risk-neutral). Several results stand out. First, all the programs manage effectively to eliminate the income risk. The procurement program has the strongest stabilizing effects on both price and income. The stocks accumulated from procurements in years of plentiful production are released in later years when shortfalls in production occur, thus lowering the price to producers in those years. As a result, producers' income with the procurement program rises by only 0.7 percent, compared with rises by 3.9 and 1.7 percent, respectively, under the minimum-price and guaranteed-income programs. On the other hand, con-

Table 4–1
Main Effects of Alternative Producers' Support Programs in a Closed Economy, No Risk Response

	Policy				
	No Intervention	Minimum Price Support	Government Procurement	Guaranteed Income	Buffer Stocks[a]
Farmers' price (Unit Value)					
Mean	103.6	106.1	102.5	104.6	101.8
Variability (CV%)	32.7	26.5	21.2	29.9	23.6
Farmers' revenues					
Mean[b]	101.4	105.4	101.6	103.1	100.3
Variability (CV%)	22.3	16.2	12.5	19.2	15.0
Risk[c]	24.4	0.0	0.1	0.0	11.0
Government expenditures[b]	0	5.5	0.4	2.3	0.9

[a]Stocks equal to 10 percent of the annual production.

[b]Expressed as percentage of the revenues from the crop in a stable year.

[c]Probability that farmers' income falls by more than 15 percent below their normal income.

sumers would benefit from the greater stability in the market price and, perhaps most important, this program requires the lowest fiscal costs.[3]

With buffer stocks equal to 10 percent of annual production, there are still considerable risks that farmers' income would fall below the level deemed necessary to secure their solvency. The costs of buffer stocks, however (which include amortization costs) are relatively small, and their desirability should be determined also by their effect on consumers (the same is true for the procurement program).

Table 4–2 summarizes the effects of the policies in an open economy. The most obvious difference between the results in this table and those in table 4–1 are the much larger stability of the open economy. The stabilizing effects of free trade would considerably reduce both the need for and the fiscal costs of producers' stabilization programs. Thus, for instance, minimum price support would reduce the coefficient of variation of farmers' income by 6.1 percentage points in the closed economy and by only 1.3 percentage points in the open economy. The fiscal costs of the program in the open economy will be less than one-quarter of their costs in the closed economy. Interestingly, however, the minimum-price program—as well as the procurement program—effectively eliminates the income risk of farmers in the closed economy, whereas in the open economy there is still a risk of 2 percent. The reason is that in the closed economy a fall in production triggers a rise in price that moderates the decline in farmers' income and (depending on the price elasticity of demand) may even raise it. In the open economy a fall in price

Table 4–2
Main Effects of Alternative Producers' Support Programs in an Open Economy, No Risk Response

	Policy				
	No Intervention	*Minimum Price Support*	*Government Procurement*	*Guaranteed Income*	*Buffer Stocks*[a]
Farmers' price (Unit Value)					
Mean	101.3	102.1	101.5	101.5	100.9
Variability (CV%)	15.2	13.6	12.7	14.8	13.1
Farmers' revenues					
Mean[b]	100.7	101.8	101.2	101.0	100.4
Variability (CV%)	11.7	10.4	10.2	11.2	10.6
Risk[c]	7.0	1.8	1.8	0.0	4.8
Government expenditures[b]	0	1.2	0.3	0.3	1.1

[a]Stocks equal to 10 percent of the annual production.
[b]Expressed as percentage of the revenues from the crop in a stable year.
[c]Probability that farmers' income falls by more than 15 percent below their normal income.

may concur with a low import price, in which case farmers' income may fall well below the critical level. These potentially destabilizing effects of free trade on farmers' income were discussed by Newbery and Stiglitz (1981) and in chapter 3. Farmers' problems may be aggravated in countries where the government subsidizes imports in order to secure low food prices to consumers. This issue is discussed later in this chapter.

Table 4–3 summarizes the effects of these policies when risk-averse producers respond to the income risks. The most noteworthy result is the considerable decline in the mean price and the rise in output as an effect of the greater stability secured by the policies. In crops for which the price elasticity of demand is greater than one, the fall in mean production as an effect of the greater stability would, however, be accompanied by a *fall* in farmers' mean income, rather than a rise—as in the present simulations. In that case the income risk would be *higher* with risk response than with risk neutrality when there is no intervention, and the fiscal costs to prevent this risk would also be higher. In the present simulations, the lower level of production under risk aversion and the resulting higher prices reduce the need for government interventions to prevent sharp falls in the price or in farmers' income.

Table 4–4 summarizes the economic gains and losses from these policies to the main sectors of the economy. Both consumers and producers appear to gain from the minimum-price-support and the guaranteed-income programs. As mentioned earlier, these programs have no direct effect on the market price, and consumers gain as a result of producers' response to the increase in

Table 4–3
Main Effects of Alternative Producers' Support Programs in a Closed Economy, with Risk Response

	Policy				
	No Intervention	*Minimum Price Support*	*Government Procurement*	*Guaranteed Income*	*Buffer Stocks*[a]
Farmers' price (unit value)					
Mean	112.6	112.2	108.1	112.3	107.7
Variability (CV%)	33.2	28.5	24.4	31.1	24.2
Farmers' revenues					
Mean[b]	107.5	108.8	105.1	107.9	104.3
Variability (CV%)	22.6	18.0	15.0	20.4	15.4
Risk[c]	15.7	0.0	0.1	0.0	8.2
Government expenditures[b]	0	3.6	0.2	1.4	0.9

[a]Stocks equal to 10 percent of the annual production.
[b]Expressed as percentage of the revenues from the crop in a stable year.
[c]Probability that farmers' income falls by more than 15 percent below their normal income.

Table 4–4
Expected Annual Economic Gains or Losses from Alternative Producers'
Support Program, No Risk Response

	Economic Sector			
Policy	Consumers	Producers	Government	Total Economy
Closed economy[a]				
Minimum price support	+ 1.9	+ 3.4	− 5.5	− 0.2
Government procurement	− 0.2	+ 0.5	− 0.4	− 0.1
Guaranteed income	+ 0.8	+ 1.4	− 2.3	− 0.1
Buffer stocks	+ 0.8	− 0.5	− 0.9	− 0.6
Open economy[b]				
Minimum price support	+ 0.2	+ 1.0	− 1.3	− 0.1
Government procurement	− 0.2	+ 1.5	− 0.3	− 0.0
Guaranteed income	+ 0.1	+ 0.2	− 0.3	0.0
Buffer stocks	+ 0.5	− 0.3	− 1.1	− 0.9

Note: Expressed as percentage of the annual expenditures on this crop.
[a]Compared with no intervention.
[b]Compared with free trade.

the mean price. Obviously, consumers' gains would be much larger with risk response since the effect of the policies on the level of output would then be much larger. The fiscal costs outweigh the economic gains of the private sector, and the economy at large would lose from all programs. With risk response, however, the economy would have net gains because of the rise in output, provided that the price elasticity of demand is less than one. The net effects of the programs on income distribution may be quite substantial. An important factor is the share of each sector in the tax burden necessary for financing these policies. In the open economy, however, the frequency and intensity of government interventions to support the producers is much smaller, and the gains or losses from the policy would therefore also be smaller.

Some Sensitivity Analysis

Table 4–5 summarizes the results of the simulation experiments with less stable production and more elastic demand. Clearly the effects of the policies are quite sensitive to the value of these key parameters. In a more stable crop, stabilization policies are, as expected, both less frequently implemented and much less costly. It should be noted, however, that the coefficient of variation in the base case, assumed to be 9 percent, is by no means high. Thus, for instance, in wheat production in the United States this coefficient is 10 percent

Table 4–5
Main Effects of Alternative Producers' Support Programs in a Closed Economy, Some Sensitivity Analysis

	Policy				
	No Intervention	Minimum Price Support	Government Procurement	Guaranteed Income	Buffer Stocks[a]
More stable crop*					
Farmers' price (unit value)					
Mean	100.1	101.7	100.8	101.2	100.5
Variability (CV %)	17.3	15.3	11.8	16.7	11.7
Farmers' revenues					
Mean[b]	100.4	101.4	100.5	100.7	100.0
Variability (CV %)	12.0	10.1	7.3	11.4	7.4
Risk[c]	8.8	0.0	0.0	0.0	2.2
Government expenditures[b]	0.0	1.4	0.2	0.4	0.9
More elastic demand**					
Farmers' price (unit value)					
Mean	100.9	101.1	100.8	100.9	100.6
Variability (CV %)	11.5	11.1	9.7	11.5	9.4
Farmers' revenues					
Mean	100.1	100.3	100.1	100.1	100.0
Variability (CV %)	2.3	2.1	2.2	2.3	2.4
Risk	0.0	0.0	0.0	0.0	0.0
Government expenditures	0.0	0.3	0.2	0.9	0.9

*Coefficient of variation in the countries production is 5 percent against 9 percent in the base case.
**Price elasticity of demand is 0.8 against 0.3 in the base case.
[a]Stocks equal to 10 percent of the annual production.
[b]Expressed as percentage of the revenues from the crop in a stable year.
[c]Probability that farmers' income falls by more than 15 percent below their normal income.

(see, e.g., Hazell 1983). The base case results and the sensitivity analysis suggest that for less stable crops these programs are likely to be considerably more effective but also much more costly, as further results presented later indeed confirm.

The results in table 4–5 also show that with higher price elasticity of demand, the price and, especially, farmers' income become more stable, and the income risk is practically zero even without any policy. These results require further clarification, however. When the price elasticity of demand is 1, farmers' income in the closed economy is completely stable. As the price elasticity rises above 1, the variability of farmers' income also rises, and it would be equal to the variability in production when demand is completely elastic. The need for stabilization programs may therefore exist for products having high price elasticity of demand, as well as for those having low price elasticity of demand.

Finally, table 4–6 summarizes the results with so-called cobweb expectations—that is, when supply is a function of last year's price only. The most striking result here is the much higher variability associated with this naive form of expectation. With no intervention, the variability of farmers' price and income is more than 100 percent higher than their variability with the adaptively rational expectations assumed in the base case (where the expected price is a simple average of the past nine prices). Another noteworthy result is the marked effectiveness of the stabilization programs, matched, however, by a somewhat less than proportional increase in government expenditures. Thus, for instance, with cobweb supply the procurement program would reduce the variability of farmers income by 68 percent at a cost equal to 1.6 percent of the total revenues from the crop. In the base case the comparable figures are 48 and 1.4 percent.

Minimum Price Support: Alternative Schemes

In an earlier section we saw that a program supporting a floor price equal to 85 percent of the average price through restitution payments may heavily tax the fiscal budget. On average, government expenditures would amount to 5.5 percent of the total normal revenues from the crop. For a country such as India, this may mean that these expenses, which do not include administrative costs, would be on average $600 billion. Since such falls in price would occur, on average, only once every three years, it means that in those years in which the price falls below the minimum level, government expenses would be approximately 17 percent of the total revenues from the crop. Again, for a country such as India the program would therefore involve fiscal costs of at

Table 4–6
Main Effects of Alternative Producers' Support Program in a Closed Economy, Cobweb Supply

	No Intervention	Minimum Price Support	Government Procurement	Guaranteed Income	Buffer Stocks[a]
Farmers' price (unit value)					
Mean	118.8	110.0	102.8	110.6	103.5
Variability (CV %)	66.0	30.9	19.5	39.1	26.6
Farmers' revenues					
Mean[b]	108.9	108.6	101.9	107.2	101.3
Variability (CV %)	42.6	18.5	13.7	24.5	17.0
Risk[c]	33.7	0.0	3.8	0.0	14.1
Government expenditures[b]	0.0	7.4	1.6	4.0	0.8

[a]Stocks equal to 10 percent of the annual production.
[b]Expressed as percentage of the revenues from the crop in a stable year.
[c]Probability that farmers' income falls by more than 15 percent below their normal income.

least $2 billion once every three years. In this section we examine three alternatives for reducing the fiscal costs of the price-support program:

1. Lowering the floor price to 80 percent of the mean price.
2. Adjusting the floor price from year to year in order to moderate the price declines rather than preventing them altogether.
3. Charging premium payments when the market price exceeds the critical price.

Under the second alternative of adjusting the floor price, the government determines the minimum price each year with the objective of moderating the fall in farmers' price rather than preventing it altogether. If, for instance, in any given year the market price is expected to fall by 30 percent below its normal level, the policy would allow the price to fall by only a fraction of this decline—say by 15 percent—rather than preventing any decline below a fixed floor price. The scheme examined here is operated according to the following linear (but still discontinuous) rule

$$P_F = \begin{cases} \beta P_c + (1 - \beta)P & : \text{if } P < P_c \\ P & : \text{if } P \geq P_c. \end{cases}$$

where P is the market price, P_c is the critical price below which support is given, P_F is the price to the farmers, and $0 \leq \beta \leq 1$. This rule has the effect of modifying the effective or the *target* demand curve that farmers face, making it more elastic at the lower segment of the price distribution below P_c. The target price elasticity of demand at that range is then given by $\eta/(1 - \beta)$, where η is the market price elasticity at that segment. In the simulation analysis in this section, the floor price, P_c, is assumed to be 85 percent of the normal price and β to be equal to 0.5. Thus a 10 percent drop in the market price below P_c would entail only a 5 percent decline in the farmers' price.

The alternative of charging premium payments from farmers in the good year has the form of an insurance program. In theory the program could be self-financed and carried out on a commercial basis. In practice, however, the capital market in the developing countries is not developed enough, and the government would have to offer these services. The scheme need not be obligatory, and farmers may be free to choose whether they want the protection of the price-support program in years of low prices at the cost of premium payments in years of high prices. In the insurance scheme considered here, the premium payments are determined by a linear rule and farmers' price is given by

$$P_F = \begin{cases} P_c & : \text{if } P < P_c \\ \mu \cdot P_c + (1 - \mu) \cdot P & : \text{if } P \geq P_c \end{cases}$$

Here, μ is the premium rate, so that when the market price rises, say, by 10 percent above P_c, the price to farmers would rise by only $(1 - \mu) \cdot 10$ percent. In the experiments presented here, the premium rates were assumed to be 10 percent in one scheme and 20 percent in another. The floor price P_c is still assumed to be 85 percent of the normal price.

This structure of an insurance scheme is obviously highly stylized, and no attempt will be made to analyze the complexities involved in crop insurance programs, including questions of moral hazard, adverse selection, the actual administration of the scheme, and so on. Instead, the objective here is to offer orders of magnitude of the savings that can be achieved through this kind of scheme and their initial effects on the farmers.

Table 4–7 summarizes the simulation results describing the effects of the various schemes. The results suggest that the insurance scheme would be preferred, by both the government and producers, over the other schemes that scale down the price-support program. Thus, for instance, with a premium rate of 20 percent, the government would be able to cover most of its expenses and at the same time eliminate the income risk of the farmers.[4] Relative to the base-case program, farmers' mean income would decline by 3.4 percent with the insurance scheme as a result of the premium payments, and by 2.3 percent with the adjusting floor-price scheme. Farmers are likely, however, to prefer the insurance scheme, for several reasons. First, the adjusting floor-price scheme would still leave an income risk equal to 6.8 percent. In other words, over the long run, once every fifteen years, farmers' income would still fall by more than 15 percent below their normal income. With the insurance scheme this risk is eliminated altogether. Given the wide difference between the interest for creditors and that for debtors, farmers

Table 4–7
Main Effects of Alternative Minimum Price Support Schemes, Closed Economy, No Risk Response

| | Guaranteed Minimum Price Scheme | | | Premium Payments | |
	Fixed Minimum Price = 85	Fixed Minimum Price = 80	Adjusting Minimum Price	Premium Rate 10%	Premium Rate 20%
Farmers' revenues					
Mean[a]	105.4	104.9	103.1	103.6	102.0
Variability (CV %)	16.2	17.7	18.6	14.4	12.7
Risk[b]	0.0	0.0	6.8	0.0	0.0
Government expenditures[a]	5.5	3.6	2.6	3.2	0.8

[a]Expressed as percentage of the revenues from the crop in a stable year.
[b]Probability that farmers' income falls by more than 15 percent below their normal income.

are likely to find it far more expensive to use their own means to protect themselves against such extreme falls in their income through savings or loans. Second, the argument in favor of a government insurance scheme would be even stronger for risk-averse farmers, who are likely to respond to the greater stability secured by the program by increasing their output. This increase would not only benefit consumers but would also moderate the decline in the farmers' mean income.

Figure 4–1 illustrates the trade-off between the level of government expenditures and the variability of farmers' income under different levels of the minimum price support. The concavity of the curve shows that increasing the stability of farmers' income by raising the minimum price involves increasing *marginal* costs for the government. Put differently, the cost-effectiveness of the program tends to decline at higher levels of the minimum price.

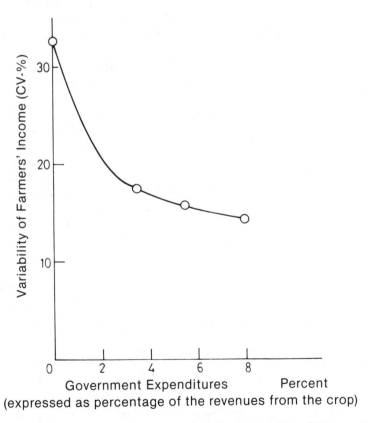

Figure 4–1. Government Expenditures and the Variability of Farmers' Income under Different Levels of the Minimum Price Support

Government Procurement

The various stabilization programs have the effect of transforming the instability of farmers' income to an instability in the fiscal budget. With the procurement program this is reflected mostly by the accumulation of large stocks that often exceed by far the amounts deemed necessary to buffer future supply shortages. The huge stocks of grain accumulated in the United States as part of the government efforts to prevent a fall in grain prices below the minimum guaranteed price is, perhaps, the most familiar example of these effects of the policy, but similar problems exist in India, Turkey, Brazil, the Common Market, and many other countries.

All too often the procurement price effectively determines the market price, considerably reduces the trading activities of the private sector, and overburdens public storage far beyond its capacity or needs. Furthermore, the administration costs involved in the procurement activities[5] may increase substantially the burden on the fiscal budget, thus making the program much less attractive than the earlier results in tables 4–1 and 4–2 suggest. In addition, the previous assumption that losses in the public storage are at an annual rate of 10 percent are rather optimistic and are more appropriate to dry or semiarid conditions. In humid or semihumid conditions these losses may be substantially higher. In this section we examine the performance of the program at different levels of the procurement price; evaluate the fiscal costs, taking into account administrative costs—assumed to add 20 percent to the direct procurement expenses (when procurements are made); and assess the cost-effectiveness of the program when the annual storage losses are 25 percent. To measure the instability introduced into the government fiscal budget by the program, we measure the *fiscal risk,* defined as the probability that government expenses on this account exceed a certain critical level, assumed to be 10 percent of the total revenues from the crop. For a country such as India, that would mean government expenses in excess of $1.5 billion.

Table 4–8 presents the simulation results summarizing the fiscal consequences of the program (assuming that storage losses are still 10 percent annually). It shows that administrative costs may add roughly 75 percent to the costs of the program and increase the fiscal risk by more than 50 percent. Thus, for instance, when the procurement price is 85 percent of the mean price, government total costs would exceed the average costs on the program by more than 1,300 percent once every fifteen years.

Figure 4–2 illustrates the trade-off between the instability of government expenditures and the variability of farmers' income that results from raising the procurement price from zero to 90 percent of the minimum price. It shows that with the rise in the procurement price and the resulting increase in the quantities procured for storage, the effects of the higher storage losses are

Table 4–8
Fiscal Expenses and the Quantities Procured at Different Procurement Prices

	Procurement Price (as Percentages of the Mean Price)			
	75	80	85	90
Government expenditures				
Average direct expenses[a]	0.1	0.2	0.4	0.8
Average total expenses[a,b]	0.2	0.3	0.7	1.3
Fiscal risk[c]				
Without administrative costs	1.3	2.6	4.8	7.6
With administrative costs	2.0	4.3	6.6	10.3
Procurement				
Average quantity procured[d]	0.9	1.3	1.8	2.5
Probability that procurement is made	17.1	23.5	31.6	38.8
Average quantity procured[d] when procurement is made	5.3	5.6	5.8	6.4

[a]Expenses as percentage of total farmers' revenue from the crop.

[b]Including administration costs that add 20 percent to the procurement expenses when procurement is made.

[c]Fiscal risk = the probability that government expenditures exceed 10 percent of total revenues from the crop.

[d]Quantities as percentage of total output in a normal year.

likely to be more significant than those of the administrative overhead costs. Nevertheless, despite the addition of overhead costs or higher storage losses, the resulting increase in the fiscal burden does not appear to make the program less desirable than the other programs; and, at least on fiscal grounds, it still seems to be more attractive than the minimum-price program. The conclusion may not be extended to countries or crops for which the administrative costs or the storage losses are even higher, as would be the case for support programs with perishable products. For food or feed grains, however, the results appear to justify the decision of many governments to resort to this program rather than to any of its alternatives.

Price and Income Effects of Price Policies on Farmers' Own Demand and Excess Supply

The various producers' support programs examined earlier, and any variations thereof, can be grouped into two categories: programs that provide direct support to farmers without changing the market price, and programs that support a prespecified target price by bringing the market price to that level. Examples of the former include price support through restitution pay-

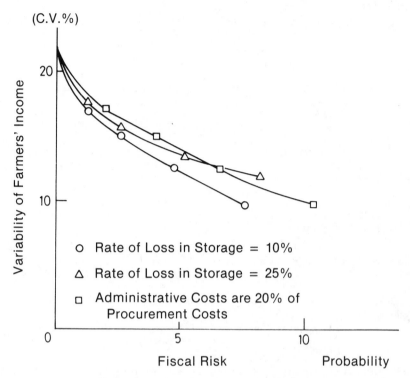

Figure 4–2. Instability of Government Expenditures and the Variability of Farmers' Income at Different Procurement Prices

ments, guaranteed income, and various crop insurance schemes. Examples of the latter include government procurement, buffer stocks, and set-aside programs (often implemented in the United States).

Programs in the first category effectively create a dual price system by introducing a wedge between the price consumers pay and the price (or the unit value) producers get. Thus, for example, with a price-support program, our earlier simulation analysis showed that farmers' mean price would be 6 percent above the market mean price. Programs in the second category maintain a unified system of prices for consumers and producers. At these prices, however, the market is no longer in equilibrium, and government purchases or sales are necessary to clear the market.

The distinction between these two categories is necessary for the analysis when farmers' own demand for the product constitutes a substantial portion of the total market demand, so that attention is then focused on their *excess* supply. The reason is that, from the point of view of the beneficiary farmers, programs in the first category have the effect of an income transfer. Raising their income via, say, the restitution payments would shift farmers' own demand curve for the product (in proportion to their income elasticity of demand) and reduce somewhat their excess supply. An equilibrium market price would then be determined, which takes into account this shift in farmers' demand.

In the closed economy and when no other policy is implemented, farmers' revenues would fall below their normal level in years when the actual output *exceeds* the average, if the price elasticity of demand for staple foods is less than 1. Guaranteed-income or price-support programs, which do not affect the market price directly, would in those years raise farmers' own demand, lower their excess supply, and thus moderate the decline in the market price. In the open economy, in contrast, prices are mostly determined by the border price for exports (FOB) or imports (CIF). Farmers' revenues are therefore likely to fall below their normal level in years when actual output falls below the average. The guaranteed-income program that raises farmers' demand in these years would have the effect of raising the market demand for imports or lowering its supply of exports.

Programs in the second category, which alter the market price, affect farmers both as producers and as consumers of the product. To examine these simultaneous effects, we analyze the consumption decisions of a farmer producing a single commodity, part of which he retains for his own consumption and part of which he sells in order to buy other products.[6] Ordinarily, the production and consumption decisions are separable; in analyzing the latter, the consumer can be regarded as having an endowment of the product. This analysis will be made in reference to figure 4–3.

In the figure, the consumer is endowed with the quantity $\overline{OW}$ of x_1 and is faced with market prices p^0, represented by the slope of the budget line $\overline{VW}$. At these prices his position at A indicates that he chooses to consume the quantity $\overline{OM}$ of his own endowment and to sell the quantity NW. When the price of x_1 rises, the new budget line would be $\overline{VW}$, at which the consumer would have a higher level of utility. This consumer-producer would therefore *gain* from a price rise for those commodities of which he has excess supply. His position at B indicates that he will increase his consumption of both x_1, for which the income effect outweighs the substitution effect, and x_2, for which the income and price effects work in the same direction. The Hicksian compensating variation for the consumer—that is, the additional endowment needed to leave him at the original level of welfare following the rise in the price of x_1—is given in the figure by $-\overline{QW}$, where the minus sign indicates that this quantity must be *subtracted* from his original endowment. $\overline{QW}$ thus measures the welfare gains of this producer following a price rise. The equivalent variation is given by $+\overline{WR}$ (or, in money terms, by $\overline{VT}$), indicating that additional endowment would have to be given to this consumer to allow him the welfare level u_1, if the price of x_1 were to fall back to its original level.

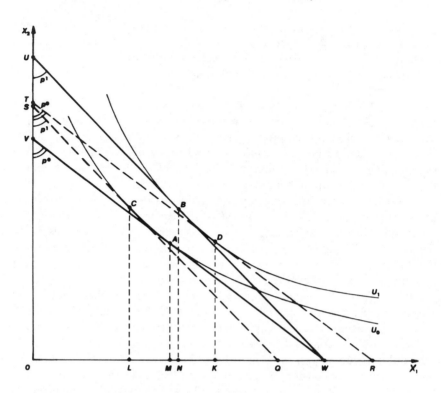

Figure 4–3. Consumption Decisions for an Agent with Commodity Income

The important point to note in this analysis is that the two simultaneous effects are already accounted for by the slope of the demand curve of these farmers. To see this, derive the Slutsky equation for these farmers who are both producers and consumers of that crop (see Bigman and Shalit 1983). Their total production consists of a bundle of products, $Q = (q_1, \ldots, q_n)$, which, at harvest time, is assumed to be fixed. Facing the prices $P = (p_1, \ldots, p_n)$, they choose their consumption basket $X = (x_1, \ldots, x_n)$ so as to maximize an increasing, strictly concave utility function $u(X)$, subject to the budget constraint

$$P(X - Q) = 0$$

Let $x(P, u)$ denote the Hicksian compensated demand curves and let $x(P, PQ)$ denote the Marshallian demand curves of a typical consumer-producer. Then,

$$\frac{dx_i(P, PQ)}{dp_j} = \frac{\partial x_i(P, PQ)}{\partial p_j} + \tag{4.1}$$

$$q_j \cdot \frac{\partial x_i(P, PQ)}{\partial Y}; i, j = 1, \ldots, n$$

where $Y = PQ$ is the consumers' nominal income. The first element on the right hand side of equation 4.1 registers the ordinary price effect on consumers' demand when income is held constant. The second element registers the income effect on a consumer endowed with the quantity q_j, when the price of that commodity rises. From the familiar Slutsky equation for an ordinary consumer, however, together with equation 4.1, we get

$$\frac{dx_i(P, PQ)}{dp_j} = \frac{\partial x_i(P, u)}{\partial p_j} \bigg|_{\bar{\mu}} \tag{4.2}$$

$$+ (q_j - x_j) \cdot \frac{\partial x_i(P, Y)}{\partial Y} \bigg|_{\bar{P}} \quad i,j = 1, \ldots, n .$$

The first element on the right hand side of equation 4.2 is the substitution effect, which is always negative for a change in the product's own price. The second element is the income effect for this consumer-producer when the price remains constant. It registers, therefore, the change in income when output is changing. If x_i is a normal good—that is, if $\partial x_i / \partial Y \geq 0$—and if the consumer-producer is a net seller of that product—that is, $(q_j - x_j) \geq 0$—the income effect would be *positive*. In that case the income effect outweighs the substitution effect, and the entire Marshallian demand curve is positively sloped. This consumer-producer thus gains from a price increase if he is an excess supplier of that product, and these income gains will allow him to increase his own consumption of the product. Bigman and Shalit (1983) have shown that these gains are already embodied in the shape of the demand curve, and have established the conditions under which the ordinary measures of this consumer-producer's surpluses via the areas under the supply and demand curves are a good approximation of the compensating and the equivalence variations. Thus, for instance, they show that if the income elasticity of demand is 2.0 or less, and the share of the product in the consumer's expenses is no more than 80 percent, then the error of approximation in using the ordinary consumer and producer surpluses is less than 4 percent. The error is 2 percent if the income elasticity is 1.0 or less, and it would be even smaller, the smaller the share and/or the smaller the elasticity.

In elasticity terms, equation 4.2 can be written as

$$\eta_{ij} = \eta c_{ij} + k_j \cdot \xi_i \qquad (4.3)$$

where η_{ij} is the price elasticity of the Marshallian demand curve, ηc_{ij} is the price elasticity of the compensated demand of the ith product with respect to a change in the price of the jth product, ξ_i is the income elasticity of demand for the ith product, and $k_j = P_j(q_j - x_j)/ Y$ is the share of the revenues from the net sales of the jth product in this consumer's total income. Let $m_i = (q_i - x_i)$ denote the producer's excess supply of the ith product. The elasticity of marketing, defined as the percentage change in excess supply when the market price rises by 1 percent, is thus given by

$$\eta m_i = \frac{dm_i/m_i}{dP_i/P_i} = \epsilon_{si}\frac{q_i}{m_i} - \frac{x_i}{m_i}\eta_{ii} \qquad (4.4)$$

where ϵ_s is the within-year price elasticity of supply of the ith product—that is, the extent to which producers can increase their output at harvest time by, say, using more labor to pick more of whatever already exists in the field. For grains this supply elasticity is almost zero; but for cash crops such as cotton, coffee, and cocoa, and for food crops such as roots (cassava, yams, and so on) and vegetables, it is likely to be nonnegligible.

The effects of a government procurement program can now be analyzed in reference to figure 4–5. In the rural sector, the Hicksian *compensated* demand curve is always negatively sloped. A rise in price also raises the producer's income and allows him to attain a higher level of utility. It is possible that the Marshallian demand curve is dominated by the income effect and is thus positively sloped even for normal goods, as is the case in figure 4–5. The excess-supply curve, denoted by *ES* in the figure, is therefore negatively sloped. Suppose that the quantity produced is Q_0. Farmers' own demand is then Q_1, and their total excess supply, $(Q_0 - Q_1)$, is equal to the demand of urban consumers, Θ_2. The market is in equilibrium. Suppose now that the government wants to raise the price to P_2. With the rise in price, the demand of rural consumers rises to Q_3, but the demand of urban consumers falls by more than that, to Q_5. The market cannot be cleared at that price, and the government has to procure and extract the quantity $(Q_4 - Q_5)$ from the market. This quantity is, however, smaller than that estimated from the demand curve of the urban sector by itself $(Q_2 - Q_5)$, since that estimate ignores the effect of the policy on the demand of rural consumers. Once this effect is recognized, the total effect of the program on incomes and demands in both sectors is fully taken into account. This effect would automatically be taken into account if the slope of the consumer-producer demand curve is the one given in equation 4.3.

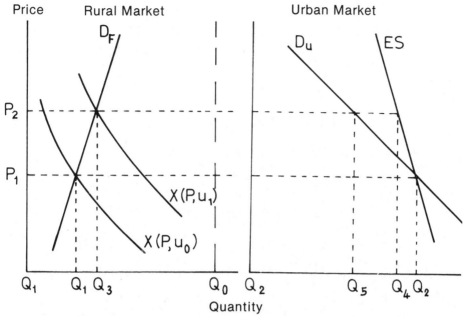

Figure 4–4. Government Procurement Program for Food

An important caveat of this analysis is the effects of fluctuations in production on farmers' income and thus also on their demand for the product. These effects are examined in figure 4–6, which maintains, for simplicity, the assumption of risk neutrality. In the figure, the quantity produced is assumed to fluctuate between Q_1 and Q_2.

Any change in output triggers a proportional change in income and thus also in the farmers' own demand for the product. The percentage change in net income when output of the ith product is changing by 1 percent is given by

$$\frac{dI/I}{dq_i/q_i} = k_i \cdot \phi_i \qquad (4.5)$$

where ϕ_i is the percentage change in net income when gross income from the ith product rises by 1 percent. When the changes in output are due to varying climatic conditions, and they do not involve changes in variable costs (that is, if the within-year supply elasticity is zero), ϕ_i would be equal to 1. This is the assumption made in the subsequent numerical analysis. The percentage change in the farmers' own consumption when output rises by 1 percent is therefore given by

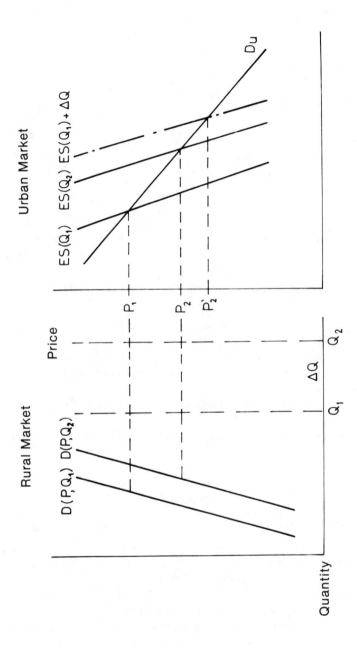

Figure 4–5. Rural and Urban Markets with Stochastic Output

$$\frac{dx_i/x_i}{dq_i/q_i} = \frac{dx_i/x_i}{dI/I} \cdot \frac{dI/I}{dq_i/q_i} = \xi_i \cdot k_i \cdot \phi_i \qquad (4.6)$$

and the percentage change in the marketed surplus is given by

$$\frac{dm_i/m_i}{dq_i/q_i} = 1 + \frac{x_i}{m_i} (1 - \xi_i \cdot k_i \cdot \phi_i) \qquad (4.7)$$

In figure 4.6 the variations in output would therefore cause the demand curves of the rural consumers to fluctuate between $D_1(P, Q_1)$ and $D_2(P, Q_2)$, respectively; in the urban market, the excess supply curves would fluctuate between $ES(Q_1)$ and $ES(Q_2)$. As a result, the market price would also fluctuate between P_1 and P_2. If there was no income effect as farmers' output changes, the excess supply curve would have fluctuated between $ES(Q_1)$ and $ES(Q_1 + \Delta Q)$, where $\Delta Q = (Q_2 - Q_1)$, and the price would have varied between P_1 and P_2'. The income effect of fluctuations in output on farmers' own demand for their products would therefore absorb much of the fluctuation in the urban market and thus also the variability in the price. The reduction would be larger the larger the share of rural consumers in total demand and the larger their income elasticity of demand.

The Programs with Farmers' Income Effect

In this section the simulation analysis is extended to products in which farmers' own consumption constitutes a considerable share of total consumption, on the basis of the behavioral relationships derived in the previous section. Variations in farmers' income caused by fluctuations in their production would in this case augment the instability of their own consumption and, therefore, lower the instability of their excess demand and of the market price. Farmers' elasticity of own consumption—that is, the percentage change in their own consumption when their output changes by 1 percent—was shown in equation 4.6 to be equal to their income elasticity of demand times the share of the net revenues from the sales of their excess supply in their total income. In the simulation analysis, the farmers' income elasticity of demand is assumed to be 0.7, and the share in income is assumed to be 50 percent in one case and 70 percent in another case. The corresponding elasticities of own consumption are then 0.35 and 0.5, respectively.

Table 4–9 summarizes the effects on farmers' own consumption and on their excess supply of different values of the elasticity of own consumption. A zero elasticity represent products of which farmers' own consumption is small. The most important result is the sharp rise in the variability of farmers' consumption and in their food insecurity. This result manifests in part, the higher risks to which monoculture farmers are exposed. It shows, however,

Table 4–9
Income Effects of Output Variations on
Farmers' Own Consumption and Excess Supply

	Elasticity of Own Consumption[a]		
	0[b]	0.35	0.5
Variability of excess supply (CV %)	10.0	6.4	4.9
Variability of the market price (CV – %)	30.2	19.6	15.1
Variability of farmers' consumption (CV – %)	8.1	11.4	12.9
Farmers' consumption insecurity (10%)[c]	7.0	16.2	19.6

[a]Percentage change in farmers' own consumption when their output changes by 1 percent.

[b]A zero elasticity indicates that farmers' own consumption of that crop is a small portion of the market consumption.

[c]Probability that farmers' consumption falls by more than 10 percent below their normal consumption.

that at the same time urban consumers enjoy a more stable flow of supply of these products. The analysis ignores measures farmers take to protect themselves against these variations in output and income, such as in-farm stocks and various forms of savings. In the following section we further extend the analysis to examine the effects of these measures.

Table 4–10 summarizes the effects of the different producer support programs with the income effects on farmers' own consumption. The reduction in the variability of the price under the income effect markedly reduces the frequency and the extent to which the market price falls below the minimum price. The frequency of government interventions to support the minimum price or to maintain the guaranteed income would therefore be much smaller. The effects of the programs on farmers' price or income would also be smaller, and government expenditures would likewise be smaller, the larger the income effects—that is, the larger the share of the farmers' own consumption in total consumption, the share of their revenues from the product in farmers' total revenues, and their income elasticity of demand.

Another effect these policies would then have is on farmers' own consumption and hence on food security in the rural sector. These effects largely depend on the market price elasticity of demand. If the price elasticity is smaller than 1, then in the closed economy a fall in output is accompanied by a rise in price and in farmers' income. Neither the price-support nor the guaranteed-income program is therefore activated. These programs are activated only in years of above-average production. As a result, the income transfers implicit in the programs would not offset the negative effect of the fall in out-

Table 4–10
**Main Effects of Alternative Producers' Support Program in a
Closed Economy with Income Effects of Output Variations on Farmers'
Own Consumption**

	Policy				
	No Intervention	Minimum Price Support	Government Procurement	Guaranteed Income	Buffer Stocks[a]
	Elasticity of own consumption = 0.35				
Farmers' price (unit value)					
Mean	101.6	102.9	102.2	101.9	101.0
Variability (CV%)	19.6	16.6	15.6	18.8	13.7
Farmers' revenues					
Mean[b]	100.3	102.2	101.5	100.7	100.2
Variability (CV%)	10.7	7.6	6.9	9.6	6.9
Risk[c]	7.6	0.0	0.0	0.0	2.3
Government expenditures[b]	0.0	0.6	0.3	0.2	1.1
	Elasticity of own consumption = 0.5				
Farmers' price (unit value)					
Mean	101.4	102.0	103.7	101.4	101.0
Variability (CV%)	15.1	13.6	11.5	15.0	11.4
Farmers' revenues					
Mean[b]	100.4	101.4	103.7	101.4	100.5
Variability (CV%)	6.1	4.7	3.8	5.9	5.0
Risk[c]	1.3	0.0	0.0	0.0	0.6
Government expenditures	0.0	0.3	0.6	0.0	1.2

Note: The elasticity of own consumption is equal to the income elasticity of demand times the share of the product in farmers' total revenues.

[a]Stocks equal to 10 percent of the annual production.

[b]Expressed as percentage of the revenues from the crop in a stable year.

[c]Probability that farmers' revenues from the crop fall by more than 15 percent below their normal revenues.

put on farmers' income and own consumption. Thus, for instance, if the minimum guaranteed income were to rise from 85 to 95 percent of farmers' normal income, the probability measure of their food insecurity would have declined from 16.0 percent to 15.2 (and government expenditures would have risen from 0.2 to 2.3 percent of total normal expenditures for the product). If, however, the market price elasticity of demand is larger than 1, then a fall in output will result in a fall in income, which in turn may trigger the guaranteed-income program. In that case the income transfers due to the program would coincide with and offset the negative income effect of the fall in output.

One further comment on the simulation results is due. These results are based on, among other things, the assumption that farmers' demand is negatively sloped (with a price elasticity of demand equal to − 0.2). This in turn implies that the substitution effect dominates the income effect. The results would possibly have been quite different had the Marshallian demand curve been dominated by the income effect and thus positively sloped. An illustration is given in figure 4–7. In the figure $D(P, Q)$ are the farmer's Marshallian demand curves if the substitution effect is dominating and $D'(P, Q)$ are the demand curves if the income effect is dominating. When the quantity produced is Q_2, the market price is P_2 and farmers' own consumption is D_2, under both assumptions. When the quantity produced falls to Q_1, the market price rises to P_1 and the demand curve shifts to $D(P, Q_1)$ or $D'(P, Q_1)$,

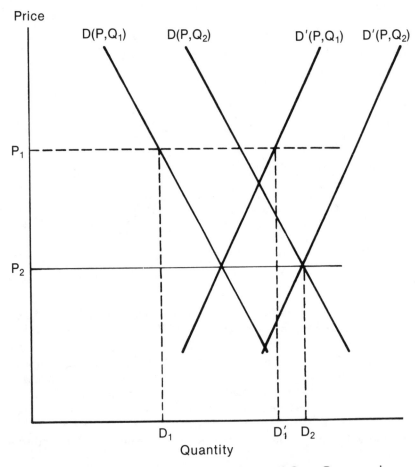

Figure 4–6. Price and Output Effects on Farmers' Own Consumption

depending on the income effect. The horizontal shift itself is of equal size under the two assumptions, representing the effect of the reduction in income as a consequence of the reduction in output. The final change in demand from D_2 to either D_1 or D_1' represents the combined effect of the change in output and the change in price. The figure illustrates that if the substitution effect is dominating—that is, the demand curve is negatively sloped—the variations in demand are larger than the horizontal shifts in the demand curve (the price and quantity effects on the quantity demanded work in the same direction) whereas if the income effect dominates—that is, the demand curve is positively sloped—the variations in demand are smaller than the horizontal shifts in the demand curve (the price and quantity effects on the quantity demanded work in opposite directions).

Farmers' Stocks and Marketing Decisions and Their Effects on Pirce Variability in Urban Markets

Although the results of the previous section, which follow directly from the standard theoretical analysis of consumers' behavior, show that farmers' income and consumption are less stable the larger the share of their own consumption, it has often been argued that in practice farm household consumption tends to vary somewhat less than production, so that fluctuations in production are magnified at the level of marketing (see, e.g., Timmer, Falcon, and Pearson 1983, p. 86). This finding can be explained by the measures farmers take to protect themselves against fluctuations in income and consumption. These measures include in-farm stocks; investments in cattle that serve as both a store of value and a store of food; and investments in machinery, gold, valuable household effects, and the like. In-farm stocks have been found to be at least six to nine months of consumption. Some studies have found stocks of one to four years of consumption in some parts of Africa.

The approach taken here to explain these consumption and marketing decisions of farmers under instability is a variant of the permanent-income hypothesis. It assumes farmers' consumption to be a function of their *long-run expected income* rather than their current income. To bridge the gap between the quantity of consumption afforded by their current income and the quantity desired on the basis of their permanent income, farmers accumulate stocks of food (or income) in years of plentiful production that would supplement their consumption in years of poor harvest. Their consumption and marketing decisions can be analyzed in reference to figure 4–8. In the rural market, $D_F(\bar{Q}, \bar{P})$ denotes the farmers' ordinary demand schedule, which determines their consumption decisions, as a function of their permanent income and thus of the long-term average output $\bar{Q}$ and the expected price $\bar{P}$. Earlier we noted that this curve, as a function of the expected price, can be positively sloped if the income effect outweighs the substitution effect.

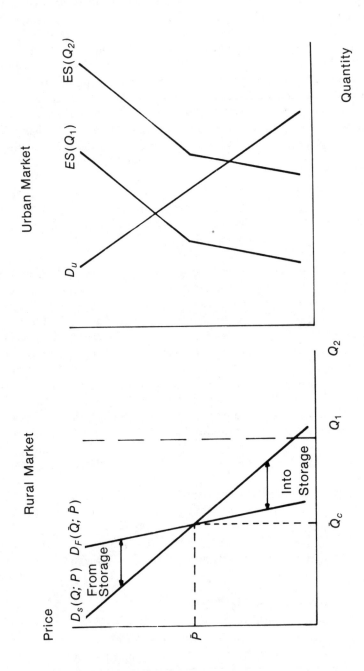

Figure 4–7. Farmers' Storage and Marketing Decisions

The slope of the curve as a function of the *current* price depends on the formation of expectations. If expectations are rational (and assuming there is no trend in prices and no serial correlation) then any deviation of the current price from the expected price would be perceived as purely random. In that case the level of the current price would have no effect on its expected level in the following period, and the $D_F(\bar{Q}, \bar{P})$ curve—as a function of P—would be completely inelastic. If expectations are adaptive or if there is a positive serial correlation, a higher-than-average price today would be expected to be followed by another high price tomorrow. In that case the $D_F(\bar{Q}, \bar{P})$ curve would be responsive to changes in the current price, as assumed in the figure. These price expectations depend primarily on farmer's expectations about the aggregate level of output in the following period, which we discuss later.

The curve $D_S(Q, P)$ denotes the farmers' speculative demand, which determines their marketing and stocks decisions as a function of *current* output Q, and *current* price P. For a given level of current output, if the current market price rises above $\bar{P}$, the farmer will release some of his stocks to take advantage of the favorable price. If the current market price falls below $\bar{P}$, he will reduce his sales and keep more in stocks in anticipation of higher prices in the future. The slope of the speculative demand curve thus depends on the expected price relative to the current price, on the storage losses, on the expected profits from alternative forms of savings, and on the farmer's degree of risk aversion. If, in addition, the farmer is risk-averse, then (prior to reaching his desired or steady-state stocks) his $D_S(Q, P)$ curve will intersect with the $D_F(\bar{Q}, \bar{P})$ curve at a price higher than $\bar{P}$. If, for example, his current stocks are lower than his desired stocks, then even in a normal year, when the current price is $\bar{P}$, the farmer would still increase his stocks in order to minimize the probability that in the future his consumption will fall below his desired consumption, $\bar{Q}_C$. The effects of these factors are further discussed later.

The effect of the level of current output on the farmer's stocks and marketing decisions depends on his expectations about the level of output in the following year. If the farmer is risk-neutral, his expectations rational, there is no serial correlation and no trend in production, then in any given year $\bar{Q}$ and $\bar{P}$ would be his most efficient estimates of the following year's output and price (see chapter 2). The farmer would therefore expect to be able to consume the desired quantity $\bar{Q}_C$ in the following year even without accumulating any stocks. Other things (including the price) being equal, plentiful output above $\bar{Q}$ in the current year would, however, induce the farmer to increase his stocks in the same way that an increase in income induces an urban consumer to increase his savings. The speculative demand curve $D_S(Q, P)$ would therefore shift to the right when production rises and to the left when production falls.

If the farmer is risk-averse, he would keep some stocks even when current consumption is $\bar{Q}$ and his expectations rational. In other words, the $D_S(Q,$

P) curve will intersect with the $D_F(\bar{Q}, \bar{P})$ at $\bar{Q}_c$ but at a price higher than $\bar{P}$. This would reflect the farmer's precautionary measures to lower the risk that in the following year he would not be able to consume the quantity $\bar{Q}_c$.

If his expectations about aggregate output in the following year are adaptive of the form

$$Q_{t+1}^{\text{exp}} = \pi Q_t + (1 - \pi)Q_{t-1} \qquad : 0 \le \pi \le 1$$

where Q_{t+1}^{exp} is the output expected at time t for time $(t + 1)$, then a fall in output below Q_{t-1} in year t raises expectations that the following year's output will rise above Q_t. These expectations can be termed *regressive*. Under this specification the expected rate of change in output is given by

$$\hat{Q}_{t+1}^{\text{exp}} = -(1 - \pi)\hat{Q}_t$$

where a hat over a variable denotes its rate of change over time—for example, $\hat{Q}_t = (Q_t - Q_{t-1})/Q_{t-1}$. Hence,

$$d\hat{Q}_{t+1}^{\text{exp}}/d\hat{Q}_t < 0$$

In words, a fall in output this year is expected to be followed by a rise in output next year. If, however, a fall in output this year is expected to be followed by another poor harvest next year, that is,

$$d\hat{Q}_{t+1}^{\text{exp}}/d\hat{Q}_t > 0$$

expectations can be termed *progressive* and can be formalized as:

$$\hat{Q}_{t+1}^{\text{exp}} = \pi \hat{Q}_t \qquad : 0 \le \pi \le 1$$

With positive serial correlation in production, even rational expectation will be progressive.

Under regressive expectations, the speculative demand curve will shift leftward when current output falls below the average; that is, less output will be put into storage or more will be released from storage when current output falls below the average in anticipation of plentiful output in the following year. The speculative demand curve will shift *rightward* when current output *exceeds* the average; that is, more output will be put into storage or less will be released from storage when current output exceeds the average in anticipation of a shortfall in production in the following year. The corresponding excess supply curve will shift in the opposite direction, thereby reducing price fluctuations in the urban market. Progressive expectations, in contrast, will *enhance* price fluctuations in the urban market. Farmers will increase their stocks and release a smaller amount to the urban market in a bad year, anticipating that another bad year will follow. They will reduce their stocks and release more to the urban market in a good year, anticipating that another good year will follow.

Farmers' stocks and marketing decisions depend also on the availability and profitability of alternative forms of savings. A heuristic representation of these decisions can be made as follows. Assume that a farmer wants to secure a certain quantity, say Q^*, to be in his command in the following year. He can either retain some of his output in stocks or sell his output and invest the money earned in financial or other assets. If he retains the food products in stocks, they will suffer some losses during the year due to rats, insects, and the like—say, at the rate of ρ percent. To have the amount Q^* in the following year, he must therefore store the amount $Q^*/(1 - \rho)$ in the current year. In addition he will have some costs for sacks, jars, the storage facility, and so on. Let c be the storage costs per unit. Total expenditures on stocks therefore consist of the direct storage costs plus the revenues foregone. Had he invested the money, he could have in the following year a sum of money equal to

$$c.Q^*/(1 - \rho) + P_t^s Q^*(1 + r)/(1 - \rho)$$

where r is the rate of interest (or the rate of appreciation of his assets—that is, the rate of change in the price of his investments—and P_t^s is the selling price at time t. With this sum of money he expects to be able to buy a quantity of food equal to

$$\frac{c.Q^*/(1 - \rho) + P_t^s \cdot Q^*(1 + r)/(1 - \rho)}{P_{t+1}^{\exp}}$$

where $P_{t+1}^{\exp}$ is the buying price expected in the following period. To ensure that the amount Q^* will be at his command, risk-averse farmers would require some safety margins. Specifically, assume them to require that the probability that the price in the following year will rise to levels that will not allow him to buy the desired quantity Q^* is smaller than a certain critical level, say α. This is essentially the Kataoka (1963)–Baumol (1963) safety-first criterion. The degree of *reliability* of his investment is therefore $(1 - \alpha)$. Symbolically, the requirement is

$$P_r \left\{ \frac{(cQ^*/(1 - \rho)) + P_t^s \cdot Q^* \cdot (1 + r)/(1 - \rho)}{P_{t+1}^{\exp}} \leq Q^* \right\} < \alpha$$

where p_r is a probability statement. In terms of the expected price, the requirement is therefore

$$P_r\{[P_{t+1}^{\exp}(c/(1 - \rho) + P_t^s(1 + r)/(1 - \rho)] \geq 0\} < \alpha$$

Assuming that the probability distribution of $P_{t+1}^{\exp}$ can be fully described by the parameters of the first two moments, we can make the transformation

$$P_r\{[P^{\exp} - (c/(1 - \rho) + P_t^s(1 + r)/(1 - \rho)] \geq 0\} =$$

$$1 - F\{[(c/(1 - \rho) + P_t^s(1 + r)/(1 - \rho)] - P^{\exp})]/\sigma_P\} < \alpha$$

where F is the distribution function of $P^{\exp}$ and σ_P is its standard deviation. From this expression we can define a constraint on $P_{t+1}^{\exp}$, given by

$$P_{t+1}^{\exp} < c/(1 - \rho) + P_t^s(1 + r)/(1 - \rho) - F^{-1}(1 - \alpha) \cdot \sigma_P$$

This is exactly Baumol's confidence criterion. For a symmetric distribution $F^{-1}(1/2) = 0$. Risk aversion is manifested when the degree of reliability required is $\alpha < 1/2$, in which case $F^{-1}(1 - \alpha) > 0$. In conclusion, if the price in the following year is expected to be lower than

$$[c/(1 - \rho) + P_t^s(1 + r) - F^{-1}(1 - \alpha) \cdot \sigma_P]$$

then the risk that the farmer will not be able to buy the desired quantity of food in the market with the money invested is smaller than α, and in this case the stocks option would be inferior to the investment option. The stocks option would be more desirable the lower the storage costs c and the rate of storage losses ρ; the lower the current selling price P_t^s and the expected yield on investments r; the higher the marketing gap between selling and buying prices; the higher the level of reliability required $(1 - \alpha)$ (that is, the higher the degree of risk aversion); and the higher the price variability σ_P.

We can now turn to a formal analysis. Consider a farmer who makes his consumption decision in period 1 and at the same time decides how much to keep in stocks and how much to market. In period 2 the farmer chooses consumption of good X, which he produces himself, and consumption of a composite of all other goods in the economy, Y, so as to maximize the following VNM utility function:

$$U(X, Y) \tag{4.8}$$

$$s.t. \ P_2 X + Y = I_2$$

where P_2 is the price of good X and I_2 is the income in period 2. The solution to this problem yields the following indirect utility function

$$V(P_2, I_2) \tag{4.9}$$

For simplicity, let us assume that the farmer produces only in period 1; thus his revenues from sales in period 1 and his stocks are his only source of income in period 2. We further assume this to be a two-period problem only. (Alternatively, we could regard $U(X, Y)$ as the reduced form of the stream of future utilities and I_2 as including also the present value of the stream of future expected incomes). The farmer's income in period 2 is thus given by

$$I_2 = (1 + r)(P_1 \cdot M - cS) + P_2(1 - \rho)S \qquad (4.10)$$

where M and S are the quantities marketed and stored, respectively. In words, the farmer's income in the second period is equal to the value at that time of his revenues from the sale of M in the previous period (compounded by the relevant interest rate) minus the expenditures on the stocks (assumed to made in the first period) but plus his potential earnings from the sale of his stocks, after taking into account the storage losses.

At the time that the farmer makes his decision how much to store and how much to market out of his excess supply in the first period, the market price P_2 is not known to him. The farmer's problem is therefore to choose M and S so as to maximize

$$E[V(P_2, I_2)] \qquad (4.11)$$

$$s.t. \ M + S = Q$$

where Q is the excess in the first period over and above the farmer's own consumption.

The first-order conditions for an interior solution to equation 4.4 are

$$E[V_I(\cdot) \cdot (1 + r)P_1] - \lambda = 0 \qquad (4.12)$$

$$E\{V_I(\cdot) \cdot [P_2(1 - \rho) - c(1 + r)]\} - \lambda = 0$$

$$M + S = Q$$

Hence,

$$P_1(1 + r) = \frac{E\{V_I(\cdot) \cdot [P_2(1 - \rho) - c(1 + r)]\}}{E[V_I(\cdot)]} \qquad (4.13)$$

Using the definition of the product of two random variables in the latter equation yields

$$P_1 = \frac{(1 - \rho)}{(1 + r)} \cdot E(P_2) - c + \frac{\text{Cov}(V_I(\cdot), P_2(1 - \rho))}{(1 + r) \cdot E[V_I(\cdot)]} \qquad (4.14)$$

If P_1 is greater than the expression on the righthand side of equation 4.14, then the farmer would prefer to sell his excess supply in the market, whereas if P_1 is smaller, he would prefer to keep it in stocks.

To analyze the covariance, differentiate the marginal utility of income, $V_I(\cdot)$, with respect to the commodity price P_2

$$\frac{\partial V_I[P_2 \cdot (1 + r)M + (P_2(1 - \rho) - c(1 + r))S]}{\partial P_2} = V_{IP2} + (1 - \rho)SV_{II}$$

$$(4.15)$$

where $V_{II} < 0$. If the farmer retains no stocks—that is, if $S = 0$—then the covariance is greater than, equal to, or less than 0 if and only if the effect of price variations on the marginal utility of income is greater than, equal to, or less than 0 (see Newbery and Stiglitz 1981). Differentiating Roy's identity, we get

$$V_{IP2} = \frac{X \cdot V_I}{I}(R - \xi) \qquad (4.16)$$

where ξ is the income elasticity of demand for commodity X and $R = -I.(V_{II}/V_I)$, is the relative risk aversion. Hence

$$R \underset{<}{\overset{\geq}{}} \xi < = > \qquad \mathrm{Cov}(V_I(\cdot), (1 - \rho)P_2) \underset{<}{\overset{\geq}{}} 0 \text{ at } S = 0 \qquad (4.17)$$

If $S > 0$, then if also $R > \xi$ the covariance can then be either negative or positive. If, however, $S > 0$ and $R \leq \xi$, then the covariance would be negative, since $V_{II} < 0$.

From equation 4.7 and the latter results we can also conclude that

$$\frac{\partial S}{\partial P_1} < 0$$

implying that the slope of the speculative demand curve $D_S(P, Q)$ in figure 4–8 is negative. An increase in r, ρ, or c would result in a shift of $D_S(P, Q)$ to the left, whereas an increase in $E(P_2)$ or R would result in a shift of $D_S(P, Q)$ to the right.

In practice we should expect the farmer to maintain stocks for his consumption in the near future, since the storage costs and losses are still small, as are the gains on financial (and other) investments. For longer time periods he would tend to switch gradually to financial investments, depending on the availability of credit market or other forms of investment, on the availability of a reliable and relatively stable food market, and on his subjective degree of risk aversion. Each of these factors will affect the slope of the speculative demand schedule $D_S(Q, P)$.

Agricultural Trade Policies

Another route for conducting the national agricultural policies, in addition to domestic price interventions, is via trade policies. In this section we examine the effects of several trade policies aimed at constraining competing imports through different forms of trade barriers in order to encourage domestic production. The specific policies examined (and their notations in the summary tables) are:

FREE: Free trade triggered by price differentials between the FOB export or CIF import price and the internal price.

TARIFF: An ad valorem tariff of 20 percent is levied on all competing food imports.

VAR-LEV: Variable tariffs is levied on both imports and exports of agricultural produce. The details of this policy were explained in chapter 3. In this section the variable import levy has the following linear form:

$$P_{IMP} = \Theta(1 + t)P_I + (1 - \Theta)\bar{P} \quad : 0 \leq \Theta \leq 1$$

where P_{IMP} is the domestic price of the imported product, P_I the CIF import price, $\bar{P}$ the domestic normal (median) price, and t the tariff rate. The import levy is thus equal to t when $P_I = \bar{P}$; it gradually declines for import prices higher than $\bar{P}$ and gradually rises for prices below $\bar{P}$. The import levy may turn into an import subsidy when

$$P_I < \frac{1 - \Theta}{1 - (1 + t)\Theta} \cdot \bar{P}$$

In the simulation analysis we assume a tariff rate t equal to 20 percent and $\Theta = 0.65$.

Exports under this policy are taxed whenever the export price (FOB) rises above the median price and subsidized whenever the export price falls below the median price, according to the following rule:

$$P_{EXP} = \alpha P_x + (1 - \alpha)\bar{P} \quad : 0 \leq \alpha \leq 1$$

where P_{EXP} is the domestic price of the exported product and P_X is its FOB price. In the simulation analysis we assume $\alpha = 0.5$.

MIN-PRICE: This policy prevents the price from falling below a certain minimum level by allowing trade to determine the domestic price but taxing imports and subsidizing exports as needed to support that price. In the simulation analysis, this policy is assumed to constrain the price from falling by more than 10 percent below the average price, where the average price is calculated as a moving average of the prices in the past nine years. This policy is thus equivalent to the minimum support price examined earlier, but the instrument now is variable import or export levies.

PROC-EXP: This policy supports a minimum price to producers through constraints on imports, procurement to government storage, or subsidies to exports.

The analysis has been conducted for three types of countries:

1. Normally self-sufficient.
2. Normally only 95 percent self-sufficient.
3. Normally only 80 percent self-sufficient.

Price elasticity of supply is assumed to be 0.25 in the base case and 0.5 in another case. The risk response elasticity is assumed to be 0.25, implying that a fall by 1 percent in the coefficient of variation of farmers' income would induce them to increase output by 0.25 percent.

Table 4–11 summarizes the results of the various trade policies in a self-sufficient country. The most outstanding result is the poor performance of the TARIFF policy, i.e., a uniform ad valorem import levy, compared to a policy of variable import and export levies. Under the TARIFF policy, the

Table 4–11
Agricultural Trade Policies in a Self-Sufficient Country
(Supply Elasticity = 0.25)

Policy	FREE	TARIFF	VAR-LEV	MIN. PRICE	PROC-EXP
Price					
Mean	103.4	109.5	106.6	103.1	106.1
CV (%)	14.9	20.3	13.8	14.3	8.4
Quantity produced	98.4	99.3	99.7	98.5	99.8
Farmers' revenues					
Mean	100.9	107.1	105.2	100.6	105.9
CV (%)	11.5	14.0	8.4	10.6	8.4
Risk (15%)[a]	6.6	4.4	1.4	6.3	1.1
Quantity imported[b]	2.7	0.8	0.2	2.7	2.0
Quantity exported[b]	1.7	2.0	2.6	1.7	3.5
Balance of trade[c]	– 1.3	+ 0.9	+ 0.9	– 1.3	+ 1.2
Quantity consumed[e]	100.0	98.7	99.1	100.1	98.9
Food insecurity (10%)[d]	1.0	9.6	1.7	0.8	0.5

[a]Probability that farmers' revenues will fall by more than 15 percent below their normal revenues.

[b]Expressed as percentage of normal annual production.

[c]Expressed as percentage of normal annual expenditures on the food product.

[d]Probability that food consumption falls by more than 10 percent below the normal consumption.

[e]As percentage of consumption under FREE TRADE.

average market price rises by almost 6 percent above its free-trade level, but its coefficient of variation rises by 36 percent. As a result, the rise in output with the TARIFF policy is less than 1 percent. Under the variable-levies (VAR-LEV) policy the average market price to rise by 3.1 percent but its variability declines by 7 percent and, as a result, output rises by 1.5 percent. The TARIFF policy also destabilizes the flow of supply to consumers. The probability of a shortfall in consumption by more than 10 percent below the normal consumption rises from 1.0 percent under free trade to 9.6 percent with a uniform tariff, but only to 1.7 percent with variable levies.

Tables 4–12 and 4–13 extend the analysis to a country that normally (that is, when production is at its long-run level) imports only 5 percent of its consumption. With the TARIFF policy, the share of imports in total consumption falls to 2.5 percent. This decline is achieved by a fall in consumption of 2.2 percent and a rise in production of 1.8 percent. In this country the TARIFF policy will have a much smaller effect on raising the variability of the price, since in most years imports will be bought despite their higher price. In the self-sufficient country, in contrast, the tariff may make imports prohibitively expensive, thereby frequently preventing imports from supplementing domestic supply in years of domestic production shortfalls.

Table 4–12
Agricultural Trade Policies in an Importing Country That is Normally 95 Percent Self-Sufficient
(Supply Elasticity = 0.25)

Policy	FREE	TARIFF	VAR-LEV
Price			
Mean	112.3	121.8	116.4
CV (%)	14.3	17.8	13.1
Quantity produced	100.6	102.4	102.0
Degree of self-sufficient[a]	94.4	98.2	96.7
Farmers' revenue			
Mean[b]	100.0	109.8	105.0
CV (%)	10.9	12.4	8.4
Quantity imported[c]	6.5	2.6	3.8
Balance of trade[d]	−6.1	−2.1	−3.4
Quantity consumed[f]	100.0	97.8	99.0
Food insecurity (10%)[e]	4.2	17.3	4.3

[a]Quantity produced as percentage of the quantity consumed.
[b]Expressed as percentage of their revenues under free trade.
[c]Expressed as percentage of normal production.
[d]Expressed as percentage of ormal annual expenditures on the food product.
[e]Probability that food consumption falls by more than 10 percent below the normal consumption.
[f]As percentage of consumption under Free Trade.

Table 4–13
Agricultural Trade Policies in an Importing Country That Is Normally
95 Percent Self-Sufficient
(Supply Elasticity = 0.5)

Policy	FREE	TARIFF	VAR-LEV
Price			
Mean	110.1	116.8	113.8
CV (%)	14.3	19.0	13.5
Quantity produced	102.6	105.1	104.5
Degree of self-sufficiency[a]	95.6	99.4	98.2
Farmers' revenue			
Mean[b]	101.8	110.0	106.5
CV (%)	10.8	13.0	8.3
Quantity imported[c]	5.4	1.7	2.8
Balance of trade[d]	− 4.8	− 0.9	− 2.0
Quantity consumed[f]	100.0	98.5	99.2
Food insecurity (10%)[e]	2.9	13.9	2.9

[a]Quantity produced as percentage of the quantity consumed.

[b]Expressed as percentage of their revenues under free trade.

[c]Expressed as percentage of normal production.

[d]Expressed as percentage of normal annual expenditures on the food product.

[e]Probability that food consumption falls by more than 10 percent below the normal consumption.

[f]As percentage of consumption under Free Trade.

The increase in the country's degree of self-sufficiency with the TARIFF policy, from 94.4 percent to 98.2 percent when supply elasticity is 0.25, and from 95.6 percent to 99.4 percent when supply elasticity is 0.5, is achieved at the expense of a large increase in food insecurity, reflected by a rise in the probability that food consumption will fall by more than 10 percent below the normal level from 4.2 percent to 17.3 percent when supply elasticity is 0.25, and a rise from 2.9 percent to 13.9 percent when the elasticity is 0.5. All the other policies considered also contribute to raising production and self-sufficiency, though at a lower rate. They do not, however, have the same negative effect, some even having a positive effect on a country's food security. The policy of variable levies, for instance, helps raise domestic production at nearly the same rate as the TARIFF policy but causes a much smaller decline in average consumption and does not increase the probability of extreme shortfalls in consumption.

Table 4–14 further extends the analysis to a country that is normally only 80 percent self-sufficient. Now the domestic price is almost always determined by the import price, and the various trade policies do not block imports but only raise their price. As a result, these policies have a much

Table 4–14
Agricultural Trade Policies in an Importing Country That Is Normally 80 Percent Self-Sufficient
(Supply Elasticity = 0.25)

Policy	FREE	TARIFF	VAR-LEV
Price			
Mean	116.5	139.2	125.8
CV (%)	12.4	12.3	9.0
Quantity produced	100.6	105.3	103.1
Degree of self-sufficiency[a]	77.8	85.9	81.7
Farmers' revenues			
Mean[b]	100.0	125.0	110.7
CV (%)	15.5	14.5	12.5
Quantity imported[c]	28.8	17.3	21.9
Balance of trade[d]	−24.3	−14.5	−18.6
Quantity consumed[f]	129.3	122.6	126.2
Food insecurity (10%)[e]	5.1	39.0	8.3
Government revenues[d]	0.0	2.9	2.6

[a]Quantity produced as percentage of the quantity consumed.
[b]Expressed as percentage of their revenues under free trade.
[c]Expressed as percentage of normal production.
[d]Expressed as percentage of normal annual expenditures on the food product.
[e]Probability that food consumption falls by more than 10 percent below the normal consumption.
[f]As percentage of consumption under Free Trade.

smaller effect on the variability of the market price, and most of their effect is on its level. The negative effects of the TARIFF policy on the variability of the price would therefore be much more modest, whereas its effect on the price level would help encourage production and self-sufficiency more than the other policies. This increase would be achieved, however, at the expense of a large increase in the country's food insecurity.

Notes

1. This estimate is obviously rather conservative, and in some areas a much larger proportion is taken by rats and insects or is spoiled in other ways. An AFO export committee estimated that storage losses for cereals were, on average, between 10 and 25 percent (see Bigman 1982, chaps. 4 and 5, for further details and references).

2. Investment costs are at 1982 prices and are calculated for warehouse storage in bags, which is more typical in developing countries (see Bigman 1982, chap. 4, app. 4, for the detailed calculations).

3. It should be noted that the fiscal costs include also the storage operating costs

and take into account the greater extent to which grains stored in open areas are likely to decay. They do not, however, include the administrative costs of the program, which may be substantial. These costs are accounted for in the fifth section of this chapter.

4. The reduction in the coefficient of variation is not an appropriate performance criterion in this case, since it reflects the reduction in the frequency of getting *high* income as a result of the premium payments.

5. The loading and unloading charges were, however, taken into account.

6. See Bigman and Shalit (1983) for the details of this analysis.

References

Baumol, W.J. 1963. An expected gain-confidence limit criterion for portfolio selection. *Management Science* 9:174–182.

Bigman, D. 1982. *Coping with hunger: Toward a system of food security and price stabilization.* Cambridge, Mass.: Ballinger.

Bigman, D., and Shalit, H. 1983. Applied welfare analysis for consumers with commodity income. *De Economist 131*:31–45.

Chibber, A. 1983. Long-term agricultural growth in developing countries: A framework for comparing the role of price and non-price policies. Unpublished ms., Agricultural Department, FAO, Rome.

Clay, E.; Chambers, R.; Singer, H.; and Lipton, M. 1981. Food policy issues in low-income countries. World Bank Staff Working Paper No. 473.

Hammer, J.S. 1983. "Subsistence first": Farm allocation decisions in Senegal. Unpublished ms.

Harberger, A.C. 1971. Three basic postulates for applied welfare economics. *Journal of Economic Literature 9*:785–797.

Hazell, P.B.R. 1983. Sources of increased instability in indian and U.S. cereal production. Unpublished ms.

Kataoka, S. 1963. A stochastic programming model. *Econometrica 31*:181–196.

Newbery, D.M.G., and Stiglitz, J.E. 1981. *The theory of commodity price stabilization.* Oxford: Clarendon Press.

Timmer, C.P.; Falcon, W.P.; and Pearson, S.R. 1983. *Food policy analysis.* Baltimore, Md.: John Hopkins University Press.

Tolley, G.S.; Thomas, V.; and Wong, C.M. 1982. *Agricultural price policies and the developing countries.* Baltimore, Md.: John Hopkins University Press.

5
Food-Distribution Policies: Price Subsidies and Income Transfers

Government interventions to secure adequate supply of staple consumption items, such as food grains, at affordable prices are virtually universal. India, Sri Lanka, Pakistan, Thailand, Turkey, Egypt, Tunesia, Nigeria, Mexico, Brazil, and Colombia are only few examples of countries whose governments are heavily involved in marketing and distributing staple foods and in which large portion of the fiscal budget is committed to food subsidies. These interventions take several forms:

1. General price subsidies to selected staples.
2. Import subsidies, either directly or through overvalued exchange rates.
3. Targeted subsidies or income-transfer programs.
4. Export constraints, through tariffs, quotas, or direct government contracts, that depress domestic prices.
5. Food-for-work programs.
6. Supplementary feeding programs.
7. Direct distribution through monopolistic parastatal agencies that assume the administrative, storage, transportation, interest, and marketing costs.

A fundamental characteristic of these interventions is the tension they create between the different objectives of the government, between different consumer groups, between producers and consumers, between growth and equity. In many countries the primary goal of public intervention in food distribution is to secure food supply and provide a cushion against inflation to urban consumers. The urban bias of these policies creates an urban-rural conflict by shifting at least part of the burden onto the rural population. Farmers and landless rural consumers are often denied the cheap food, especially when the food is imported, their own revenues are cut by forced procurement, and their food security is reduced as they are forced to absorb much of the instability in production so that a stable flow of supply to the urban market is secured.

Another cost of low food prices is a growing dependence on food imports and concomitantly lower rates of agricultural growth. Further, the pressures of the food problems of today divert attention from longer-term priorities of economic growth in general and of agricultural development in particular, by demanding a large share of the fiscal budget, by worsening the balance-of-payments position of many countries, and by distorting resource allocation between agriculture and industry and within the agricultural sector between different crops.

One purpose of this chapter is to highlight the trade-offs involved in government distribution policies. The chapter concentrates on subsidy and on income- and food-transfer programs targeted on poor urban consumers. The first section examines the long-term effects of alternative schemes via comparative static analysis and compares their cost-effectiveness. The second section extends the theoretical analysis to a stochastic environment and defines measures of food security when production, prices, and incomes are unstable. The third section examines the effects of targeted subsidy programs under instability in a general analytical model in order to highlight the basic trade-offs involved. The next two sections examine the direct and indirect effects of alternative distribution schemes via simulation analysis of the sectorial model, which was extended to distinguish between different income groups. The sixth section examines more specifically the urban-rural trade-off associated with the targeted distribution programs. The final section examines these trade-offs in an open economy and also demonstrates the trade-off between food security and balance-of-payments position.

The Cost-Effectiveness of Alternative Target-Group Transfer and Subsidy Programs

The economic justification for commodity subsidy programs largely draws on Musgrave's (1959) merit-good argument, which distinguishes certain goods whose consumption is supposed to be meritorious from a social point of view. Pazner (1972) and Wenzel and Wiegard (1981) have presented models wherein the quantities consumed of these goods enter the social-welfare function directly, not through the individual utility function. The failure of market mechanisms to supply these goods in adequate quantities justifies public intervention.

In many cases, however, the failure of the market lies not in the adequacy of total supply but in its distribution. Production may be efficient and supply plentiful, but the existing distribution of income and wealth may still affect those segments of society who lack what Sen (1981) has termed the "exchange entitlement"—the purchasing power to buy goods such as staple foods in quantities that are deemed adequate or necessary from a social point of view. Any form of public intervention aimed at securing a more favorable distribution of the available supply would, however, be inconsistent with the Pareto-optimality principle and, under the ordinary assumptions about the community's preference ordering or the welfare function, is likely to involve net welfare losses.

Nevertheless, public interventions through cash transfers, through food stamp programs, through general or target-group subsidy programs, or through direct public distribution via ration shops and supplementary feeding programs are widely practiced in almost all countries. These programs are generally centered on staple foods, and their objective is to improve the nutritional standard of certain groups of the population who are either chronically or temporarily undernourished. The wide application of these policies in both rich and poor countries provides vivid proof that the elimination of hunger is indeed socially meritorious, if not morally dictated.

In the following analysis we examine the effects of some of these programs on the market price, on income distribution, and on the fiscal budget in a partial-equilibrium framework of the specific commodity under consideration—assumed to be staple food. In particular, we concentrate on two target-group policy options: income transfers and a targeted price subsidy. In many ways all other programs, such as food stamps, income transfers through payments in kind, and direct public distribution, share the basic characteristics of one of these two programs. Of the two, traditional welfare economics has always emphasized the superiority of direct cash transfers, which allow consumers a greater freedom of choice. Targeted subsidy programs may, however (depending on the price and income elasticities), encourage the consumption of the merit good at considerably smaller fiscal costs.[1]

Group-Target Subsidy Program

Consider first a price-subsidy program targeted on poor consumers. Market-clearing conditions for the food product under consideration are given by:

$$D_r(P) + D_p[P(1 - \theta)] = S(P) \tag{5.1}$$

where P is the market price and $P_s = P(1 - \theta)$ is the subsidized price that applies to the poor consumers (group p) only, θ being the subsidy rate; D_r and D_p are the demands of the rich and the poor consumers, respectively; and S is total supply (domestic and imported) of the commodity. By taking the logarithmic differential of equation 5.1, we can express the market-clearing conditions in terms of rates of change, as

$$- \eta_p w_p \hat{P}_s - \eta_r w_r \hat{P} = \epsilon \hat{P} \qquad (5.2)$$

where a hat over a variable denotes its rate of change or its logarithmic derivative; for example, $\hat{P} = dP/P$, $\eta_i (i = r, p)$ is the price elasticity of demand of the corresponding consumer group, w_i is the weight of the group in total demand for that product, and ϵ is the price elasticity of supply.

By solving the latter equation for $\hat{P}$, we can express the resulting changes in the market and the subsidized prices, noting that $\hat{P}_s = \hat{P} - 1/(1 - \theta)$,

$$\hat{P} = \frac{+ w_p \eta_p}{(1 - \theta)(\epsilon + \eta)} > 0 \qquad (5.3)$$

$$\hat{P}_s = \frac{-(w_r \eta_r + \epsilon)}{(1 - \theta)(\epsilon + \eta)} < 0 \qquad (5.3')$$

where $\eta = w_r \eta_r + w_p \eta_p$.

The rise in the market price and the fall in the subsidized price with a rise in the subsidy rate are the very changes that enable the program to achieve the desired redistribution of the available food supply. The rise in the market price forces the nonbeneficiary consumers to give up some of their food consumption (the amount foregone depending on their price elasticity of demand), whereas the fall in the subsidized price allows the poor consumers to increase their consumption. The extent to which the nonbeneficiary consumers cut their food consumption in order to allow the poor to increase theirs, measures the real trade-off involved in the program, given by

$$\frac{\hat{D}_r}{\hat{D}_p} = \frac{- \eta_r w_p}{(\eta_r w_r + \epsilon)} < 0 \qquad (5.4)$$

The nominal trade-off or the change in relative prices is given by:

$$\frac{\hat{P}}{\hat{P}_s} = \frac{- \eta_p w_p}{\eta_r w_r + \epsilon} < 0 \qquad (5.4')$$

The fall in consumption of the nonbeneficiary consumers and the rise in their price would be smaller the larger the price elasticity of supply, since a smaller portion of the poor's additional consumption would then come from intragroup transfers and a larger portion from the increase in supply. The wedge created by the program between subsidized and market prices would also be smaller the larger the price elasticity of supply. If supply is infinitely elastic, there would be no need for intragroup transfers of food consumption, and no price differentials would be created. This would be the case if at least part of the supply can be imported with no rise in price.[2]

The fiscal costs of the subsidy program are given by:

$$FC = \theta \cdot P \cdot D_p \tag{5.5}$$

Obviously, the larger the subsidy rate, the higher these costs would be. Assume now that the objective of the program is to raise the consumption of the target population by a given percentage, say α, in order to bridge the gap between their present consumption and the minimum consumption required for adequate nutrition. Hence,

$$\hat{D}_p = -\eta_p \cdot \hat{P}_s = \alpha$$

From the foregoing results, we can calculate the subsidy rate necessary to achieve this nutrition objective, given by

$$\theta = \frac{(\alpha - \eta_p)(w_r \eta_r + \epsilon) + w_p \eta_p \cdot \eta_p}{\alpha(\epsilon + \eta)} \tag{5.6}$$

Given this subsidy rate, together with equation 5.5, it is possible to calculate the fiscal costs involved. These costs are calculated here as percentage of national income and are given by:

$$FC^N = \theta \cdot s_p \cdot \gamma_p = \frac{[(\alpha - \eta_p)(w_r \eta_r + \epsilon) + w_p \eta_p^2] \cdot s_p \cdot \gamma_p}{\alpha(\epsilon + \eta)} \tag{5.7}$$

where $s_p = (P \cdot D_p / I_p)$ is the share of food expenditures in the poor's income denoted by I_p, and γ_p is the share of the poor's income in total national income. Superscript N denotes the value of the corresponding variables as percentage of national income.

The following conclusions emerge from equation 5.7: First, the larger the price elasticity of supply, the smaller the subsidy rate and the smaller therefore also the fiscal costs. Hence, if the nutritional objective can be achieved by supplementing the diet of the poor with any one of various alternative food products that are close substitutes in terms of the resulting calorie and protein intake as well as the nutritional habits, the government should focus its subsidy program on that product having the highest supply elasticity. Second, for a country in which the product can be imported with no further rise in price, the fiscal cost would be:

$$FC^N = \frac{(\alpha - \eta_p)}{\alpha} \cdot s_p \cdot \gamma_p$$

Thus, the higher the price elasticity of demand of the poor consumers, the smaller the fiscal costs.

Income-Transfer Program

The effect of income transfers to poor consumers on their level of consumption is moderated somewhat by the simultaneous increase in the market price. The rate of change in the consumption of the poor as an effect of the change in their income is given by

$$\hat{D}_p = \xi_p \hat{I} - \eta_p \hat{P} \tag{5.8}$$

where ξ_p is the income elasticity of demand of group p. The first element on the righthand side of the equation measures the income effect when the price is held constant. The second element accounts for the effect of the change in price. By inserting the market clearing conditions into equation 5.8, we can determine the change in the market price as an effect of the transfer program, given by:

$$\hat{P} = \frac{\xi_p}{\eta + \epsilon} \cdot w_p \cdot \beta > 0 \tag{5.9}$$

where β is the rate of change in the income of the poor as an effect of the program. Equations 5.8 and 5.9 yield the resulting rate of change in the poor's consumption, given by:

$$\hat{D}_p = \beta \cdot \xi_p \frac{(\eta_r w_r + \epsilon)}{(\eta + \epsilon)} \tag{5.10}$$

Suppose, as before, that the objective of the program is to increase the poor's consumption at a rate of α percent. Inserting this target into equation 5.10 implies that the transfer should raise the poor's income at the rate of

$$\beta = \frac{\alpha \cdot (\eta + \epsilon)}{\xi_p \cdot (\eta_r w_r + \epsilon)} \tag{5.11}$$

By combining equations 5.10 and 5.11, we can see that an income transfer of that amount would cause the market price to rise by

$$\hat{P} = \frac{\alpha \cdot w_p}{\epsilon + w_r \eta_r} \tag{5.12}$$

and this rise is exactly equal to the rise in price under the subsidy program. This result is quite obvious since the increase in consumption of the poor can be achieved only by an increase in the market price that forces other consumers to forego some of their consumption and encourages producers to increase their production. As long as the consumption objective for the poor remains the same (and provided there is no rationing and no exogenous increase in supply), the rise in the market price would have to be the same under all policies.

The fiscal costs in this case are simply the income transfers to the poor consumers. Normalized by national income, these costs are given by:

$$FC^N = \frac{\gamma_p \cdot \alpha}{\xi_p \cdot [1 - \frac{w_p \eta_p}{(\eta + \epsilon)}]} \tag{5.13}$$

By comparing equation 5.13 with equation 5.7, we can compare the expected fiscal costs of the two programs and determine their cost-effectiveness in achieving the goal of raising the food consumption of the poor by α percent. The results of the comparison show that the larger the price elasticity of supply the more cost-effective is the subsidy program relative to the income-transfer program. When supply is completely elastic—for example, when any additional supply of the product can be imported at the current market price—the subsidy program is the more cost-effective one for $\alpha > \eta_p$, but the income transfer is the more cost-effective one for $\alpha < \eta_p$. When supply is completely inelastic, then the subsidy program will be the more cost-effective one only for small changes in the poor's consumption. For representative values of the parameters (which have also been used later in the simulation analysis), it was found that only for an increase of 8 percent or less in the poor's consumption the subsidy program is the more cost-effective one, whereas for larger increases the income-transfer program is more cost-effective. The important point to note, however, is that the two programs are interchangeable; therefore, it is always necessary to examine which of the two is more effective in any given application.

The reason that the subsidy program may, in certain cases, be more costly than the income-transfer program is that when the poor's demand for the product is very inelastic and the share of their expenditures on the product in their income very large, the subsidy program would require a large drop in the subsidized price and hence large subsidy payments. If, in these cases, the income elasticity of demand is sufficiently high, the income-transfer program may be more cost-effective.

Transfers in Kind

Transfers in kind programs include the increasingly popular food-for-work program, where the payment in kind is made against work (this work is assumed, however, *not* to contribute immediately to the food supply—for example, public works). The unique feature of this program from the point of view of the market as a whole (as opposed to the ordinary income-transfer program) is the addition it makes to total food supply. Although at the national level this addition may be very small, at the regional level it may be more significant.

We review first the effect of the program from the point of view of an individual consumer, assuming that the program offers a net transfer and does not substitute any other income-generating activity. In other words, in the absence of the work he is given through the program, the consumer would be unemployed. This review will be made in reference to figure 5–1.

In the figure, X represents the food product under consideration and Y the aggregate of all other commodities (or money income). Initially the individual has a money income of $\bar{Y}_0$, and at the retail price P he can buy the quantity $\bar{X}_0$ of commodity X. In this case the individual is assumed to choose the bundle (X_0, Y_0) at point A. Suppose the individual receives payments in kind equal to ΔX. At the prevailing retail price, his actual budget line would be $[\bar{X}_1, B, \bar{Y}_2]$. If, however, he can sell the product only at a price lower than the retail price (for example, the farm gate price), his actual budget line would be $[\bar{X}_1, B, \bar{Y}_1]$, where the distance from the origin to X_3 is exactly equal to ΔX. It is further assumed in the figure that X is a normal good, in which case the consumer will increase his consumption as an effect of the payment in kind. This payment will, however, have an effect identical to that of a rise in income from $\bar{Y}_0$ to $\bar{Y}_2$. The consumer will then move to point B, where he chooses the bundle (X_1, Y_1). He will increase his consumption of X from X_0 to X_1, but *decrease* his purchases of that commodity from X_0 to X_2 (where $\Delta X = X_1 - X_2$). By saving his expenses on X, the consumer will be able to increase his consumption of the other commodities from Y_0 to Y_1, along the budget line $[\bar{X}_1, B]$ where the opportunity cost is still P.

If the consumer is also a producer of that commodity (for example, part-time farmer), producing, say, the amount X_2, then previously he bought the amount $(X_0 - X_2)$ at the retail price P. With the payment in kind of ΔX, he can become self-sufficient in X. Note, however, that this payment should be *larger* than his previous purchases of that commodity, since the money previously spent on X, equal to $P(X_0 - X_2)$, will now be spent on other commodities, equal to $(Y_1 - Y_0)$.

When analyzing the effect of the program on the demand of the beneficiary consumers, we have to take into account the effect of the additional supply on the market price, together with the income effect on

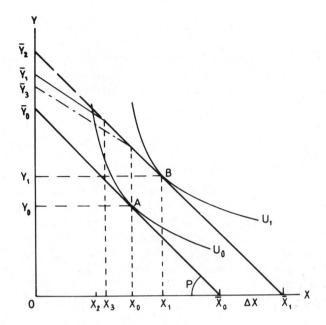

Figure 5–1. The Income and Consumption Effects of Payments in Kind

demand. It is thus assumed that the payments in kind are made in products obtained outside the existing supply system—for example, via foreign food aid. The combined effect on the market price can be calculated, taking the linear approximation of the demand and supply schedules, and is given by:

$$\hat{P} = \rho \cdot \frac{(\xi_p \cdot s_p - 1)}{(\eta + \epsilon)} < 0 \qquad (5.14)$$

where $\rho = \Delta S/S$ is the rate of increase in supply. Since the marginal propensity to spend the additional income on food is less than 1, the price under this program will necessarily fall as an effect of the additional supply that is brought to market. The resulting increase in consumption of the beneficiary consumers is calculated by taking the total differential of the demand function, given by:

$$dD_p = \left. \frac{\partial D_p}{\partial I_p} \right|_{\bar{p}} \cdot \frac{\partial I_p}{\partial S} \cdot dS + \frac{\partial D_p}{\partial P} \cdot \frac{\partial P}{\partial s} \cdot dS$$

The first element on the righthand side of the equation measures the income effect of the transfer in kind; the second element measures the price effect of the increase in supply. The resulting increase can thus be calculated from equations 5.8 and 5.14 to yield:

$$\hat{D}_p = \rho \left[\xi_p \cdot w_p \cdot s_p + \frac{\eta_p (1 - s_p \xi)}{(\eta + \epsilon)} \right] \tag{5.15}$$

In this case the income effect and the price effect work in the same direction to raise the poor consumers' demand. The decline in price will benefit nonbeneficiary consumers also but will cause losses to producers and over the long run may have a larger deterrent effect on producers than that recorded by the short-run elasticity. Suppose, as before, that the target of the policy is $\hat{D}_p = \alpha$. The payments in kind necessary to secure this target require an increase in supply at the rate of

$$\rho = \frac{\alpha(\eta + \epsilon)}{\xi_p \cdot s_p [w_p (\eta + \epsilon) - \eta_p] + \eta_p} \tag{5.16}$$

The fiscal costs of the policy can now be calculated. An important factor determining these costs is the price the government pays for the quantities distributed under the program. The government can buy these quantities at the going market price, it can obtain them through forced procurement at a lower price, or it can get them very cheap or even free from aid programs. By definition, these costs are given by:

$$FC = P^* \cdot \Delta S \tag{5.17}$$

where P^* is the price paid by the government for the additional supply. Thus, by normalizing these costs by the national income, we get

$$FC_{Tk}^N = \frac{P^*}{P} \cdot \mu \cdot \rho \tag{5.18}$$

where μ is the share of the sector in the GDP. When the objective is to raise the poor's consumption by α percent, the fiscal costs of the transfer in kind program would be:

$$FC_{Tk}^{N} = \frac{P^*}{P} \cdot \mu \cdot \alpha \cdot \frac{(\eta + \epsilon)}{\xi_p \cdot s_p \left[w_p \left(\eta + \epsilon \right) - \eta_p \right] + \eta_p} \tag{5.19}$$

By comparing the latter result with that in equation 5.13 we can see that the fiscal cost of the income-transfer program would be lower than those of the transfer-in-kind program if and only if

$$\frac{P^*}{P} > \frac{\gamma_p \xi_p \cdot s_p \cdot \left[w_p \cdot \left(\eta + \epsilon \right) - \eta_p \right] + \eta_p}{\xi_p \cdot \mu (\epsilon + w_r \eta_r)} \tag{5.20}$$

For representative values of the parameters, the ratio on the right hand side of equation 5.20 is of the order of magnitude of 0.5. Hence, only if the cost of the food to the government is half the market price will the transfers in kind be more cost-effective than the income transfers. Moreover, the price, P^* in this evaluation should be the effective cost or, when relevant, the *opportunity* cost, at the point of distribution. It should thus include all shipment and distribution costs as well as the administrative costs involved. It is, therefore, highly questionable whether these programs, despite their popularity, are indeed more cost-effective than the more conventional programs which do not require the physical transfer of food products.

Reutlinger (1983) raised serious doubts about the cost-effectiveness of transfers in kind via food-aid programs conducted when there is no shortage of supply. Even without taking the supply response into account, his estimates suggest that the value of wheat transfers to beneficiary consumers in Egypt is only one-quarter of their cost. In India and Pakistan the ratio is one-half. In other words, the (P^*/P) ratio for wheat is about 4 in Egypt and 2 in India and Pakistan. For corn, Reutlinger estimates the ratio at 3 in Egypt, around 2 in Pakistan, and around 1.5 in India. These ratios are far too high to justify the program on economic grounds under any reasonable set of parameters.

At the same time, however, two arguments should be mentioned in support of this type of program. First, for the recipient country, the actual costs of the food purchased or obtained as aid for these transfers may well be very small (the costs, however, can be substantially higher for the donor country or institution). Equally important, the recipient country cannot expect nearly as much financial support for an income-transfer program even when the latter is more cost-effective. Second, the foregoing analysis does not take into account the large administrative costs that are likely to be involved in the income-transfer program and that may become prohibitive if the program is widely abused.

Nonmarket Programs

Our analysis so far has focused on programs and forms of intervention that operate largely within the framework of the market system. Other programs work through rationing, enforced procurement, and strict curtailment of the market and any interpersonal exchanges. Superficially, these programs may seem attractive because they appear to involve much lower fiscal costs and to offer the most direct way of securing the desired distribution of the available food supply. Indeed, many governments in developing countries that have refrained from full-scale central planning have considered at one time or another implementing this type of program.

In some cases, such as extreme supply shortages, enforced rationing and procurement may be necessary. In most cases, however, past experiences clearly prove that government efforts to control the market have brought more harm than good and sometimes led to disastrous consequences. Poor administration and widespread abuses on the one hand, and strong negative reaction of the market participants on the other not only defeated the attempt to achieve the desired distribution but also had lasting adverse effects on production. In 1973, for example, the government of India took over the entire wholesale wheat trade. Despite extensive legal and administrative preparation, the plan failed badly and had to be withdrawn hastily. Wheat procurement under the government takeover fell far short of the statewide operational targets and was much lower than even that of the previous year. This, combined with the very low level of stocks and the high world prices of food grains, produced an unbearable strain on the working of the public distribution system and brought the experiment to an early end.[3]

The theoretical analysis in this chapter, although neceassarily stylized, still cannot offer a general recommendation as to which program is the most desirable on welfare grounds or the most cost-effective on fiscal grounds. It does indicate, however, that these programs can indeed substitute for one another and that the selection of the most efficient one depends on the specific economic environment in which they operate. The choice of a particular policy instrument for a country is, therefore, largely a matter for an economic evaluation of its cost-effectiveness that should not be biased by any prejudice, conventional wisdom, or past habits.

Measures of Food Insecurity under Instability

The policies analyzed in the previous section are designed to cope with chronic undernutrition of vulnerable population groups. Another dimension of the food problem is that associated with temporary aberrations in food supply due to erratic weather conditions, price fluctuations, policy changes, and the like. These aberrations not only aggravate the situation of the chronically undernourished but also expose other groups, who do manage to support themselves in normal times, to temporary undernutrition or even outright famine.

The measure of the dimensions of the food problem in a stochastic environment must reflect the effects of temporary fluctuations in food consumption as well as those of chronic undernutrition. In chapter 1 it was noted that common measures such as the average per capita calorie intake are inappropriate in this case, both because they fail to take into account the distribution of the food consumed between different income groups and therefore are likely to bias downward the true dimensions of the food problem, and because they average out year-to-year fluctuations in food supply and thus ignore years in which the food problem is worsened as the incidence of undernutrition is both deepened and widened with shortfalls in supply and mounting prices.

In this section we examine several measures of food insecurity in an unstable environment. Our starting point, however, is the axiomatic approach developed by Sen (1976, 1981) for measuring poverty in a stable environment.

Let T denote the set of all chronically undernourished persons in a country, those whose calorie intake is below the minimum subsistence level D^*. The *food gap* of a chronically undernourished individual is given by

$$G_i = D^* - D_i \qquad : i \in T \tag{5.21}$$

where D_i is their actual calorie intake. The total food gap in that country is given by

$$G = \sum_{i \in T} G_i \tag{5.22}$$

The standard measures of food insecurity is the number of undernourished persons, or their ratio in the population, given by

$$N = \frac{m}{n} \tag{5.23}$$

where m is the number of individuals in T and n is the total number of individuals in that country. Another widely used measure is the absolute food gap, G, or the food gap ratio given by

$$I = G/(m \cdot D^*) \tag{5.24}$$

A unique feature of these two measures is that they define the food problem as a characteristic of the undernourished persons only. To use Sen's terminology, these two measures satisfy the *focus* axiom (F).

To assess the degree to which these or other measures succeed in describing the severity of the problem, Sen defined two other "axioms of legitimacy," namely, two desired properties of the measures of poverty, or, in the present context, of food insecurity:

1. *The monotonicity axiom (M):* Other things being equal, a reduction in food consumption of a chronically undernourished person must increase the food insecurity measure.
2. *The weak-transfer axiom (T):* A transfer of food from one person to another whose calorie intake is both smaller than that of the donor and below D^* (but without changing the overall number of the chronically undernourished) must reduce the food insecurity measure.

The latter axiom, which is a direct product of the assumption of decreasing marginal utility of food consumption, implies that, given the total food supply, the more equitable its distribution, the smaller the degree of food insecurity.

The two measures N and I do not have these desired properties (M) and (T). N violates both axioms. I satisfies the monotonicity axiom but violates the weak-transfer axiom. Thus, for example, a food transfer from a person having a small food gap to another person having a large food gap would not change the global food gap and thus would also leave unchanged the measure I. Equally important, a *reverse* food transfer from a person having a large food gap to another having a smaller food gap—for example, a transfer from rural consumers to poor urban consumers as an effect of urban-biased government policies—will also leave unchanged the measure of food insecurity. In Sen's words, these two measures are "blind to distribution among the poor" (1981, p. 186).

As temporary shortfalls in food consumption occur from time to time, both the number of individuals in T and their calorie intake (and thus also their food gap) become stochastic variables, as illustrated in figure 5–2. In the figure the population is divided into five income groups and the calorie intake per capita is measured for each group, at two different time periods. The minimum calorie intake per capita is determined at Q_c. In the first period, marked in the figure by the solid lines, groups 1 and 2 only suffer from undernutrition, although the deficiency of group 1 is much larger. The food gap in that period is the shaded area under Q_c line and above the horizontal solid lines. In the second period, marked in the figure by the broken lines, per capita consumption of all groups decreases, though at different rates. In the second period, groups 1, 2, and 3 suffer from undernutrition. The food gap

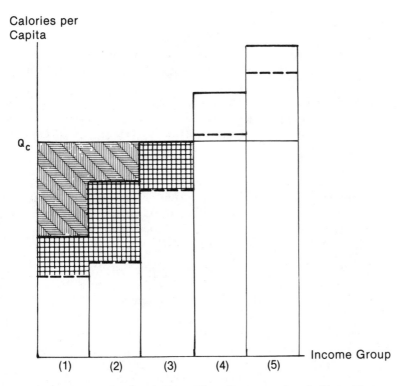

Figure 5–2. The Food Gap When Consumption Is Unstable

in that period is the entire shaded area under the Q_c line and above the broken lines. The expected food gap is the average gap over all time periods.

Temporary undernutrition is the result of fluctuations *over time* in food prices, food supply, or income, which may leave certain subgroups of the population undernourished in some years, although most of the time they may be adequately fed. To measure this dimension of food insecurity, the axiomatic approach must be extended to a dynamic setting. Axioms (*M*) and (*T*) would then characterize the desired properties of a food insecurity measure within each period, and another axiom would describe its desired properties with respect to consumption *sequences* over time. This is given by

3. *The intertemporal-transfer axiom (S):* A transfer of consumption from a good year—one in which $D_i(t) > \bar{D}_i$, where $\bar{D}_i$ is the average con-

sumption of person i—to a bad year—one in which *both* $D_i(t) < \bar{D}_i$ and $D_i(t) < D^*$—must reduce the food insecurity measure.

The requirement that in a bad year $D_i(t) < D^*$ guarantees the consistency of this axiom with the focus axiom (F). In other words, the measure of food insecurity focuses on all individuals who suffered from undernutrition in some—though not necessarily all—years.

A straightforward extension of the previous two food-insecurity measures to a stochastic framework is to take their *expected* values. The measure $E(N)$ would then measure the number of persons whose *average* consumption is below subsistence. This measure is completely blind to temporary shortages and thus violates axiom (S). It also violates the other (static, or within-period) axioms not only for the reasons mentioned earlier but also because it ignores individuals who suffer from undernutrition in some years although on average they manage to subsist. Nevertheless, this is the most widely used measure in empirical studies and policy position papers.

The expected food gap is measured as follows. Let

$$G_i = \begin{cases} (D^* - D_i) & : \text{if } D_i < D^* \\ 0 & \text{Otherwise} \end{cases} \tag{5.25}$$

Then

$$E(G) = \sum_{i=1}^{n} \int G_i f(D_i) dD_i \tag{5.26}$$

where $f(D_i)$ is the frequency distribution of D_i. This measure would record a reduction in food insecurity provided that even after the transfer from the good year to the bad, food consumption in the good year still exceeds D^*. It therefore ignores intertemporal transfers of the chronically undernourished from good to bad years.

Bigman and Reutlinger (1979a, b) defined the measure of food insecurity in a country as the probability that in any given year, food consumption of low-income consumers (only) falls below a certain critical level. The critical level itself can be the minimum subsistence level D^* or a fraction of that level. If the critical level is D^*, the measure would violate both the monotonicity axiom (M) and the weak-transfer axiom (T); it will satisfy the intertemporal axiom (S) for the normally subsistence consumers only (for whom $\bar{D}_i > D^*$). If the critical level is a fraction of D^*, then the probability measure may exhibit a reduction in food insecurity as required by the three axioms in some cases. An illustration is given in figure 5–3. In the figure, F_1 is assumed to be the lower half of the probability distribution of the quantity consumed by the poor, D_p, when no policy is implemented. The intercept of F_1 with the Y axis

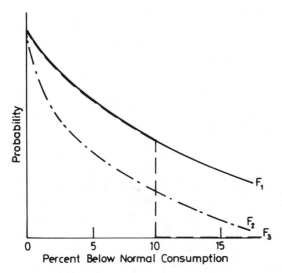

Figure 5–3. Probability That Actual Consumption of the Poor Falls below the Prespecified Level

thus measures the probability that the poor's consumption falls below D^*. Let F_2 and F_3 be the lower halves of two probability distributions of D_p generated by two alternative stabilization policies. Suppose also that the critical level of consumption is determined as a fraction, say 90 percent, of D^*. Under this assumption, F_3, which reduces the probability of a consumption shortfall below the critical level to zero, would be ranked higher than F_2. If, on the other hand, the critical level is assumed to be 95 percent of D^*, F_3 would appear to have no effect at all on the level of food security; F_2 would be ranked higher. The expected food gap is the area under the curve of the probability distribution.

To overcome these deficiencies, the probability measure can be extended as follows: Let D_p^1 and D_p^2 be two consumption sequences of low-income consumers. The sequence D_p^1 is said to reduce food insecurity more than D_p^2 if and only if there is $0 < \tilde{\Theta} \leq 1$ such that

$$P_r(D_p^1 < \tilde{\Theta}D^*) < P_r(D_p^2 < \tilde{\Theta}D^*)$$

and if, for any other $0 < \Theta \leq 1$,

$$P_r(D_p^1 < \Theta D^*) > P_r(D_p^2 < \Theta D^*)$$

then $\Theta > \tilde{\Theta}$.

In words: The probability of having a food shortage in excess of $\tilde{\Theta}D^*$ is smaller under D_p^1 than under D_p^2, and if at any other level of consumption ΘD^*, D_p^1 provides *less* food security (in probability terms) than D_p^2, then the shortage at that level is not as extreme as that at $\tilde{\Theta}D^*$. It is easy to verify that this measure would satisfy all three axioms.

The simple probability measure of Bigman and Reutlinger has the attractive feature of providing a clear and understandable measure of insecurity—namely, the probability that an extreme shortage may develop. It assumes however, that the target group on which attention is focused can be clearly identified. In theory, at least, the target group may be the group of all consumers, because in theory there might be an extreme combination of events—however small its probability may be—under which the entire population would suffer from temporary undernutrition. If, however, the target group is extended to normally subsistence consumers, then the probability measure will no longer exhibit the problem of chronic undernutrition, which may affect only a subgroup of the target group.

The approach taken in this study is to present both the probability measure of food insecurity and the expected food gap for each income group separately. Consumption sequence x would then be said to provide greater food security than consumption sequence y if it reduces the level of food insecurity—as measured by either one of these measures—for at least one of the consumer groups without raising this level for any of the other groups. When the level of food security of one group is raised at the expense of that of another group—via, say, a target subsidy program—the trade-off between the level of food security of the two groups would be presented.

Food-Distribution Policies under Instability

When production, prices, and incomes are unstable, distribution policies typically play the dual role of securing the desired distribution of the average food supply on the one hand, and stabilizing the consumption of the target population on the other hand. To see this, consider the subsidy program specified earlier. The effects of this program can be analyzed as having two entirely separable and essentially unrelated components. One is the permanent component, which registers the effects on the expected price; the other is the transitory component, which registers the effects on the year-to-year disparity between the actual price and the expected price. The first component is the one analyzed in a comparative static analysis in the first section. The second component, which becomes relevant in a stochastic environment, summarizes the *stabilizing* effects of the subsidy program.

To illustrate the basic issues concerning food security and food policies in a stochastic environment, consider a linear version of the partial-equilibrium model of the first section. The demand and supply functions are then given by:

$$D_r(P) = a_r - b_r P$$
$$D_p(P) = a_p - b_p P$$
$$S(P) = c + dP + u$$

where D_r and D_p are the demands of the effluent and poor consumers, respectively, and S is the total supply. The random disturbances in supply, u, are assumed to be symmetrically distributed with zero mean, finite variance σ^2, and no serial correlation.[4]

The equilibrium market price thus varies together with the variations in supply, and its variability is given by:

$$\text{Var}(P) = \frac{\sigma^2}{(d + b_r + b_p)^2} \tag{5.27}$$

With these variations in the market price (and when there are no compensating income transfers), food consumption of the two groups would also vary. In times of price rises, low-income consumers may be priced out of the market because of the reduction in their purchasing power. The food deficiency of the chronically undernourished would then become more acute, and consumers who merely subsist in normal years may suffer from temporary undernutrition. Especially vulnerable are farmers and rural landless workers, whose income may fall further as a result of the decline in output and employment in the agricultural sector.

Bigman and Reutlinger's probability measure of food insecurity, focused on the food consumption of the poor consumers. In the present model this measure is given by:

$$P_r(D_p < D^*) \tag{5.28}$$

where D_p is the food consumption of the poor consumers, D^* is the minimum subsistence level,[5] and P_r is a probability statement. In the linear model this probability is equal to

$$P_r(u_t < u^*) \tag{5.29}$$

where $u^* = -(\bar{D}_p - D^*) \cdot (d + b_r + b_p) \, b_p$, is the corresponding shortfall in supply, $\bar{D}_p$ being the average food consumption of the poor. In theory—that is, under the ordinary assumptions about u, for *every* predetermined finite u^*, however small, it is *always* the case that $P_r(u < u^*) \geq 0$. In other words, there is *always* a nonzero probability that in one of the years, however remote in the future, an extreme shortage—in the sense of the definition in equation 5.28—may develop.

Policy that can truncate the distribution of D_p to the extent that the food insecurity is completely eliminated is said to be one that provides *complete* food security. At least in theory, such policy may require prohibitively high fiscal costs. The only practical approach is therefore to design food policies that can provide a predetermined or *desired* degree of food security—or, tolerable degree of food *insecurity*.

Suppose that the probability measure of food insecurity is required not to exceed a tolerance level v. By definition,

$$p_r(D_p < D^*) = F\left\{\frac{(D^* - \bar{D}_p)}{(\sigma_{Dp})}\right\} = v \qquad (5.30)$$

where F is the cumulative probability distribution of D_p, and σ_{Dp} is its standard deviation. From equation 5.30 we can develop an expression for σ_{Dp}, given by:

$$\sigma_{Dp} = \frac{(D^* - \bar{D}_p)}{F^{-1}(v)} \qquad (5.31)$$

For a symmetric distribution $F^{-1}(1/2) = 0$. In practice, however, the tolerance level of the food insecurity would have to be much lower than 50 percent; therefore, $F^{-1}(v) < 0$. This definition implies that if the poor can support themselves in normal years (if $\bar{D}_p > D^*$), then food security can be achieved by just stabilizing their food consumption. If, however, the poor are chronically undernourished, food security would be strengthened by *destabilizing* their food consumption. In the following analysis we will make the former assumption in order to concentrate on the stability effects of the various programs.

Consider first a target-group subsidy program similar to the one discussed in the previous section; that is, the subsidized price the poor pay is some fraction $(1 - \Theta)$ of the market price, $P_s = (1 - \Theta)P$. In this specific program the transitory component has element of an insurance scheme. The poor consumers enjoy a price lower than the market price (or, if there is already a subsidy program in effect, receive a higher subsidy rate) during bad years, but pay a premium (or get a lower subsidy rate) during years of plentiful supply. In the vast majority of cases, however, the subsidy program is one-sided in the sense that it is activated or intensified by the government during the shortage period—along the upper tail of the price distribution—without being trimmed during periods of plentiful supply. The program is widened, in terms of both the population covered and the subsidy rate, when the market price rises above its normal level, without any significant offsetting reduction in benefits when prices are falling.

In the two-sided, insurance type of subsidy program, the expected market price is given by:

$$E(P) = \frac{a_r + a_p - c}{b_r + (1 - \Theta)b_p + d} \qquad (5.32)$$

and its variability by

$$\text{Var}(P) = \frac{\sigma^2}{[b_r + (1 - \Theta)b_p + d]^2} \qquad (5.33)$$

Hence both the variability of the market price and its expected level are rising with increases in the subsidy rate. Since both the spread and the mean are rising with Θ, however, a more relevant indicator would be the change in the coefficient of variation. From equations 5.32 and 5.33 it can be observed, however, that the coefficient of variation of the market price does not depend at all on Θ and therefore remains unchanged.

The variability of the subsidized price is simply $(1 - \Theta)^2$ times the variability of the market price, and one can easily verify that this variability *declines* as the subsidy rate is raised. The coefficient of variation, however, remains unchanged.

The standard deviation of the quantity consumed by the poor consumers is given by:

$$\sigma_{Dp} = \frac{(1 - \Theta) \cdot b_p}{b_r + (1 - \Theta)b_p + d} \sigma \qquad (5.34)$$

If the goal of the subsidy policy is the one specified in equation 5.31, then the subsidy rate that provides this level of food security is given by:

$$\Theta = 1 + \frac{k(\bar{D}_p - D^*)(b_r + d)}{b_p[\sigma + k(\bar{D}_p - D^*)]} \qquad (5.35)$$

where $k = 1/F^{-1}(v) < 0$.

Given that subsidy rate, the expected fiscal costs can be calculated, yielding

$$E(FC) = E(\Theta P \cdot Dp) \qquad (5.36)$$
$$= \Theta E[P(a_p - b_p(1 - \Theta)P)]$$
$$= \Theta\{a_p E(P) - b_p(1 - \Theta) \cdot [\text{Var}(P) + E^2(P)]\}$$

By inserting the earlier results into equation 5.36, the expected fiscal budget for the program can be calculated as a function of all the model's parameters.

Even more important, however, than the *expected* fiscal burden of the subsidy program is the instability introduced by the program to the fiscal budget and the risk that in any given year the subsidy costs will be so high that they will disrupt the entire fiscal system. We can term this probability the *fiscal risk*. The difficulty of financing large government expenditures in years of extreme shortage exists because insurance markets in these countries are incomplete or even absent, so that the government cannot finance its additional expenses in bad years through loans that would be repaid in good years, and the extra financing may have to be inflationary.[6]

There is an obvious technical difficulty in measuring the fiscal risk even in a simple theoretical model with linear demand and supply functions and a symmetric distribution of additive random disturbances in supply. Even in this model, the frequency distribution of *FC* is no longer symmetric. An analytical solution is even more difficult if not impossible to get when the policy decisions are contingent on and respond to the actual events taking place in that year. Food distribution programs are, however, of this type. The subsidy program is intensified considerably when the market price is rising; income transfers and, even more so, transfers in kind are often implemented only when the regular sources of income of the target population are severely eroded. In all these cases the decision is discontinuous in the sense that it takes place only at one tail of the relevant probability distribution. To allow a more thoroughgoing analysis of government food distribution policies under instability, we examine in the next sections these policies via simulation analysis of the food grain market.

Simulation Analysis: Data, Parameters, and Policy Rules

The simulation analysis is based on the sectorial model and the solution method detailed in chapter 2 and applied in chapters 3 and 4. The following modifications have been made:

1. Consumers are divided into three income groups. A separate demand function is specified for each group, and total demand in the country is the sum of the demands of the three groups. The demand function of each group is assumed to be kinked-linear, becoming less elastic at the higher segment of the price distribution.[7] The specific demand parameters assumed in the simulation analysis are listed in table 5–1.

2. The distribution programs are targeted on one group only—group 1, assumed to be the group of poor consumers. In the version of the model examined in the fifth section of this chapter, the target group is assumed to be the group of poor consumers in *urban* areas only. The relatively high price elasticity of demand of consumers in this group is due to the high proportion

Table 5–1
Demand Parameters in the Country

	Consumer Groups			
	Group 1 (Target Group)	Group 2 (Farmers)	Group 3	Population
Share of the group in total normal consumption	25%	50%	25%	100%
Price elasticity of demand at the mean				
$P > \bar{P}$	0.5	0.15	0.20	0.25
$P < \bar{P}$	0.5	0.30	0.30	0.35
Income elasticity of demand	0.7	0.70	0.40	

of their income allocated to staple foods. Their demand is therefore dominated by the income effect.

3. Group 2 is assumed, in the versions of the model presented in the fifth section and in subsequent chapters, to be the group of rural consumers. Their low price elasticity of demand, especially at high prices, is due to the income effect on their excess supply, which moderates, if not entirely outweighs, the substitution effect.[8] In addition to price, income part of which the derive from food production, also affects the demand of these consumers. Weather-induced variations in food production would thus cause their income, and with it their consumption, to vary. The size of the variations depend on the share of their revenues from these products in their total income—assumed in these experiments to be 70 percent—and on their income elasticity of demand—assumed to be 0.7. In a normal year their own consumption of the food products is assumed to be half their production. Under these assumptions a 1 percent change in output would cause their own consumption to vary by 0.25 percent.

4. Group 3 represents the group of middle- to high-income consumers, especially in urban areas.

5. The share of each group in total consumption is likely to be substantially different from its share in the population. Specifically, the share of the low-income group in consumption is much smaller than its share in the population, thus representing the initial inequalities in the distribution of income and of food consumption.

6. Supply is determined as a log-linear, constant-elasticity function of the expected price. The price elasticity of supply is assumed to be 0.25. When noted, producers are assumed to be risk-averse and to respond to the variability in *income* by constraining their production. The risk-response elasticity is assumed to be 0.25. An increase in the income variability by 1 percent would then cause a reduction in planned output of that product by 0.25 percent.

7. The other parameters of the model—the variability in production, the variability of the world price, and so on—are the same as those assumed in chapter 4.

We can now turn to the specific decision rules of the policies under consideration.

Subsidy Program

This program has the basic structure of the subsidy program examined in the previous section (see also Bigman 1982, chap. 5). Food is distributed at a discount price to the target population, and some form of rationing is implemented to guarantee that only eligible consumers can enjoy the discount price. There is no quota constraint, however, on the quantity eligible consumers can buy at the discount price. The subsidy program, which becomes active only when the market price rises above a prespecified threshold price, is aimed at moderating the price of food paid by the poor consumers or even preventing that price from rising and their food consumption from falling below a prespecified minimum level. The subsidized price is assumed to be determined by the following linear (though discontinuous) rule

$$P_s = \begin{cases} \Theta \hat{P} + (1 - \Theta)P & : \text{if } P \geq \bar{P} \\ P & : P \leq \bar{P} \end{cases}$$

where P and $\bar{P}$ are the actual and the median price, respectively, and $0 \leq \Theta \leq 1$. The threshold price that triggers the subsidy program is thus assumed to be the median (or the normal) price, which is also the price in a stable year. This rule has the effect of specifying a Harbergerian type of target demand function for the target population, its elasticity being $(1 - \Theta)$ times the original elasticity of the group. In the simulation analysis that follows, several values of the parameter Θ and thus also several target elasticities have been examined. Under the other parameters and in the absence of a subsidy program, a rise in price by 10 percent above the normal price would force poor consumers to cut their consumption by 5 percent. An equal rise in price would cause their consumption to decline by only 2.5 percent when $\Theta = 0.5$—that is, when the target elasticity is 0.25—and by 1 percent when $\Theta = 0.8$—that is, the target elasticity is 0.1. When $\Theta = 1$ (the target demand curve becomes completely inelastic above the median price), any decline in the poor's consumption below their normal consumption is prevented.

Income Transfer Program

This program transfers money income to the target population in order to increase their purchasing power and hence their food consumption. Transfers are repeated every year in order to maintain their income at the target level. Here these targets are specified as percentage increases in their income—for example, income transfers that would raise the income of the target population by 5 or 10 percent above its present level and maintain it at that higher level throughout the twenty-year period of the program. That target can also be specified in terms of the increase in food consumption. Transfers are assumed to be made every year and are not contingent on any specific events.

Buffer Stocks

This program stabilizes the flow of supply to the general population and is not specific to the target group. Nevertheless, by smoothing out the flow of supply, it reduces the risk that an extreme shortage, by which poor consumers would be hurt the most, may develop. Storage decision rules are specified by a price band and by the storage capacity. In the program considered here, the price band is 20 percent above and below a reference price. This reference price itself is calculated as a moving average of the market prices in the past nine years. The price band therefore does not remain fixed but gradually floats with the long-run moving average, adjusting itself to long-run changes in the price level due to risk response, policy changes, and so on.[9] The storage capacity is assumed to be 10 percent of the annual production of food grains. Storage costs include operating and amortization costs. Investment in a storage facility is assumed to cost $150 per MT (at 1982 prices), to be amortized over twenty years.

The performance measures used in the analysis are denoted and defined as follows:

1. *Food insecurity* ($X\%$): The probability that food consumption of the group under consideration falls by more than X percent below their normal consumption. Their minimum or subsistence consumption is thus assumed to be $(1 - X)$ percent of their normal consumption. For poor urban consumers, minimum consumption is assumed to be 95 percent of their normal consumption; for rural consumers it is assumed to be 90 percent of their normal consumption.

2. *Expected food gap:* Expected gap between the group's actual consumption in years of supply shortages and their subsistence consumption. The gap is thus calculated only in years when the group's actual consumption falls below subsistence. For the target group, subsistence consumption is assumed here to be their normal consumption. For the second group, subsistence consumption is assumed to be 90 percent of their normal consumption.

All value measures are given as percentages of the annual expenditures on food grains in the economy in a normal year, and all quantity measures are given as percentages of total production in a normal year.

Simulation Results: The Base Case

In the base case we consider a prototype model of the food grains sector in a closed economy. This should not mean the absence of any trade. Instead, it means that all trade activities are either regulated or directly carried out by the government according to its own policy objectives, rather than being determined endogenously by market forces according to the difference between the border price and the internal price. The main reason for selecting the closed economy as the base case is to isolate the net effect of each policy and program. With free trade, the results will register the combined effect of the policy under consideration and of trade. The effects of the policies under free and constrained trade are subsequently examined.

Table 5–2 presents the main economic and food security effects of the three types of distribution policies considered: (1) a subsidy program targeted on the group of low-income consumers, (2) income transfers to this group, and (3) buffer stocks that stabilize food grains supply to the general population. Under the subsidy program, both the mean and the coefficient of variation of the market price are rising. The added demand of the target population, permitted by the program, bids up the price; and, by stabilizing the consumption of the target population, the program narrows the incidence of production instability to the nonbeneficiary consumers only, thereby destabilizing their consumption. The income-transfer program, in contrast, which is not state-contingent,[10] causes only the mean price to rise without affecting its variability. The slight reduction in coefficient of variation noted in the table is due to the rise in mean production as the price is rising.

The rise in price is the mechanism that permits the redistribution of supply, since it forces the nonbeneficiary consumers to forego some of their consumption. For example, under the subsidy program with a target elasticity equal to 0.1, the market price rises by 4.3 percent. As a result, consumption of the nonbeneficiary consumers declines by 0.6 percent, and output rises by 1 percent. This allows the consumption of the target group (whose share in total consumption is assumed to be 25 percent) to rise by 5.7 percent. Moreover, since the program is activated only when the market price exceeds the median price, the rise in the poor's consumption *in those years* is, on average, 11.4 percent. With an income-transfer program that raises the poor's income by 10 percent, their mean consumption also rises by 5.7 percent. (The effect of the increase in income is, obviously, moderated by the rise in the market price by 3.1 percent.) But the increase is the same in both the good and the bad years (unless these consumers themselves take measures to save part of the added income in good years to finance their higher expenditures in the bad years). This income-transfer program would therefore provide *less* food security than the subsidy program, even though the two require the same fiscal budget. Indeed, with the subsidy program considered, the expected food

Table 5–2
Main Economic and Food Security Indicators of Alternative Food-Distribution Policies: Base Case (Closed Economy: No Risk Response)

| | | Policy | | | | |
| | | Targeted Subsidy: Target Elasticity | | Income Transfer: Rate of Income Change | | |
Performance Measure	No Intervention	0.25	0.1	+5%	+10%	Buffer Stocks[a]
Market price						
Mean	102.2	104.5	106.6	103.9	105.4	101.6
CV (%)	30.2	35.1	39.7	30.0	29.7	22.8
Consumption of target group						
Δ %Mean[b]	—	+3.2	+5.7	+2.8	+5.7	+0.1
Insecurity (5%)[c]	37.4	29.5	15.8	31.6	26.7	32.0
Expected food gap[d]	6.7	4.1	1.9	5.5	4.5	4.7
Government expenditures						
Mean[e]	0	1.5	3.6	1.8	3.6	0.9
Risk[f]	0	0.9	14.8	0.0	0.0	0.5
Economic gains or losses due to policy						
Target group	—	-1.4	+2.5	+1.5	+2.7	-0.1
Other consumers	—	-1.9	-3.5	-1.7	-2.9	+0.1
Producers	—	+1.8	+3.3	+1.6	+3.2	-0.1
Government	—	-1.7	-3.6	-1.8	-3.6	-0.9
Total economy	—	-0.4	-1.3	-0.4	-0.6	-1.0

[a]Buffer stocks equal to 10 percent of normal annual production. Expenditures include amortization costs.

[b]Percentage change in mean consumption due to policy.

[c]Expressed as percentage of total annual production.

[d]Probability that consumption of the target group falls by more than 5 percent below their normal consumption.

[e]Expressed as percentage of total annual expenditures on the product.

[f]Probability that government expenditures exceeded 10 percent of the annual expenditures on the product.

gap would be reduced from 6.7 to 1.9 percent of the annual production, whereas with the income transfer program considered, the gap would be reduced to 4.5 percent only. The assumption implicit in the latter conclusion is that consumers cannot substitute for the food products whose price has risen other products (domestically produced or imported) whose price remained unchanged. If substitution opportunities exist, the income-transfer program would provide much more food security than what the foregoing partial-equilibrium analysis suggests.

One disadvantage of the subsidy program is its destabilizing effect on the fiscal budget. In the program under consideration, once every 6.5 years government expenditures on subsidies would exceed three times their average level. The subsidy program also involves much higher deadweight losses; and, over the long run, the economic gains of the target group from the program would be smaller than those under the income-transfer program. The small economic losses resulting from the income-transfer program, however, do not take into account the potential adverse effects of government taxes and expenditures on labor supply, inflation, and so on.

A comparison between these two programs on the basis of the simulation results summarized in table 5–2 would therefore lead to mixed conclusions as to which of the two is preferable. Each program has its weaknesses and its strengths. The choice between the two should be based on the relative weight of each of these in the overall government policy objective. In making this choice, several other points should be taken into account.

1. The income-transfer program is much more susceptible to fraud and abuse. The subsidy program—through food stamps, rationing, and the like— is also frequently abused, and even in countries such as the United States a considerable number of recipients are not in fact eligible for the program. To minimize this damage and lower the costs of widespread abuse, the program can be constrained to a small number of commodities that are the customary diet of the poor. In the Fair Price shops in India, for example, the quality of the rice distributed is considerably lower than that in the regular retail outlets, and the quality difference serves to deter the more affluent consumers much more effectively than formal rationing would. In other countries the program can reach the target population by concentrating on low-grade commodities such as millet, sorghum, root crops, lower-quality products, and so on.

2. The cost-effectiveness of the program, especially in the developing countries, largely depends on the extent to which it can effectively identify and be constrained to the target population. In many countries the entire population enjoys the subsidized price on a wide variety of food and some nonfood items. Egypt, Tunisia, Turkey, and Israel are only a few examples of countries where the government subsidizes many consumer goods at extremely high fiscal and foreign-exchange costs. When the program is not

targeted on any specific subgroup of the population, it cannot, of course, secure adequate consumption through redistribution. The only way for the government to supplement the domestic supply is through subsidized imports. In the following chapters we examine this policy in detail.

3. The targeted subsidy program destabilizes not only the market price but also farmers' revenues. Under the subsidy program with a target elasticity of 0.1, for instance, the coefficient of variation of farmers' revenues rises by 40 percent. If farmers are risk-averse, they would react to the growing instability by switching to other, more stable crops. This response may reduce the effectiveness of the program and require much larger fiscal costs to achieve the food-security goals. Table 5–3 summarizes the economic and food-security effects of the programs with risk response. Several results stand out. First, with risk response, mean output is 2.3 percent lower and mean price 8.0 percent higher than their corresponding values under risk neutrality. As a result, the probability that food consumption of the low-income consumers would fall below subsistence is 26 percent higher and the expected food gap is 37 percent higher than their levels under risk neutrality. Second, the destabilizing effects of the subsidy program on risk-averse producers moderate (and may even reverse) the price effects on output. Thus, for instance, under a subsidy program with target elasticity of 0.1, mean output rises by only 0.5 percent (compared with a rise of 1 percent under risk neutrality) even though the mean price rises by 9.1 percent; the reason is the simultaneous rise in the variability of farmers' income. As a consequence, most of the additional consumption of the target population would have to come at the expense of the food consumption of the other consumers; government expenditures would have to be much higher (by close to 50 percent under the aforementioned program), and the income transfers implicit in the program and measured by the economic gains or losses to the various sectors would be much larger. Third, under these circumstances stabilizing policies such as buffer stocks (or, in an open economy, variable import levies) would be much more attractive. Thus, for instance, with buffer stocks equal to 10 percent of annual production, the expected food gap would decline by 27 percent compared with a decline of 36 percent under a subsidy program with a target elasticity of 0.25. The fiscal costs of the stocks program would, however, be only one-third of those of the subsidy program. There are limits however, to the effectiveness of buffer stocks and other general stabilization policies and to their ability to reach the target population without distribution measures. Thus, for instance, further reductions in the expected food gap via buffer stocks would require rapidly rising costs, which may well become higher than the costs of alternative programs before the food security objectives are reached.

The results presented in this section further emphasize the tradeoffs involved in the various food distribution programs and thus the political,

Table 5–3

Main Economic and Food-Security Indicator of Alternative Food-Distribution Policies, with Risk Response

	Policy			
		Targeted Subsidy: Target Elasticity		
Performance Measure	*No Intervention*	*0.25*	*0.1*	*Buffer Stocks*[a]
Market price				
Mean	110.3	115.4	120.3	107.5
CV(%)	29.2	34.2	38.8	22.9
Consumption of target group[b]				
Δ% mean[c]	—	+3.8	+7.2	+1.7
Insecurity (5%)	47.3	40.7	24.9	44.4
Expected food gap	9.2	5.9	2.9	6.7
Government expenditures				
Mean[e]	0	2.5	5.3	0.9
Risk[f]	0	1.8	23.3	1.0
Economic gains or losses due to policy[e]				
Target group	—	+1.6	+2.7	+0.1
Other consumers	—	−3.6	−6.1	+1.2
Producers	—	+3.5	+6.8	−0.8
Government	—	−2.5	−5.3	−0.9
Total economy	—	−1.0	−1.9	−0.4

[a]Buffer stocks equal to 10 percent of normal annual production. Expenditures include amortization costs.

[b]Percentage change in mean consumption due to policy.

[c]Expressed as percentage of total annual production.

[d]Probability that consumption of the target group falls by more than 5 percent below their normal consumption.

[e]Expressed as percentage of total annual expenditures on the product.

[f]Probability that government expenditures exceeded 10 percent of the annual expenditures on the product.

economic, and budgetary difficulties of implementing them. Figures 5–4, 5–5, and 5–6 present these trade-offs under the targeted subsidy programs with different target elasticities. Completely inelastic target demand curve defines a program that prevents *any* fall in the consumption of the target population below the minimum level.

Figure 5–4 demonstrates that increasing the food security of the target population would involve raising prices to levels that may actually jeopardize the food security of the other consumers. As noted earlier, the minimum subsistence level of the second income groups is 90 percent of their normal consumption. The results presented in figure 5–5 show that as the expected food gap of the target population is lowered, the consumption of the second

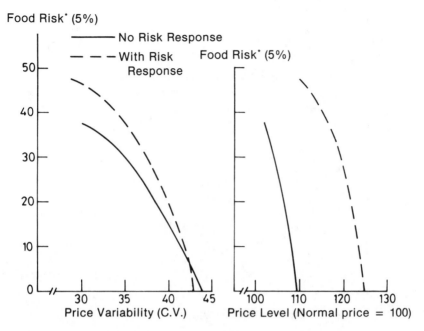

*Probability that food consumption of the target group falls by more than 5% below their normal consumption.

Figure 5–4. Trade-off between Food Security and the Level and Variability of the Market Price under the Subsidy Program

group falls more and more frequently below their subsistence level such that the expected food gap of this group rises up to 1.3 percent of the annual production (2.2 percent when there is risk response) when the food gap of the target population is completely eliminated. It should be emphasized, however, that *any other* distribution program that works via the market system would involve *identical* trade-offs between the food security of the two groups. The reason is that the added consumption of the target population can only come at the expense of the consumption of the other consumers. The question is, therefore, which of the programs is more cost-effective—that is, can achieve the desired level of food security for the target population at the least possible costs. The fiscal implications of the subsidy program are presented in figure 5–6.

The trade-off between food security of the target population and that of the other consumers is especially significant in the controversy over the urban bias of government price policies, since most distribution programs are targeted on the urban population. We examine this issue further in the next section.

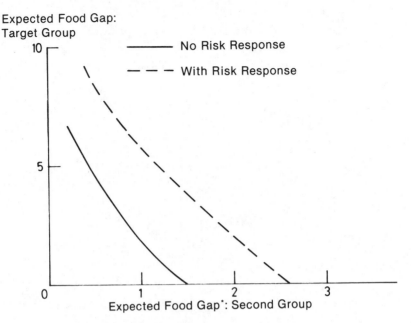

*Expressed as percentage of total annual production.

Figure 5–5. Trade-off between Expected Food Gap of Target Group and Expected Food Gap of Second Income Group as an Effect of Targeted Subsidy Program

Distribution Programs Targeted on Urban Consumers and Their Effects on Rural Consumers

In this section the second consumer group, which constitutes 50 percent of the population, is assumed to be the group of rural consumers—farmers and landless rural workers. Food consumption of this group, as a function of food prices and income, varies from year to year with variations in their income resulting from weather-induced fluctuations in output and from fluctuations in prices. Price variations themselves are caused both by the changes in output and by the policies implemented. In chapter 4 we saw that these variations in farmers' own consumption considerably reduce the variability of their excess supply and thus also the fluctuations of the price in urban markets. We have also noted, however, that farmers take a wide variety of measures including on-farm stocks, investments in cattle, machinery, gold, and the like, to protect themselves against these variations in income and moderate the fluctuations in their consumption.

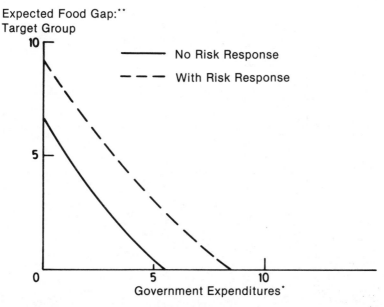

*Expressed as percentage of total expenditures on the crop.

**Expressed as percentage of total annual production.

Figure 5–6. Trade-off between Food Security and Government Expenditures on Subsidies

Nevertheless, income and consumption of small farmers and landless rural workers are subject to considerable fluctuations—the more so the smaller is their crop variety and the more constrained is their access to the credit market. In the present analysis the parameters of the model imply that a 1 percent change in food production results in a 0.25 percent change in their own consumption of these food products. Tolley, Thomes, and Wong (1982, pp. 123–135) estimate that in Korea a 1 percent change in production is transmitted into a $0.366\xi_f$ perent change in own consumption, where ξ_f is the farmers' income elasticity of demand (i.e., a 0.27 percent change in own consumption when $\xi_f = 0.7$). Distribution policies targeted on urban consumers, which have the effect of destabilizing the price of the nonbeneficiary consumers, would therefore further erode food security in rural areas.

Table 5–4 summarizes the economic and food security effects in rural and urban areas of food distribution programs targeted on poor urban consumers. The much smaller variability of the price in the urban markets due to the income effect on farmers' own consumption considerably reduces the food insecurity of poor urban consumers. Thus, for instance, the expected food gap of these consumers is 6.7 percent of normal production when there

Table 5–4
Main Economic and Food-Security Indicators of Alternative Food-Distribution Policies, with Income Effects on Farmers' Own Consumption

Performance Measure	No Intervention	Targeted Subsidy: Target Elasticity		Income Transfer: Rate of Income Change		Buffer Stocks[a]
		0.25	0.1	+5%	+10%	
Market price						
Mean	101.4	102.9	104.2	103.4	105.5	101.0
CV (%)	15.1	17.7	20.2	15.0	15.0	11.4
Consumption of target group[b]						
Δ %Mean[c]	—	+1.6	+2.8	+2.4	+5.2	+0.4
Risk (5%)	48.2	46.6	3.6	19.2	13.0	22.7
Expected food gap[d]	3.4	2.0	1.0	2.4	1.1	2.5
Consumption of real consumers						
Insecurity (10%)[d]	19.6	20.8	21.6	20.0	20.0	19.0
Expected food gap[c]	1.3	1.6	1.8	1.4	1.4	1.0
Government expenditures						
Mean[e]	0	1.0	1.9	1.8	3.6	1.2
Risk[f]	0	0.0	2.9	0.0	0.0	0.2
Economic gains or losses[e] due to policy						
Target group	—	+0.8	+1.3	+1.6	+2.8	0.0
Other consumers	—	-1.5	-2.5	-2.1	-3.5	+0.1
Producers	—	+1.2	+2.3	+2.0	+3.3	+0.1
Government	—	-1.0	-1.9	-1.8	-3.6	-1.2
Total economy	—	-0.5	-0.8	-0.3	-1.0	-1.0

[a]Buffer stocks equal to 10 percent of normal annual production. Expenditures include amortization costs.
[b]Percentage change in mean consumption due to policy.
[c]Expressed as percentage of total production.
[d]Probability that consumption of the target group falls by more than 5 percent below their normal consumption (10% for the rural consumers).
[e]Expressed as percentage of total annual expenditures on the product.
[f]Probability that government expenditures exceed 10 percent of the annual expenditures on the product.

is no income effect on farmers' own consumption and only 3.4 percent when the income effect causes farmers' own consumption to change with changes in output. The coefficient of variation of farmers' consumption is, in the latter case, 12.9 percent, whereas the coefficient of variation of their excess supply is only 4.9 percent. Government interventions to prevent the consumption of the target population from falling below subsistence would not have to be as extensive, nor the fiscal costs as high. A subsidy program with a target elasticity of 0.1 would almost eliminate the probability of food insecurity—from 48.2 to 3.6 percent—and reduce the expected food gap by 70 percent. The income-transfer program—with transfers that raise the poor's income by 10 percent—would not perform as good as the subsidy program even though its fiscal costs are almost twice as much. Although the income transfers would raise the average consumption of the poor by 5.2 percent, compared with 2.8 percent with the subsidy program, they are much less effective in preventing acute shortfalls in the poor's consumption.

Buffer stocks would stabilize the consumption of both urban and rural consumers. A storage facility with capacity equal to 10 percent of annual production would reduce the expected food gap of the target population by 26 percent and of the rural population by 23 percent. Further increases in the storage capacity would, however, contribute much less to food security. Moreover, by reducing the price variability by 25 percent, the public stocks would reduce the incentives for private stock holdings. Public stocks would, therefore, partly substitute for farmers' private stocks, and their net effect on food security in the rural areas is likely to be somewhat smaller than that recorded in the table.

Figure 5–7 illustrates the trade-off between the food security of the target population and that of the rural population, which results from the targeted subsidy program. Put differently, it illustrates the urban bias of the subsidy program. Thus, for instance, preventing any food deficiency of poor urban consumers would involve an increase by 53 percent in the expected food gap of rural consumers. It should be noted, however, that the negative effects of the subsidy program are somewhat moderated by the resulting increase in production.

Distribution Programs in an Open Economy

International trade allows the country to supplement consumption of the target population with imported food instead of enforcing transfers from the other consumers. The ability to mobilize foreign exchange has, however, become a prior condition for the implementation of the program, since the effects of the additional food imports on the country's overall balance-of-payments position may become a more serious problem than the effects on

Expected Food Gap:**
Target Urban
Consumers

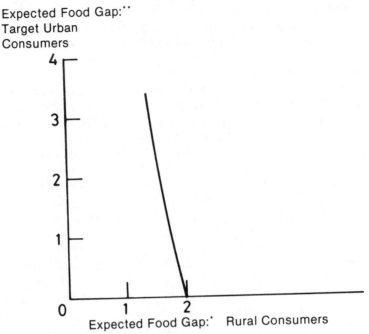

Expected Food Gap:*   Rural Consumers

*Probability that food consumption of the group falls by more than the prespecified percentage below its normal consumption.

**Expressed as percentage of total annual production.

Figure 5–7. Trade-off between Urban and Rural Food Security under a Subsidy Program Targeted on Poor Urban Consumers

the fiscal budget. Having at least part of the imported food from aid, would enable the government in many developing countries to carry out distribution programs that may not otherwise be possible because of economic or political constraints.

When food is imported by a government agency or donated to the government through a foreign-aid program, it can be distributed directly to the target population through government distribution outlets or through supplementary feeding programs. When food is imported by the private sector and trade is triggered by price differentials, the added demand of the target population permitted by the distribution programs is met at least in part by imports. Either way, the extra supply moderates the price rise in the domestic market.

In the simulation analysis in an open economy, the following assumptions have been added: The country is self-sufficient in the product under consideration in a normal year, and the domestic price is equal to the world price so that there is no incentive for trade. Stochastic variations in domestic supply and in the world price, however, would create price gaps that in turn trigger trade activities. Transportation costs are equal to 15 percent of the price of the product per metric ton (MT). (Transportation costs for wheat would therefore be approximately $25 per MT in 1984 prices.)

Table 5–5 summarizes the effects of the distribution programs under consideration in an open economy. The most important observation is that free trade itself has a strong stabilizing effect on the economy. By comparing the results in this table with those in table 5–2, we can see that the coefficient of variation of the price declines from 30.2 percent in the closed economy to 12.8 percent in the open economy. As a result, the expected food gap of the target population declines from 6.7 percent of the annual production in a closed economy to 3.3 percent under free trade. The arbitrage activities, triggered by the price differential between the domestic and the world markets, help moderate price rises in the bad years by allowing extra imports, and price falls in the good years by siphoning the excesses to exports.

In the open economy, the targeted subsidy and income-transfer programs would require much smaller transfers of food, and indirectly also of income, from the other consumers; and their economic losses from the programs will therefore be much smaller. Consequently, their objection to the program may also be much smaller. Producers' gains from the programs will also be much smaller, since the rise in the market price as an effect of the program would be much smaller in the open economy. Thus, with a subsidy program with a target elasticity of 0.1, the quantity imported will rise by 22 percent, whereas with an income-transfer program, with transfers equal to 10 percent of the poor's income, the quantity imported will rise by 27 percent. There is, however, a significant difference between the two programs in their effect on exports. Both distribution programs will cause the price and thus also the output to rise (though at a much lower rate than in the closed economy). The income-transfer program that raises the consumption of the target population in both bad and good years will divert this additional output as well as a portion of exports to these consumers. The subsidy program in contrast raises their consumption only in the bad years, while in the good years exports will not be affected by the program. Thus, exports rise by 15 percent with the subsidy program as an effect of the expansion of output but *decline* by 21 percent with the income-transfer program. On average the subsidy program will have very little effect on the balance of trade, whereas the income-transfer program will create a trade deficit equal to 1 percent of total annual expenditures on food.

Figure 5–8 demonstrates that increasing food security in the country and closing the food gap can only be achieved at rapidly rising fiscal costs and, when free trade is permitted, at rising foreign-exchange expenditures on imports. Significantly, however, the fiscal costs are markedly smaller in the open economy, and much of the burden is shifted to the foreign sector. When

Table 5-5
Main Economic and Food Security Indicators of Alternative Food Distribution Policies in an Open Economy

| | | Policy | | | | |
| | No Intervention | Targeted Subsidy: Target Elasticity | | Income Transfer: Rate of Income Change | | Buffer Stocks[a] |
Performance Measure		0.25	0.1	+5%	+10%	
Market price						
Mean	102.3	103.1	103.1	103.0	103.6	101.9
CV (%)	12.8	12.7	12.6	12.8	12.7	11.2
Consumption of target group						
Δ %Mean[b]	—	+1.2	+2.4	+3.2	+6.5	+0.4
Insecurity (5%)[d]	27.4	11.0	0.1	15.2	7.5	25.8
Expected food gap[c]	3.3	1.7	0.7	1.8	0.9	2.9
Government expenditures						
Mean[e]	0	0.9	1.5	1.8	3.6	1.2
Risk[f]	0	0.0	0.1	0.1	0.0	0.1
Balance of trade						
Imports[c]	1.8	2.0	2.2	2.0	2.3	1.6
Exports[c]	2.6	2.8	3.0	2.3	2.1	2.2
Balance of payments[e]	0.4	0.3	0.3	-0.1	-0.6	0.3
Economic gains or losses due to policy[e]						
Target group	—	+0.4	+0.8	+1.6	+3.2	0.0
Other consumers	—	-0.8	-1.3	-0.8	-1.6	+0.1
Producers	—	+0.9	+1.3	+0.8	+1.4	-0.1
Government	—	-0.9	-1.4	-1.8	-3.6	-1.2
Total economy	—	-0.4	-0.6	-0.2	-0.6	-1.2

[a]Buffer stocks equal to 10 percent of normal annual production. Expenditures include amortization costs.

[b]Percentage change in mean consumption due to policy.

[c]Expressed as percentage of total production.

[d]Probability that consumption of the target group falls by more than 5 percent below their normal consumption (10 percent for the rural consumers).

[e]Expressed as percentage of total annual expenditures on the product.

[f]Probability that government expenditures exceeded 10 percent of the annual expenditures on the product.

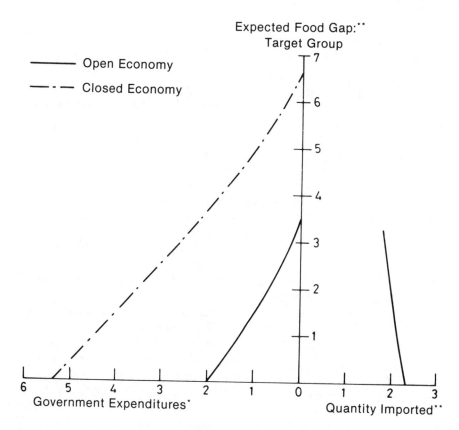

*Expressed as percentage of total annual expenditures on food.
**Expressed as percentage of annual food production.*

Figure 5–8. Trade-off between the Expected Food Gap and between the Quantity Imported and Government Expenditures under Alternative Subsidy Programs

foreign exchange is constrained, the extra imports required to supplement the consumption of the target population may have to come at the expense of other imports. The imports of investment goods may have to be cut down and some investments plans postponed. The investments foregone as a result of the food-distribution programs, and the potential adverse effects on the growth prospect of the economy, represent the trade-off resulting from budgetary and foreign-exchange constraints between the food security of the present generation and that of future generations. They also represent the contribution of aid programs in food, in investment funds, or in foreign exchange to the food security of the country's present and future generations.

Concluding Remarks

The basic thesis underlying the analysis of food distribution policies under instability is as follows: The goal of these policies is to secure adequate food consumption for the population vulnerable to undernutrition. In a closed economy this can be achieved only if the available supply is redistributed by forcing other consumer groups to forego some of their consumption (and encouraging producers to increase their output), and transferring these quantities to the target population. In an open economy this can also be achieved by supplementing domestic supply with imports. Redistribution of the available supply is the key to the solution not only of chronic undernutrition but also of temporary food shortages. Obviously, the available supply will not always suffice to feed the entire population. In cases of extreme shortage, only additional supply from outside the country or the region can alleviate the situation. In most cases, however, the shortage is not that extreme. Nevertheless, even milder shortages can deprive population groups who already live at the margins of subsistence of their ability to purchase enough food, and can deepen the deficiency of the chronically undernourished. In these cases, government interventions that redistribute the available supply more evenly can secure the availability of sufficient food for all.

These interventions can be carried out via the market system or by a system of direct government procurement and distribution. Via the market system, these policies work by increasing the purchasing power (or the exchange entitlement) of the target population through income transfers, targeted or general price subsidies, etc. Consumers maintain, however, their sovereignty in the market, given the new system of prices and incomes. Nonmarket policies are aimed at directly distributing the food products to the target population. In this chapter we have examined intervention measures via the market system; in chapter 8 we examine nonmarket distribution policies.

Notes

1. Moreover, in many developing countries cash transfers are almost impossible to implement, or they may involve prohibitive administrative costs, a large part of which may be due to fraud.

2. If the country is large—that is, its excess demand or supply has an effect on the world price—additional demand generated by the subsidy program may cause the world price to rise (in which case consumers in other countries would have to forego some of their consumption).

3. See Wall (1978) and Bigman (1982, chap. 3) for further details.

4. We assume additive disturbances here to simplify the computation, although multiplicative disturbances obviously are more appropriate for agricultural produce. The latter assumption is the one adopted in the subsequent analysis.

5. In this discussion we disregard the ongoing controversy over whether there is any minimum subsistence level of consumption and, if so, what it is.

6. External financial assistance can play an extremely important role in supporting this policy.

7. See chapter 2 for a discussion of the reasons for selecting this specification.

8. See chapter 4 for a detailed discussion of these two effects on farmers' consumption of their own produce.

9. See Bigman (1982, chap. 4) for the comparison between fixed and adaptive price bands.

10. It should be noted, however, that to any state-contingent subsidy program corresponds a state-contingent income program (a program that transfers income only when the price rises above its normal level) that has the *same* effects. This increase in income of the ith consumer group is given by

$$\frac{dI_i}{I_i} = \frac{\xi_i}{\eta_i} \cdot \frac{dP}{P}$$

where ξ_i and η_i are the price and income elasticity of the ith consumer group dP/P is the percentage rise in price and dI_i/I_i is the percentage change of income.

References

Bigman, D. 1982. *Coping with hunger: Toward a system of security and price stabilization*. Cambridge, Mass.: Ballinger.

Bigman, D., and Reutlinger, S. 1979a. National and international policy toward food security and price stabilization. *American Economic Review* 69:63–159.

———. 1979b. Food price and supply stabilization: National buffer stocks and trade policies. *American Journal of Agricultural Economics* 61:67–657.

Musgrave, R.E. 1959. *The theory of public finance*. New York: McGraw-Hill.

Pazner, E. 1972. Merit wants and the theory of taxation. *Public Finance* 27:72–460.

Reutlinger, S. 1983. Project food-aid and equitable growth income transfer efficiency first. Discussion Paper ARU 13, World Bank.

Reutlinger, S., and Selowsky, M. 1976. *Malnutrition and poverty: Magnitudes and policy options*. World Bank Occasional Paper No. 23. Baltimore, Md.: Johns Hopkins University Press.

Sandmo, A. 1983. Ex-post welfare economics and the theory of merit goods. *Economica* 50:19–33.

Sen, A.K. 1976. Poverty: An ordinal approach to measurement. *Econometrica* 44: 219–231.

Sen, A.K. 1981. *Poverty and famine: An essay on entitlement and deprivation*. Oxford: Clarendon Press.

Tolley, G.S.; Thomas, V.; and Wong, C.M. 1982. *Agricultural price policies and the developing countries*. Baltimore, Md.: Johns Hopkins University Press.

Wall, J. 1978. Foodgrains management in India: Pricing, procurement, distribution, import and storage policy. World Bank Working Paper No. 279.

Wenzel, H.D., and Wiegard, W. 1981. Merit goods and second best taxation. *Public Finance* 36:40–125.

Appendix 5A: List of Symbols

D_i = demand of the ith group (the subscript i denotes the ith consumers' group: $i = r, p$.

η_i = price elasticity of demand.

w_i = D_i/D = share of the ith group in total consumption of product.

ξ_i = income elasticity of demand.

S_i = PD_i/I_i = share of expenditures on the product in consumers' total income.

γ_i = I_i/I = share of the income of the ith group in total national income.

ϵ = price elasticity of supply.

μ = weight of the food sector in GDP.

Θ = subsidy rate.

α = target rate of growth in the poor's consumption.

ρ = rate of growth of supply.

ν = the tolerance level of food insecurity.

β = rate of change in the poor's income.

6

Grains Price Stabilization and Food-Security Policy in Turkey

Price policies for food and feed grains in general, and for wheat in particular, touch the vital interests of most Turkish households. The following statistics are indicative: Roughly 60 percent of the Turkish population works in the agricultural sector, most of them producing some grain for sale or for home consumption; value added in grains makes up about one-third of Turkey's agricultural GDP; wheat alone occupies about 45 percent of the total sown area and accounts for 19 percent of the wholesale price index; and bread accounts for 11 – 12 percent of the consumer price index.

The primary goals of the extensive government involvement in the wheat market are to maintain wheat prices at levels that would remunerate producers for their production costs, ensure a more desirable wheat distribution between surplus and deficit areas, and prevent sharp increases in consumer prices. The Turkish government has tried to achieve these goals through the direct regulation of commodity prices; by providing fertilizers, capital, and other farm inputs at subsidized prices; by establishing and providing marketing services such as transport, storage, and processing; and, by regulating imports and exports.

The ultimate responsibility for those programs is vested in the Council of Ministers. The ministries of Commerce, Agriculture and Forestry, and Finance as well as the State Planning Organization, concerned parastatals, sales cooperatives, and other agencies act in an advisory capacity to the council on various aspects of policy, particularly the annual exercise to determine farm procurement prices. Various State Economic Enterprises (SEE) and Unions of Sales Cooperatives carry out the procurement and marketing of the commodities concerned. Thus the Soil Products Office (TMO) and SEE, which operates under the nominal control of the Ministry of Commerce, intervene in grains on behalf of the government.

This chapter is based on the World Bank AGREP Division, Working Paper No. 66, 1983. I would like to acknowledge the contribution of Richard Bunkrof to this chapter.

Although the share of TMO purchases in total wheat production represents an average of only 10 percent (but up to 20 percent in some years), or about one-third of the marketed surplus, their role in the wheat market is pivotal. The basic procurement price, which the government announces each June, becomes the effective support price for producers since the TMO is required to procure any quantity at the announced price. The procurement price, therefore, is a major factor affecting the entire market each year. Sales of the TMO to local millers, at reduced prices, are made on an allocation basis and are mostly, if not solely, designated for bread production. The sale price may be subsidized at times. This affects the price of bread to consumers, especially in urban areas. In 1974–1975, for instance, the TMO sale price was 40 percent and in 1978–1979 it was 20 percent below the support purchase price. Losses suffered by TMO are covered by the government and effectively can be regarded as subsidies to bread. Since 1980, however, the government's intentions are to set the sale price above the procurement price, thereby abolishing this direct subsidy. Nonetheless, there is still an indirect element of subsidy in TMO sales through its storage and transport operations and its access to Central Bank rediscounts at highly preferential rates.

Trade and trade policies in agricultural commodities have always been a major concern of the Turkish government. Wheat exports became fairly significant in the mid- to late 1970s as wheat production was deliberately encouraged following the trauma of the worldwide wheat shortage in 1972–1974. In 1978 and 1979, for instance, Turkish wheat exports were around 2 million MT, or about 15 percent of total wheat production. These subsequently were curtailed with the onset of the economic and political crisis of the early 1980s; the country became a net importer, though marginally so, in 1981 and 1982. Export and import operations have been carried out with the primary intention of ensuring adequate stocks so that government agencies will be able to perform the function of regulating and stabilizing the domestic market. Although private exports of wheat has been authorized in 1983, TMO will remain involved in wheat trade and the government will secure its goals through tariffs, subsidies, or quota restrictions.

The Model, Parameters, and Policy Rules

This chapter evaluates the specific price policies and other interventions currently practiced in Turkey and examines alternative policy regimes. This analysis is based on actual 1981 production and price figures as well as on the estimated growth rates for wheat production, per capita wheat consumption, and population. The (real) rate of interest in all the financial calculations is assumed to be 5 percent. The values of the behavioral parameters in the model are generally based on estimates obtained in previous studies on the

Turkish wheat sector (Imrohonglu and Kasnakoglu 1980; Gurkan 1979; Somel 1979); estimates prepared for a World Bank report (IBRD 1983);[1] and TMO estimates.

Consumers in the country are divided into three income groups (low-income urban consumers, middle- and high-income urban consumers, and rural consumers). A separate demand function is specified for each group, and total demand is the sum of the demands of the three groups. Table 6–1 lists the specific demand parameters assumed in the simulation experiments. Population is assumed to grow at an annual rate of 2.1 percent.

Producers determine the area cultivated on the basis of the expected price. They are also assumed to be risk-averse, and respond adversely to the risk associated with *price* variability (see Just 1975; Bigman 1982). Mean production is 14 million MT (roughly the 1981 figure). The coefficient of variation at the mean is 11 percent. Price elasticity of supply at the mean is 0.25, and the risk-response coefficient is assumed to be 0.25. Wheat production is growing at an annual rate of 1.7 percent.

International trade is triggered by price differentials between the import or export price and the domestic price, subject to volume or price constraints enforced by government policies. Mean world price is $155 per MT, or approximately TL 17 per kg according to the official 1981 exchange rate. Transportation costs are $16 per MT on wheat imports and $8.25 per MT on wheat exports, reflecting the fact that wheat is generally imported from the United States whereas wheat exports go mostly to the Middle East or Eastern Europe.

The government of Turkey, mostly through TMO, has intervened in nearly every aspect of Turkey's domestic and external wheat markets. The TMO procurement price effectively sets the price of wheat to producers while the TMO sales price, along with price-ceiling restrictions, sets the price of

Table 6–1
Wheat Demand Parameters in Turkey

	Low-Income Urban Consumers	Middle- and High-Income Urban Consumers	Rural Consumers	Total Population
Mean quantity consumed as percentage of total consumption	20	30	50	100
Price elasticity of demand at the mean price				
Upper segment – $P > \bar{P}$	.40	.10	.30	.26
Lower segment – $P < \bar{P}$	.55	.20	.30	.32

Note: $\bar{P}$ is the mean price.

bread to consumers. Table 6–2 provides some quantitative measures for TMO activities in the wheat market over the four-year period 1978–1981.

Internal trade in grains is quite free, however, and TMO's share in the market is usually within the range of 10–12 percent of total wheat output. Nonetheless, producers typically wait for the government to announce the grain prices before they offer their crops to the market, since these prices guarantee their floor price. Until 1981 TMO was also actively involved in stabilizing the price to consumers and preventing sharp rises in bread prices, mainly through concessional sales to local millers on an allocation basis. Typically, the price of bread was determined by coordination committees, and the TMO sales at a discount price were designed to secure the profitability of the local millers. Table 6–3, which shows TMO procurement and sale prices for bread wheat, offers an indication of the subsidy element contained in this segment of its operations.[2] In 1982, however, the government dissolved the coordination committees and announced that bread prices would

Table 6–2
TMO Purchases and Sales of Wheat
(in million MT)

	1978	1979	1980	1981
Quantity purchased in domestic market	3.20	1.64	1.65	1.05
Quantity imported	—	—	—	0.34
Quantity sold in domestic market	2.74	2.34	1.74	1.15
Quantity exported	2.09	0.79	0.38	0.30
Quantity in storage	3.17	1.65	1.16	1.07

Source: TMO.

Table 6–3
TMO Bread Wheat Prices
(TL/kg)

	Procurement Price	Sale Price
1976–1977	2.65	2.50
1977–1978	2.90	2.60
1978–1979	3.30	2.60
1979–1980	4.90	4.30
1980–1981	10.25	10.75
1981–1982	18.75	18.00

Source: TMO.

be determined in the future without any restrictions and in accordance with free-market economy conditions.

In modeling the various intervention practices existing in Turkey, foreign-trade activities are not assumed to be carried out exclusively by TMO. Although such trade was a complete government monopoly until 1982, private traders are now allowed to operate in the international market subject to existing government trade policies in the form of taxes, tariffs, or quantity constraints.

The various elements of the government's price stabilization and food-security policies in Turkey consist of a package of decisions in four main areas: producer prices, storage decisions, consumer prices, and the nature of interventions in foreign grain trade. A particular package of decisions is termed a *policy* and includes a set of decisions that apply to all the aforementioned areas. The policy that represents the present policies of the Turkish government is denoted *TUR*. Following is a description of these decision rules under different contingencies and their modeling for the simulation analysis.

Procurement Decisions

Each year (typically in June) the government determines the wheat procurement price, which then becomes the floor price for the farmers. The main considerations in determining this price are production costs and world prices; therefore, the procurement price is likely to change from year to year. In modeling this policy, the following specific assumptions have been made:

1. The government supports the producers' price only if the free-market price falls below a predetermined trigger price denoted by P_m. If the free-market price rises above P_m, the government does not intervene to raise producers' price or income further.
2. If the free-market price falls below P_m, the government intervenes by procuring and removing the excess grain from the market.

The actual procurement price may also be affected by the level of production at that season, largely due to TMO's budgetary constraints. Thus, for instance, in a year of bumper harvest the TMO has often lowered the announced procurement price in order to reduce the quantities that would otherwise have to be procured. Nevertheless, within its budgetary capabilities (which are substantial), the TMO has always intervened to prevent too sharp a fall in wheat price to farmers.

The procurement decisions are modeled as follows: The trigger price is TL 18.75 per kg in 1981 prices. If the market price falls below that level, the government, through the TMO, procures the excess from the market within its budgetary capability at the time of procurement, with the objective of moderating the decline in price rather than preventing it altogether.[3] As noted in chapter 4, this pattern of intervention is roughly consistent with setting a target demand curve that effectively determines the price to farmers, its slope being more elastic than that of the market demand curve (i.e., without intervention). In the simulation analysis it is assumed that the price elasticity of target demand is three times larger than that of market demand, implying that the actual decline in producers' price below the trigger price is only one-third of the decline that would have occurred in the absence of government intervention. In addition to budgetary constraints on TMO's procurement operations, the use of *quantity* constraints is also considered a procurement option. These constraints are set to model an alternative policy wherein the total amount procured is not allowed to exceed a certain percentage of realized production.

Storage Activities

The TMO's storage decisions are largely the result of its procurement operations and thus principally of the government's support-price decisions. Once the procurement price is announced, there is usually no quantity limit on the amount procured, and all grains of suitable quality delivered to TMO by farmers are purchased (unless a constraint is set on these quantities, as noted earlier). An important part of TMO operations—and budget—involves the maintenance of grain in storage. A minimum level of stocks deemed necessary to prevent shortages and sharp rises in price is usually maintained by the TMO. These, however, are mostly operating stocks aimed at regulating their domestic and foreign sales during the year, whereas the level of TMO's carry-over of buffer stocks is usually of the order of 1.1–1.6 million MT. Covered storage capacity of TMO is somewhat less than 2 million MT. The grains procured in excess of this amount in years of bumper harvests are stored in open storage—on the open ground, covered with polyethylene and soil.

The storage costs include handling charges and other operating expenses, amortization of the storage facilities, and rent on operational buildings. The entire yearly operating expenses are estimated to be TL 600 per MT.

Although the emphasis in this chapter is on management of buffer stocks aimed at stabilizing year-to-year price fluctuations, a comment is needed on the TMO storage operations *during* the year and in particular on the effects of these operations on private stock holdings. Although the data about private stock holdings are incomplete, a fairly large portion of TMO storage operations appears to substitute for private stocks rather than add to the country's overall stocks. This is evident from table 6–4, which summarizes the main TMO procurement, domestic sales, and storage operations on a quarterly basis. The table indicates a well-defined seasonal pattern in TMO's

Table 6–4
Wheat Procurement, Storage, and Sales by TMO
(by quarters in million MT)

Year	Quarter	Procurement	Domestic Sales	Carryover from Previous Period
1978	I	0.0	0.64	4.94
	II	0.5	0.68	3.78
	III	2.7	0.48	2.89
	IV	0.0	0.80	4.44
1979	I	0.0	0.86	3.13
	II	0.4	0.70	2.45
	III	1.1	0.25	1.44
	IV	0.1	0.44	2.18
1980	I	0.0	0.52	1.69
	II	0.4	0.39	1.08
	III	1.3	0.17	0.82
	IV	0.0	0.55	1.84
1981	I	0.0	0.39	1.23
	II	0.1	0.33	0.51
	III	0.9	0.09	0.25
	IV	0.0	0.32	1.02

Source: TMO.

procurement and domestic sales operations. Most of the wheat is procured during the crop season—toward the end of the second quarter but mostly during the third quarter—whereas the bulk of the domestic sales take place four to eight months later. During the crop season itself, TMO's domestic sales are particularly low, indicating that much of the domestic supply during these months comes from private traders. In later months, however, TMO's share in total supply sharply increases and can be as high as 40 percent (even more in certain areas), compared with an annual average of 10–12 percent.

This pattern of TMO versus private sales and stock holding has important implications with respect to the subsidy element contained in TMO's operations. It suggests that a simple comparison between TMO procurement and sale price does not provide a full account of the subsidy element. The TMO procurement price should be compared with the sale price *plus* appropriate storage and financial costs, since the procurement and the sale take place at different times.

Consumer Subsidies

In the past the government has generally refrained from subsidizing wheat prices to consumers directly, but there have been a number of exceptions. In 1974 a massive intervention prevented a sudden, sharp increase in consumers' prices. The element of subsidy contained in the various TMO distribution and stocks operations has also been noted. In the analysis of the present wheat policy, no direct subsidy to consumers of any form is assumed, in keeping with TMO's intention to discontinue the supply of subsidized urban grain rations. In the analysis of alternative policy options, three variations of possible government subsidy schemes have been considered:

1. A general subsidy to the entire population: Specifically, it was assumed that the subsidy element contained in the TMO operations works to lower the market price to all consumers by an average of 5 percent.
2. A ceiling price to consumers: If the price rises above a certain critical level because of a domestic crop failure or a sharp rise in the world price, the government would maintain the ceiling price either by more stringent export restrictions, or by a more precipitate release from storage, or through imports even at a subsidized price.
3. Target subsidy to low-income consumers only.

Trade

Export activities can be carried out either by the TMO or by private traders. Export taxes are the main instrument for regulating the export activities of private traders, although quantity restrictions can also be imposed. Imports are largely a government monopoly, even though considerations about whether and how much to import are quite similar to those of private, profit-oriented traders. Figures 6–1 through 6–4 illustrate the interaction between the different policy measures of the TUR policy package as they were modeled for the simulation analysis.

Export Subsidy, Procurement, and Consumers' Subsidy. In figure 6–1, Q_0 is the quantity produced in a given year. Producers' price—determined by the target demand curve T—would then be P^T. At that price, the quantity Q_2 is sold in the market by private traders and the quantity $(Q_0 - Q_2)$ is procured by the government. Consumers' price, determined as a fraction of the market price, would then be P^S, reflecting a subsidy of $(P^T - P^S)$. At that price, consumers purchase the quantity Q_1 and the rest is exported. If the export price is P^X, then exports can only be assured by a subsidy of $(P^T - P^X)$. The subsidy costs of these exports are in fact the losses of the government agencies in charge of procurement and export. If the government maintains buffer stocks also, then the excess supply $(Q_0 - Q_1)$ is used first to fill the storage facility up to capacity, and only the excess beyond that is exported.

Procurement, Storage, and Consumers' Subsidy. In figure 6–2 the quantity produced is Q_0. Producers' price is determined at P^T and consumers' price at

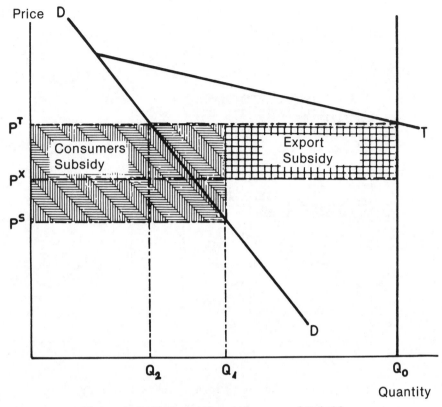

Figure 6–1. Exports' Procurement and Subsidy

P^S. The quantity Q_2 is sold in the open market and the quantity $(Q_1 - Q_2)$ procured by the government. To assure availability of the quantity Q_1 to consumers, the quantity $(Q_1 - Q_0)$ is released from storage. In that year no exports are allowed, regardless of the export price. If the amount in storage does not suffice to supplement supply up to Q_1, the government imports the extra amount needed by subsidizing imports according to the difference between the import price (P^I in the figure) and the consumers' price (P^S).

Storage, Procurement, and Imports. This policy becomes effective in years that the country imports food grain to supplement domestic supply. In figure 6–3 suppose that P^I, the import price, is lower than the domestic price without government intervention; Q_1 is then the quantity available for consumption, and $(Q_1 - Q^*)$ or $(Q_1 - Q^{**})$ are the quantity that would have been imported according to whether domestic supply in that year is S^* or S^{**}. A support-price policy is, however, implemented to raise producers' price. The

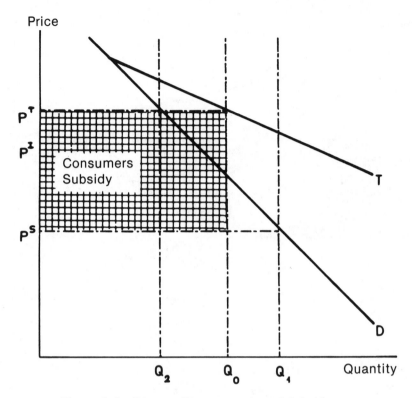

Figure 6–2. Storage, Procurement, and Subsidy

policy instruments are import tax or government procurement and storage, and the decision is determined by the target curve T. If domestic production is Q^*, an import tax of $(P^T - P^I)$ is levied, and the quantity imported is reduced from $(Q_1 - Q^*)$ to $(Q_1 - Q_2)$. If domestic production is Q^{**}, imports are banned altogether and the quantity $(Q^{**} - Q_2)$ is stored. If sufficient vacant capacity exists, the excess amount is stored in the main storage facility; if the vacant capacity available is smaller than $(Q^{**} - Q_2)$, then the storage authority is permitted to import food grain to fill the storage facility in order to be better prepared to meet shortages that may occur in the future.

Storage, Procurement, and Exports. This policy is effective in years when the country exports food grains. In Figure 6–4, suppose that P_1^X, the export price, is higher than the market price without government intervention P_3. Q_1 is the quantity that is then available for domestic consumption, and $(Q_3 - Q_1)$ the quantity exported. Suppose now that the support-price program is activated to raise the price to P_1^T and that the policy instrument is an export

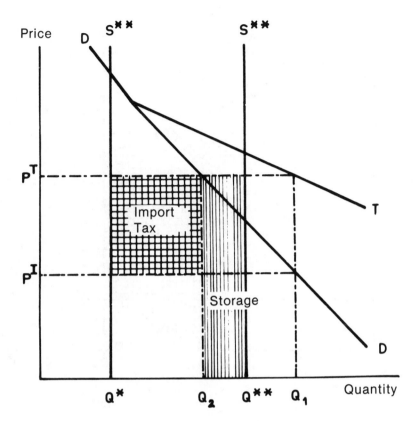

Figure 6–3. Storage, Procurement, and Imports

subsidy equal to $(P_1^T - P_1^*)$. As a result, the quantity exported rises to $(Q_3 - Q_2)$, and the quantity consumed in the country falls to Q_2.

If the export price is P_2^X, no export would normally take place and the domestic price would be P_3. The support-price program is then activated, its objective being to raise the price to P_1^T. The policy instrument now is storage. (An export subsidy can also be given in this case.) The quantity $(Q_3 - Q_0)$ is put into storage. The main storage facility is filled first, and the excess is stored in temporary facilities. The grains stored in temporary facilities suffer from faster deterioration than those in the regular storage facility.

So far we have described the modeling of the TUR policy package. A variant of the TUR policy assumes, in addition, that the government maintains a ceiling on the price to consumers through export restrictions, domestic procurement, and imports. This policy is denoted *TUR(MAX-PRICE)*.

Still another variant of TUR allows free imports and removes the import

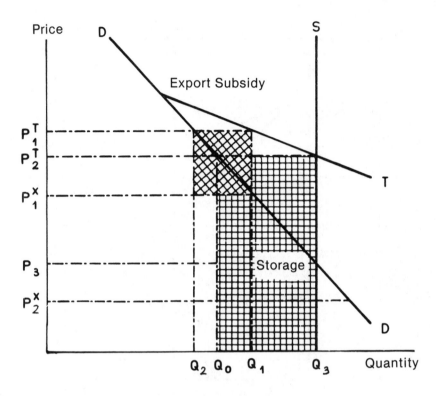

Figure 6–4. Storage, Procurement, and Exports

tariff that is imposed under the TUR policy. This variant is denoted *TUR(F-IMP)*.

Against these policies we consider several conventional market policies of the type examined in the previous chapters. They include the following individual policies or any combination thereof:

FRE = free trade.

STAB = variable export or import taxes levied to stabilize the domestic price and domestic consumption (see chapter 3).

SUB = subsidy program targeted on low-income consumers in urban areas only.

SUP = government procurement and price-support program of the type examined in chapter 4.

Simulation Results

The main conclusion emerging from the simulation analysis is that *on average* (though not necessarily in any specific year), the present price policies and interventions practiced in Turkey appear to fall far short of achieving the objectives for which they were established. They do not provide more, or as much, security and stability to consumers and producers as a policy of no intervention and free trade would offer; and there are alternative policies that are likely to perform better and be less costly. The analysis suggests also that the present price policies have substantial negative impact in a number of areas not directly related to, but nonetheless affected by, government decisions. These effects appears to be disregarded in the decision-making process, although they must be reckoned with in a complete policy evaluation.

Table 6–5 demonstrates the stability effects of four of the policies under consideration. It shows that despite the floor-price guarantee provided by the TUR policies, price variability for both producers and consumers is higher by 85 percent under the TUR policy and by 50 percent under the TUR(F-IMP) policy than under free trade. This is largely the result of insulating the economy and ensuring the government procurement operations by prohibiting free exports or by preventing the export price from affecting the domestic price via a shield of export taxes.

The variability of farmers' income, as measured by the coefficient of variation, appears to be somewhat smaller under the TUR policies. The table shows, however, that although the frequency distribution of farmers' income is more condensed under the TUR policy, it is concentrated more at the lower tail of the frequency distribution. As a result, the probability that farmers'

Table 6–5
Main Stability Indicators

		Policies		
	FRE	*TUR*	*TUR(F-IMP)*	*FRE + SUP*
	Coefficient of variation			
Consumers' price	8.5	15.7	12.8	2.7
Producers' price	8.5	15.6	12.7	2.7
Domestic consumption	1.5	2.9	2.2	1.4
Farmers' income	9.2	9.1	9.7	9.8
Insecurity measures	Probability of falling below critical level			
Total consumption (5%)	0.2	10.3	3.1	0.0
Low-income consumption (5%)	2.3	12.5	3.9	0.2
(10%)	0.0	1.0	0.1	0.0
Farmers' income (15%)	10.0	10.6	6.8	6.9

income falls below a predetermined critical level is higher under TUR than under any of the other policies. Part of the problem is the constraints imposed on imports under this policy. When the import tariff is removed under the TUR(F-IMP) policy, the probability of an extreme drop in farmers' income is markedly reduced. Table 6–6 shows, however, that under the TUR policy, farmers' income is, on average, 2.5 percent higher than under the TUR(F-IMP) policy. Figure 6–5 shows that, after accounting for the change in the average level of farmers' income, they are subject to roughly the same level of insecurity under the TUR as under the TUR(F-IMP) policy, and that both provide a somewhat greater security than free trade. This same comparison shows that the (FRE + SUP) policy performs better by far than all the other policies in guaranteeing a minimum income to farmers. On average, farmers' income under this policy is 10 to 13 percent higher than under the other policies.

Table 6–7 summarizes the economic gains and losses to the various sectors and to the economy at large. The results, given in TL billions in 1981 prices, register the net effect of the policies under consideration compared with free trade (FRE). Interestingly, government net expenditures under the three policies are roughly the same. Nevertheless, the (FRE + SUP) policy, which provides greater security and stability, also involves much smaller losses to the economy at large than does either of the TUR policies. Moreover, these net welfare losses may turn into net gains if the risk response is in fact higher than the one assumed in the simulation analysis. Nevertheless, this policy involves massive income transfers from consumers to producers

Table 6–6
Short-Run Economic Indicators
(annual averages in 1981 prices)

	Policies			
Indicators of Expected	*FRE*	*TUR*	*TUR(F-IMP)*	*FRE + SUP*
1. Consumers' price (TL)	17.1	18.0	17.3	18.7
2. Producers' price (TL)	17.1	18.1	17.4	18.7
3. Quantity of wheat produced (MMT)	14.2	14.1	14.2	14.8
4. Farmers' revenue (TL billion)	242	249	243	273
5. Government procurement (MMT)	—	1.1	1.2	—
6. Support payments to farmers (TL billion)	—	1.4	0.7	—
7. Quantity imported (MMT)	0.2	0.1	0.2	0.1
8. Quantity exported (MMT)	1.2	1.1	1.2	1.7
9. Balance of payments (TL billion)	17.1	16.6	16.3	26.1

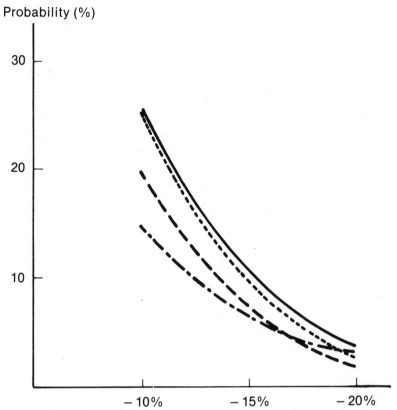

Probability (%)

Percentage Fall in Farmers' Income Below its Expected Level

Note: Probability that farmers' income falls by more than the specified percentage below its expected level.

Figure 6–5. Farmers' Income Insecurity under Different Price Regimes

Table 6–7
Welfare Indicators: Annual Gains (+) or Losses (−) from Policies
(in 1981 billion TL)

	TUR	TUR(F-IMP)	FRE + SUP
Consumers	− 10	− 2	− 20
Producers	+ 5	+ 1	+ 27
Government	− 11	− 12	− 12
Total economy	− 17	− 13	− 5

and, therefore, considerable changes in the distribution of income, largely due to the rise in average grain prices as an effect of the procurement scheme.

Table 6–8 presents the main long-run effects of the various policies in a dynamic and growing economy. The analysis is carried out over a period of thirty years, from 1981 through 2010. The two main assumptions in this analysis are that wheat production will grow at an annual rate of 1.7 percent and that the population will grow at an annual rate of 2.1 percent. It should be noted also that the simulation model generates results for each year sequentially. As a result, policy decisions at any point in time are likely to have an effect on subsequent years, with their impact magnified over time.

The dynamic analysis shows that as excess wheat production per capita diminishes (since population is expected to grow more rapidly than wheat production), the country may have to rely more heavily and more frequently

Table 6–8
Main Long-Run Effects of Policies over Thirty Years

	Policies		
	FRE	TUR	TUR(F – IMP)
Annual growth rates		Percentage	
Quantity available for consumption	1.90	1.87	1.90
Farmers' revenue	0.91	1.05	0.93
Balance of trade		TL billion	
1981[a]	+ 13	+ 17	+ 16
2010	+ 4	+ 5	+ 3
Insecurity measures		Percentage	
Market price[b] (– 20%)			
1981[a]	0	6	4
2010	0	11	7
Farmers' income[b] (– 15%)			
1981[a]	10	11	7
2010	7	14	15
Balance of payments[c] (+ 20%)			
1981[a]	9	6	8
2010	23	17	20

[a]The base year for this calculation is 1980.
[b]Probability that variable falls by more than the specified percentage below its expected level.
[c]Probability that the value of wheat imports exceeds 20 percent of total annual expenditures on wheat.

on wheat imports. The wheat trade surplus is expected to shrink from TL 13–17 billion in 1981 (depending on the specific simulation) to TL 3–5 billion (in 1981 prices) by the year 2010. As a result, the probability of a large trade *deficit* in any particular year due to a domestic crop failure will rise substantially. Thus, for instance, the probability of having a trade deficit in excess of 20 percent of total annual expenditures on wheat may rise from 6–9 percent in the mid-1980s to 17–23 percent by the year 2010.

The results of the simulations indicate that the different policies are likely to lead to different growth patterns in several respects: Under TUR, farmers' income is likely to rise at a slightly higher rate than under free trade, reflecting the protracted effects of the producers' support program, which prevents sharp drops in price. At the same time, however, price instability and the instability of farmers' income is likely to increase under TUR but to decline under free trade. Thus, for example, the probability of a drop in farmers' income by more than 15 percent below its expected level will increase under TUR from 11 percent to 14 percent, but will decline under FRE from 10 to 7 percent.

To examine further the effects of alternative policy options, we analyze their short-run effects under three different scenarios: (1) The country is generally exporting, (2) the country is self-sufficient, and (3) the country is generally importing. Indeed, if present trends in production and population continue, Turkey may become a net importer in the year 2020 (or even sooner if the transition to cash crops is accelerated), so that each of these scenarios will be relevant during a certain period of time. In the simulation analysis it has been assumed that, under free trade, the generally exporting country exports on average 10 percent of its output, whereas the generally importing country imports on average 10 percent of its consumption. The main comparison is between the TUR policy and the STAB policy of variable import and export levies. The results are presented in table 6–9.

The most obvious result is the large differences in the performance of the policies in the three different scenarios. When the country is generally exporting, the TUR policy works to lower the domestic price by constraining exports. The trade barriers would, however, cause a large increase in the price variability and an increase in food insecurity, measured here by the probability that consumption would fall below trend consumption by more than 5 percent. The rise in instability and the drop in producers' price in the generally exporting country would cause the quantity produced to fall by 4.6 percent below its free-trade level, compared with a rise by 2.2 percent under the STAB policy. When the country is self-sufficient, output under the TUR policy would still fall below its free-trade level as a result of the larger instability and despite the rise in the average price.

Table 6–9
Main Stability and Economic Indicators in Three Country Scenarios

Policy	Generally Exporting		Self-Sufficient		Generally Importing	
	TUR	STAB	TUR	STAB	TUR	STAB
	Coefficient of variation					
Variability indicators						
Consumers' price	18.6	3.0	15.4	3.9	10.0	3.8
Producers' price	16.5	3.0	13.8	3.9	9.4	3.8
Farmers' income	5.9	10.8	7.4	9.9	9.5	11.0
	Probability of falling below critical level					
Insecurity indicators						
Total consumption (5%)	18.9	0.0	15.4	0.0	5.7	0.1
Low-income consumption (5%)	25.3	0.4	29.7	0.4	15.4	1.1
(10%)	14.7	0.0	8.0	0.0	2.6	0.0
Farmers' revenues (15%)	22.0	9.3	22.6	9.3	15.2	12.2
	Percentage change of outcome compared with free trade					
Consumers' price	−6.8	+0.9	+5.1	−1.2	n.a.	n.a.
Producers' price	−3.8	+0.9	+6.3	−1.2	n.a.	n.a.
Farmers' revenues	−6.3	+5.2	+3.5	+0.3	n.a.	n.a.
Quantity of wheat produced	−4.6	+2.2	−1.9	+1.9	n.a.	n.a.
	Percentage of normal supply					
Quantity imported	0.8	0.5	3.7	4.4	n.a.	n.a.
Quantity exported	5.7	14.1	1.4	3.7	n.a.	n.a.

Conclusions

The analysis in this chapter represents an extension of the methodology to the pattern intervention of the government of Turkey in the wheat market. The findings, however, are by no means unique to Turkey, nor is the Turkish pattern of intervention unusual. In the drive for food grains self-sufficiency and food security that such interventions endeavor to provide, many countries have assumed that the direct management of procurement and distribution and a national stockpile by the government is a necessary concomitant, and thus a TMO type of operation has been put into place. In the process, the responsible agencies have tended to use very simple performance measures of the levels of security achieved—namely, a comparison of actual farmgate and consumer prices with administratively determined reference prices; the availability of domestically produced or imported grain to maintain reference levels of per capita consumption; and so on. Within the limitations of such indicators, the resource cost of the system and the effects of the institutional setting, including the abuse of the system, are frequently ignored.

The results of the analysis are striking and indicate that the basic TUR policies perform less efficiently over the long-run than do policy variants that feature considerably less intervention in external and internal markets. This applies most explicitly to the efficiency of risk management and the price and income stabilization gained thereby. Ironically, by reducing the cumulative effects of risk on producers' income, the analysis also suggest that the less interventionist policies are likely to increase expected wheat production above levels projected for the TUR interventions, even though these primarily emphasize producer incentives. Moreover, the results are robust and are not altered by the net external trade positions assumed over the projection period—for example, whether the country remains a net exporter of wheat, becomes basically self-sufficient, or turns into a net importer.

Notes

1. These estimates have been prepared by Haluk Kasnakoglu, Tercan Baysan, and Aslan Gurkan of the Department of Economics, the Middle East Technical University, Ankara, and World Bank staff.

2. In addition to the direct price subsidies indicated for all years except 1980–1981, the TMO enjoyed substantial financial subsidization through very favorable Central Bank discounts.

3. It is assumed that the TMO acts as neither a simple nor a discriminating monopolist, but simply buys what it can afford at any particular moment in the grain procurement cycle.

References

Bigman, D. 1982. *Coping with hunger: Toward a system of food security and price stabilization.* Cambridge, Mass.: Ballinger.

———. 1983. Turkey: Price stabilization and food security policies in grains. IBRD, AGREP Division Working Paper No. 66.

Gurkan, A.A. 1979. Aspects of a statistical analysis of some selected agricultural price policies in Turkey: 1950–1973. Unpublished Ph.D. dissertation, School of Economic Studies, University of Leeds.

International Bank for Reconstruction and Development (IBRD). 1983. Turkey—Agricultural development alternatives for growth with exports. Report No. 4202-TU. Europe, Middle East and North Africa Project Department, Annex 5–10.

Imrohonglu, S., and Kasnakoglu, H. 1980. Supply response in Turkeish agriculture. *METU Studies in Development* 6:327–339.

Just, R.E. 1975. Risk response models and their use in agricultural policy evaluation. *American Journal of Agricultural Economics, 57:*863–843.

Somel, K. 1979. Agricultural support policies in Turkey: A survey of literature. *METU Studies in Development* 6:275–323.

7
Nonmarket Policies: An Illustration for Pakistan

Nonmarket policies refer to policies in which the government determines prices that are different from the equilibrium prices and secures the market-clearing conditions via forced allocation and rationing. The rationed quantities are thus the main signals for economic activities (production and consumption), rather than the price system. Forced procurement, for example, requires producers—by law—to sell some or all of their output to the government agent at a price lower than the market price. If the policy is effectively enforced, then the quantities procured determine the farmers' excess supply. The difference between the low procurement price and the high market price is, however, a strong incentive for smuggling, bribery, corruption, and the like.

In this section we analyze the effects of forced procurement and public distribution policies. This analysis assumes that the allocation and rationing system can be enforced effectively, although the administrative costs involved are taken into account. In the first section these policies are examined in a prototype model of the food grains sector and are compared with market policies—that is, government interventions through the price system. The second section analyzes procurement and price policies in Pakistan.

Alternative Distribution Programs: A Comparative Evaluation in a Prototype Model

Modeling The Policy Rules

The formulation of the forced procurement and public distribution policy in this section is not designed to describe the exact practices existing in any specific country. Nevertheless, we shall see that it captures the basic structure of the actual policies practiced in many developing countries. The main decision rules of the policy are as follows:

1. At the beginning of each year the government determines the issue

price at the public distribution outlets. If the market price during the year is lower than the predetermined issue price, no subsidy is given. The difference, if one exists, between the price at the regular retail outlets and that at the public distribution outlets would then reflect mostly quality differences. If the market price rises above the normal price, the government would subsidize the price at the public distribution outlets. The rule for determining the subsidized price is the same as the subsidy rule described in chapter 5, and is formulated as

$$P_s = \begin{cases} (1 - \alpha)P + \alpha \bar{P} & : \text{if } P > \bar{P}; \ 0 \leqq \alpha \leqq 1 \\ \\ P & : \text{if } P \leq \bar{P} \end{cases}$$

where P_s is the subsidized price, P the market price, and $\bar{P}$ the normal price above which the subsidy is given. As noted earlier, this rule effectively determines a Harbergerian target demand curve for the beneficiary consumers, its elasticity being $(1 - \alpha)$ times their ordinary demand curve, at the upper segment of the price distribution. A target elasticity of $\eta_T = 0.0$ (for which $\alpha = 1.0$) means that the government does not allow any rise of the subsidized price above the normal price. This, of course, would prevent the consumption of the target population from falling below their normal consumption. A price elasticity of $\eta_T = 0.1$ ($\alpha = 0.8$) means that a 10 percent rise in the market price brings to a rise in the subsidized price by 2 percent so that the quantity demanded by the target population, whose ordinary price elasticity of demand is assumed to be 0.5, falls by 1 percent. In the latter case the government allows the issue price to rise with a rise in the market price, though at a lower rate, in order to lower the fiscal costs of the public distribution system and to lower the gap between the free market price and the issue price, thus reducing the incentive to abuse the rationing system. In the analysis it is assumed that the rationing system can be effectively enforced. Sales of the subsidized product to noneligible consumers, which may significantly raise the costs of the system, would not be taken into account. The target population consists of poor consumers in urban areas only, whose share in total consumption in a normal year is assumed to be 25 percent (although their share in the population is considerably higher).

2. The government mobilizes the quantities distributed to the target population from three sources: forced procurement, imports, and storage. It is assumed here that forced procurements are made only when the other two sources do not suffice to supply the needs of the public distribution system.

3. Forced procurements are made on a quota basis, and farmers are required to sell a portion of their output to the government agency at the announced procurement price. Sales to the government can also be made by the millers; but from the point of view of the farmers the result would be identical.

The procurement price is essentially equal to the issue price (except perhaps for some cost margins to cover the expenses of the government agency). Farmers' direct losses and their revenues foregone as a result of forced sales to the government at lower prices can effectively be regarded as income transfers from the farmers to the target population.

4. The costs to the government of the entire program consist of the administrative costs involved in the procurement and distribution activities; of the storage direct and indirect costs and of the import subsidies. The administrative costs are assumed to be proportional to quantities procured and distributed when procurement is made, and they do not include the fixed costs involved in erecting the system. Direct storage costs consist of handling, amortization, and storage losses. Indirect storage costs are the revenues foregone on account of the sales through the public distribution system at a price lower than the market price.

5. Grains are imported when their market price is higher than their import price. Imports, however, are a government monopoly. The grains imported are first allocated to the public distribution system; only the excess is sold in the free market.

6. Grains are released from public storage when their market price rises by more than 10 percent above the average price; grains are put into storage when their market price falls by more than 10 percent below their average price. The average price itself is calculated as a moving average of the market prices in the past five years. The price band thus floats together with the average price itself.

7. When the market price falls below a minimum price (assumed here to be 85 percent of the normal price), the government supports the price by procuring and extracting the excess from the market into storage. These procurements obviously are not enforced, and this program is the same as the procurement program examined in chapter 4. When this program is implemented together with the forced procurement program, it is noted in the tables that follow that procurements are for distribution *and* price support.

Simulation Results

The procurement and distribution program works by extracting a certain portion of the food supply from the market and distributing it to the target population on a rationed basis whenever the market price exceeds the mean price. As a result, both the mean of the market price and its variability would rise. Farmers' income and average unit value would rise only if the increase in the market price compensates them more for the income foregone due to the forced procurement. Figure 7–1 illustrates the changes in the market price

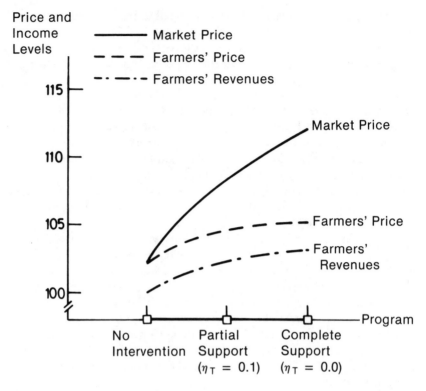

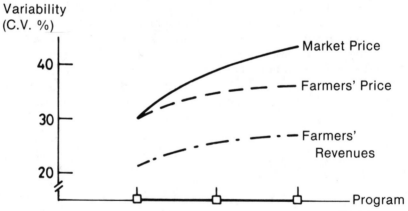

Figure 7–1. Product Prices and Farmers' Revenues Under Forced Procurement and Public Distribution Programs

and in farmers' unit value (or price) and income under different procurement-distribution programs. These programs differ only by the degree to which they stabilize the consumption of the target population. With the parameters assumed in the model, farmers' price and income are rising as an effect of the program. At the same time, however, the variability of the farmers' prices and revenues is also rising. The total effect on output thus depends on the farmers' price elasticity of supply and on their degree of risk aversion. The effect on the consumption of the rural population depends on their price and income elasticity of demand. Figures 7–2a and 7–2b describe the trade-off between food security of urban and rural consumers as an effect of the program.

Table 7–1 summarizes the effects of alternative market and nonmarket policies on the main economic indicators. The focus of the comparison is on the effects of the forced procurement program compared with those of the targeted subsidy program. Both eliminate the food gap of the target population, but the target subsidy program does so at higher fiscal costs. The rural population, on the other hand, suffers welfare losses due to the forced procurement program equal to 2.0 percent of the total expenditures on food grain, compared with *gains* equal to 1.2 percent under the targeted subsidy. These welfare losses represent the income transfer from the rural to the target population forced by the procurement and distribution program. If the government substitutes the targeted subsidy program for the forced procurement program, rural consumers will gain. The eligible urban consumers will not be affected since both programs stabilize their flow of consumption in the same way. The main effect will thus be the increase in government expenditures and in the fiscal risk associated with the transition to a target subsidy program.

Figure 7–3 illustrates the trade-off between rural and urban food security under the two alternative policies. The two policies would reduce the food gap of the target population at the expense of the rural consumers and the nonbeneficiary urban consumers. The subsidy program, however, would lead to a much larger increase in the farmers' price, which in turn would prompt an increase in output and in farmers' income. As a consequence, the rural population would suffer a *smaller* decrease in their food security under the subsidy program.

Figure 7–4 illustrates the rise in government expenditures that allows the decline in the expected food gap of the target population with either one of the distribution programs. These expenditures include the costs of administering the forced procurements and public distribution. When these indirect costs are taken into account, the savings offered by the forced procurement program are much smaller than those calculated on the basis of the direct costs only.

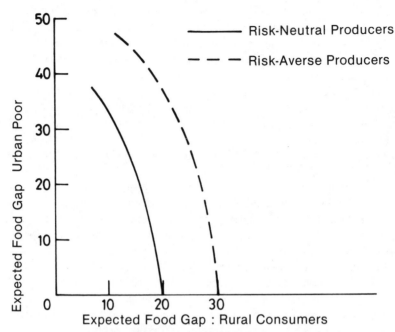

**Figure 7–2a. Trade-off between Urban and Rural Food Security under
Forced Procurement and Distribution Programs**

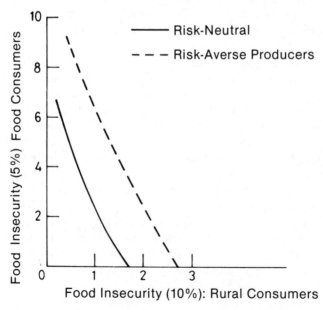

**Figure 7–2b. Trade-off between Urban and Rural Food Security under
Forced Procurement and Distribution Programs**

Table 7-1
Main Economic and Food-Security Effects of Alternative Procurement and Distribution Programs

| | No Intervention | Nonmarket Policies | | | Market Policies | |
		Enforced Procurement	Procurement and Buffer Stocks	Procurement for Distribution and Price Support	Targeted Subsidy	Buffer Stocks
Expected food gap, target population	6.7	0.0	0.0	0.0	0.0	4.7
Expected food gap, rural population	0.2	1.7	0.7	1.1	1.5	0.1
Rural Food Insecurity (10%)[a]	7.0	20.1	10.2	10.2	18.3	2.7
Farmers' income risk (15%)[b]	21.5	24.6	13.0	0.0	27.7	12.0
Quantity procured[c]	—	10.8	11.8	11.8	0.0	0.0
Government expenditures[d]	—	4.3	4.9	4.7	5.4	0.9
Government budget risk[e]	—	16.8	13.2	13.2	22.3	0.5
Economic gains or losses due to policy[d]						
Urban target consumers	—	3.5	2.2	1.6	3.6	−0.1
Other urban consumers	—	−2.0	−1.2	−1.4	−1.2	+0.1
Rural consumers-producers	—	−2.0	−1.2	−0.3	+1.2	−0.5
Government	—	−4.3	−4.9	−4.7	−5.4	−0.9
Total economic gains	—	−4.8	−5.1	−4.8	−1.8	−1.4

[a]Probability that food consumption of the rural population falls by more than 10 percent below their normal consumption.
[b]Probability that farmers' revenues fall by more than 15 percent below their normal revenues.
[c]Expressed as percentage of total normal production.
[d]Expressed as percentage of total normal expenditures on foodgrains.
[e]Probability that government expenditures on the programs would be higher than 10 percent of the total normal expenditures on food grains.

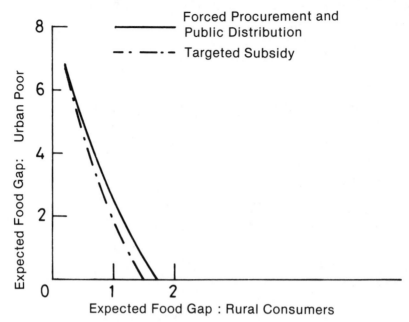

Figure 7–3. **Trade-off between Urban and Rural Food Security under Alternative Programs**

Government Procurement and Distribution of Wheat in Pakistan

In Pakistan, agricultural policies in general and food policies in particular have three main components.[1] One is support-price programs for each of the four major crops—wheat, rice, cotton, and sugar cane—which together account for 55–60 percent of the value added in agriculture. The second is a subsidy scheme for food products consisting of public distribution at controlled prices in ration shops, forced procurement, subsidized imports, export levies, overvalued exchange rate, and other trade restrictions aimed at lowering the domestic price on such exportables as rice and cotton. The third is a subsidy scheme for agricultural inputs such as fertilizers, irrigation water, and credit, aimed at securing the solvency of the farmers and the profitability of producing those crops the prices of which are being held down for the benefit of consumers.

The primary goals of these policies are to secure adequate food consumption of low-income consumers, especially in urban areas, at affordable prices; to help maintain low wages and thereby improve the competitive position of the local industry; to secure stable prices for both consumers and producers; and to achieve food self-sufficiency.

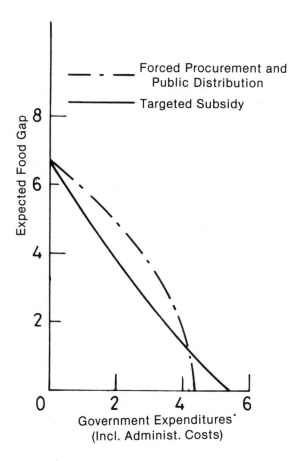

*Expressed as percentage of total expenditures on food grains.

Figure 7–4. Trade-off between Food Security and Government Expenditures under Different Programs

The institutional setting of these policies has its origin in the preindependence era and is quite similar to the one in India, despite changes during the nationalization period and in the early 1980s. The support price is announced in October, at the beginning of the planting season. The Agricultural Prices Commission (established in 1981) is the advisory body under the Ministry of Food and Agriculture, responsible for advising the government on setting prices for agricultural inputs and outputs. Its guidelines are to set prices that would cover production costs and assure a fair return. Its recommendations have to be approved by the cabinet.

Purchases of wheat for distribution in the ration shops and for storage are made by either the Provincial Food Departments or the Pakistan Agricultural Storage and Supply Cooperation. Farmers often prefer to sell their produce at lower prices to middlemen who carry the wheat to the procurement centers. Since the procurement price is fixed, most of the sales to the government are made immediately after the harvest, since farmers have no price incentive to hold stocks.[2] The wheat procured and imported by the government is sold at fixed prices through the privately owned ration shops to ration card holders. All distribution and storage costs, however, are borne by the government.

Until 1968 sales from ration shops were almost entirely of wheat imported under the P.L. 480 program. The large increase in wheat production in the late 1960s made Pakistan nearly self-sufficient, and the government met its ration shop requirements through grain purchases from domestic producers. At that time a procurement program was established to support the price received by farmers. By maintaining a fixed and relatively low issue price, however, the government incurred increasing deficits on the procurement and distribution program. To contain these deficits, a mandatory wheat procurement scheme was imposed in FY 1972–1973, which required growers to hand over a portion of their wheat at well below the world price.

The political repercussions of the forced procurement program made it necessary for the government to raise the procurement price by 65 percent (from Rs. 22.5/maund to Rs. 37.0/maund) in the following two years in order to adjust the domestic price to the rising world price (see table 7–2).[3] Poor harvests in 1973–1975 and a growing demand brought a substantial increase in wheat imports, which during these years accounted for 15 percent of total consumption. The result of the increase in wheat imports, the quadrupling of world prices, and the efforts to insulate the domestic market from the external turbulence was a sharp rise in both the food import bill and the budget allocated to wheat subsidies. In FY 1972 and 1973 wheat subsidies accounted for approximately 2 percent of the fiscal budget (excluding development expenditures); in 1974 and 1975 their share rose to 20 percent.[4]

Nevertheless, the effect of the forced procurement was that most wheat subsidies were actually paid by the farmers through low procurement prices. Gotsch and Brown (1980) estimated that on average over 50 percent (up to 70 percent in 1970) of total subsidy transfers to consumers on wheat can be attributed to price protection. Their results are summarized in table 7–3. After allowing also for the subsidies to what growers on fertilizers, Gotsch and Brown found that the net tax imposed on farmers as an effect of the various components of the wheat procurement and distribution policies accounted on average for 40 percent (up to 74 percent in 1974) of their total revenues from its production. The results are summarized in table 7–4. These estimates can only be regarded as first-order approximations because they count only the price changes but do not take into account the quality changes due to the response of both consumers and producers.

Table 7–2
Wheat Prices, Procurement, Imports, and Production in Pakistan

Fiscal Year	Procurement Price (Rs./md)	Ration-shop Price[a] (Rs./md)	Wholesale Price[b] (Rs./md)	Procurement (MMT)	Imports (MMT)	Production (MMT)
1968	17.0	17.25	19.3	0.8	1.1	6.3
1970	17.0	15.0	17.6	1.0	0.2	7.2
1972	17.0	17.0	20.5	0.2	0.7	6.8
1973	22.5	17.0	21.5	1.3	1.4	7.3
1974	23.5	21.5	27.5	1.2	1.2	7.5
1975	37.0	32.0	42.2	1.2	1.2	7.6
1976	37.0	32.0	37.4	2.3	1.2	8.5
1977	37.0	32.0	57.0	1.7	2.2	8.3
1979	46.6	40.6	58.2	2.4		10.9
1980	54.1	45.4	63.8	3.0		11.5
1981	54.1	55.4	70.5	4.0		11.4

Source (1968–1977): C. Gotsch and G. Brown, "Prices, Taxes and Subsidies in Pakistan Agriculture, 1960–1976," World Bank Staff Working Paper No. 387, Washington, D.C., 1980.
(1979–1981): M. Thobani, "Pakistan: An Analysis of Agricultural Pricing Policy," Unpublished ms., 1983.
[a]The price at which wheat is provided to the mills for grinding into flour (atta) for distribution to government-controlled ration shops. The actual ration-shop price of flour (in wheat equivalent) is 8–10 percent higher as a result of milling and distribution charges plus the costs of bags.
[b]Harvest time (April–June) price in Lyallpur.

Figure 7–5 demonstrates another aspect of the wheat subsidy provided to consumers (and the implicit tax imposed on producers) due to the government exchange rate and import policy. The figure presents the nominal protection coefficients (NPCs) and the estimated effective protection coefficients from 1960–1961 to 1980–1981 (EPCs). It shows that until 1972–1973 wheat imports were subsidized mainly through an overvalued exchange rate; since then wheat imports were directly subsidized by the government, and the subsidies were included in the fiscal budget. One objective of the mandatory procurement program was to lower the government expenses on wheat subsidies in the postdevaluation era. The subsidy rate implicit in the import price to domestic consumers varied widely from year to year, reflecting government efforts to protect the domestic consumers when world prices were rising. The effective protection coefficient was less than 1 during most of the period, implying the wheat prices to consumers and even more so to producers were lower than the world price. These protection rates represent the urban bias of the government trade policy.

The purpose of this section is to evaluate the performance of the procurement and distribution policy for wheat in Pakistan. The analysis is made via

Table 7-3
Direct and Indirect Consumers' Subsidies on Wheat
(*Rs. million*)

	1970	1972	1973	1974	1975	1976
1. Value of consumption at domestic prices[a]	1,257	1,587	2,313	2,664	3,950	4,161
Government-procured, including imports	568	414	1,629	1,677	2,398	3,532
Wholesale market purchases	689	1,173	684	987	1,552	629
2. Value of consumption at world price	2,035	2,073	2,982	4,885	7,072	6,311
3. Subsidy transfers to consumers[b]	895	583	1,053	2,750	3,780	3,280
Price protection[c]	710	328	446	1,495	2,089	1,540
Direct subsidies[d]	185	255	607	1,255	1,691	1,740
Price protection as percentage of total subsidies (%)	79	56	42	54	55	47
Total subsidies as percentage of expenditures on wheat consumption (3/1 - %)	71	37	46	103	96	79

Source: C. Gotsch and G. Brown, "Prices, Taxes and Subsidies in Pakistan Agriculture, 1960–1976," World Bank Staff Working Paper No. 387, Washington, D.C., 1980.

[a]Marketed protection plus imports at domestic prices.

[b]Calculated as [(2) − (1)] plus handling, storage, and related costs borne by the government.

[c]The indirect subsidy implicit in the procurement program, calculated as the difference between farmers' revenues on the marketed wheat and its value at world price.

[d]Government budget cost of consumer subsidies, based on the difference between the price at which wheat flour is sold at ration shops and the price at which the wheat is bought from domestic producers and imports.

Table 7-4
Direct and Indirect Producers' Taxes on Wheat

	1970	1972	1973	1974	1975	1976
1. Revenues from marketed wheat (m.Rs.)	1,152	1,267	1,493	1,844	2,778	2,986
Government procurement	463	95	809	857	1,226	2,357
Wholesale market sales	689	1,172	684	987	1,552	629
2. Value of marketed wheat at world market price	1,862	1,596	1,940	3,339	4,866	4,526
3. Implicit tax (2–1)	710	329	447	1,495	2,088	1,540
4. Direct subsidies[a]	59	40	104	139	163	303
5. Net taxes on wheat production (3–4)	651	289	343	1,356	1,925	1,237
6. Net taxes as percentage of revenues (5/1)(%)	57	23	23	74	69	41
7. Domestic price as percentage of world price	62	79	77	55	57	66

Source: C. Gotsch and G. Brown, "Prices, Taxes and Subsidies in Pakistan Agriculture, 1960–1976," World Bank Staff Working Paper No. 387, Washington, D.C., 1980.

[a]Mostly subsidies on fertilizers.

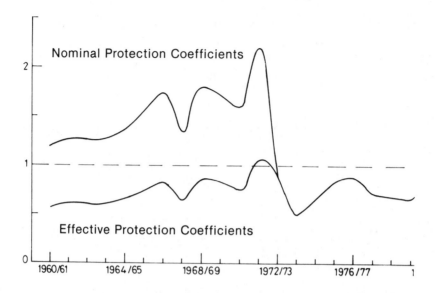

Figure 7–5. Nominal and Effective Protection Coefficients in Pakistan

the simulation model after adjusting the sectorial model to the wheat sector in Pakistan and modeling the policies appropriately. The parameters of the model are based on estimates made by Thobani (1979, 1983); Gotsch and Brown (1980); Squire, Little, and Durdag (1979); McCarthy and Taylor (1981); and World Bank Country Reports.

The Policy Rules

The policy rules for the simulation analysis have the following components:
   1. The procurement price is determined each year according to the rule

$$P_t^f = \theta \, P_c^f + (1 - \theta)P_{t-1}^I$$

where P_t^f is the farmers' procurement price at time t, P_c^f is the procurement price in a normal (stable) year, and P_{t-1}^I is the import price CIF evaluated at the effective exchange rate at time $(t-1)$. The procurement price is thus allowed to rise gradually with rises in the import price. In the base case α is assumed to be 0.7, implying that only 30 percent of the variations in the world price are allowed to be passed on to producers. Within the year the procurement price does not vary, and all the weather-induced price variations are absorbed by the government agency.
   2. The procurement price is also the one that is relevant to rural consum-

ers, on the basis of which they determine not only their production but also their own consumption and the quantities marketed. Procurements are not forced by the government, and farmers are free to sell their wheat at the procurement price to either a government agent or a private trader.

The market price of wheat in the urban centers is 25 percent higher than the farm-gate prices, reflecting the inland transport costs. Given the procurement price, the market price in urban areas can be determined. These two prices in turn determine the quantity consumed by the rural consumers, the quantity consumed by the nonbeneficiary urban consumers, and the quantity procured by the government.

3. The subsidy program has both transitory and permanent components, and the price in the public distribution system is determined according to the rule

$$P_t^s = \beta[\gamma \bar{P} + (1 - \gamma) P_t]$$

where P_t^s is the subsidized price and P_t the market price at time t, and $\bar{P}$ the normal (stable) market price. In a normal year the subsidized price is thus determined as a fraction β of the normal market price. In any other year the subsidized price is allowed to rise or fall with rises or drops in the market price, though at a lower rate. The variability of the subsidized price is therefore $\beta^2 \cdot (1 - \gamma)^2$ times the variability of the market price.

In the simulation analysis the permanent component β is assumed to be equal to 0.85 in the base case version and to 1.0 in another version. In the latter version, the subsidy program is a purely stabilizing program. In the two versions the transitory component γ is assumed to be 0.5, thus allowing only 50 percent of the variations in the market price to pass on to the beneficiary consumers.

4. Given the subsidized price, the quantity consumed by the poor is then determined. If the quantity procured exceeds the quantity distributed to the poor by the public system, the excess is stored up to capacity and exported if the surplus exceeds capacity and the world price allows exports. Because Pakistan is only 85 percent self-sufficient, however, exports will occur only rarely.

If the quantity procured falls short of the quantity distributed to the poor, the difference is released from storage to the extent available, and the rest is imported.

5. The government maintains a storage facility with a capacity equal to 3 million MT. Both the handling and operating costs and the amortization costs are being borne by the government.

The policy package consisting of all these rules and parameter values is denoted by *PAK* in the following analysis. This is the base case version of the

model. The second version of the model is the one in which the subsidy program is purely stabilizing and is denoted by *PAK-1*.

Against these two policies we examine three market policies:

FREE: Free trade and no government intervention.

SUP: This policy shifts the emphasis from consumers onto producers by
supporting a minimum price to producers. In addition to this program,
the government maintains also buffer stocks with a capacity of 3 MMT.

SUP + TARIFF: This policy further promotes production by imposing
an import tariff of 20 percent.

The goal of the last two policies is to lower the import dependence in
order to realize the goal of food self-sufficiency. The benchmark for evaluating the performance of the two policies that emphasize consumers' needs and
the two policies that emphasize producers' needs is thus the policy of free
domestic and international trade, *FREE*.

Simulation Results

Table 7–5 summarizes the main economic indicators under the five policies.
The policy package *PAK* raises the level of the market price (the price paid by
urban consumers at the usual retail outlets) by 15 percent but lowers its vari-

Table 7–5
Alternative Food Policies in Pakistan: Main Economic Indicators

	Policy				
	PAK	*PAK-1*	*FREE*	*SUP*	*SUP + TARIFF*
Market price:					
Mean (Rs./md)	50.0	50.0	43.2	43.0	50.2
CV%	3.2	3.2	9.8	8.8	10.1
Quantity produced (MMT)	10.2	10.2	10.4	10.4	10.9
Quantity consumed (MMT)	11.9	11.6	11.8	11.8	11.5
Degree of self-sufficiency	85.7%	87.9%	88.1%	88.1%	94.8%
Food insecurity (10%) - All Consumers[1]	1.2	4.2	4.8	4.3	17.4
Urban consumers					
Expected food gap (MMT)	0.1	3.4	1.7	1.5	6.7
Food insecurity (5%)[1]	1.0	4.9	12.7	9.6	63.8

[1]Probability that food consumption falls by more than the prespecified percentage below normal
consumption.

ability by 65 percent. Farmers' price is, however, 20 percent lower than the market price (see table 7–6). The decrease in farmers' price (by 8 percent) under *PAK* outweighs the risk-response effect (due to the decrease in the variability of farmers' income by 11 percent), and the result would therefore be a small decrease in the quantity produced under *PAK* compared to that under *FREE*.

The *PAK* policy effectively eliminates the food gap of 1.7 MMT that exists under *FREE*, and prevents food shortages of the target population in excess of 5 percent of their normal consumption. In the absence of government interventions such shortages would occur on average once every eight years.

A change in the food policy from *PAK* to *PAK-1*, canceling the permanent component of the subsidy program by setting $\beta = 1$, thus allowing it to stabilize only the consumption of the target population, would raise the expected food gap of urban consumers considerably. This rise, however, reflects a rise in the frequency of relatively mild shortages, whereas the frequency of extreme shortages would fall from once every eight years under *FREE* to once every twenty years under *PAK-1*.

Among the two producer-oriented policies, the minimum price plus stocks program denoted by *SUP* lowers the variability of the market and the farm-gate price by 20 percent. The stabilizing effect on production would contribute to lower somewhat the expected food gap and the probability measure of food insecurity. The 20 percent import tariff under *SUP + TARIFF* would raise the farm-gate price by 15 percent. As a result, domestic production would rise by 5 percent, and the degree of self-sufficiency would

Table 7–6
Alternative Food Policies in Pakistan: Effects on the Rural Sector

	Policy			
	PAK	*FREE*	*SUP*	*SUB + TARIFF*
Farmers' price:				
Mean (Rs./md)	40.0	43.2	43.0	50.2
CV (%)	3.2	9.8	8.8	10.1
Farmers' income:				
Mean (million Rs.)	14,940	16,635	16,605	20,155
Risk (15%)[1]	51.1	26.3	25.7	1.9
Farmers' food insecurity (10%)[2]	18.1	22.4	21.8	24.8
Farmers' expected food gap (MMT)	0.8	1.0	1.0	1.2

[1]Probability that farmers' income falls by more than 15 percent below their normal income.
[2]Probability that farmers' food consumption falls by more than 10 percent below their normal consumption.

rise from 88.1 percent under *FREE* to 94.8 percent under *SUP + TARIFF*. The constraint on imports would, however, take its toll in the form of a large increase in food insecurity and in the expected food gap. Table 7–8 shows that farmers' food insecurity would, however, rise only marginally as an effect of the import tariff and the resulting rise in price. The reason is the compensating increase in their income. However, farmers are then likely to divert some of their purchases from more expensive wheat to cheaper food products, and the result of the policy may well be an increase in the farmers' overall food security.

The *PAK* policy lowers farmers' average income by 10 percent. Despite the increase in their own consumption of wheat due to the fall in its price, farmers may be forced to lower their consumption of other food products as their income declines so that their overall food security may not increase.

Table 7–7 summarizes the effects of the policies on the balance of payments. The *PAK* policy package is seen to raise the food import bill by 25 percent. Once every three years the food import bill would exceed Rs. 3.5 billion, compared with once every four years under *FREE*. A change in the subsidy program from *PAK* to *PAK-1* would prevent most of the increase in the food import bill and in the foreign-exchange risk.

The 20 percent import tariff would cut the average food import bill by more than half and reduce the frequency of an import bill in excess of Rs. 3.5 billion from once every four years under *FREE* to once every eighteen years under *SUP + TARIFF*. The tariff would also generate revenues to the government equal to Rs. 198 million.

Table 7–8 summarizes the effects of the policies on the fiscal budget. The *PAK* policy package thus requires direct subsidies of Rs. 1.7 billion. An adjustment of the subsidy program in *PAK-1* would reduce these expenses to Rs. 703 million, half of which are storage costs. Canceling the permanent component of the subsidy program would cause the average price of wheat to

Table 7–7
Alternative Food Policies in Pakistan: Effects on the Balance of Payments

	Policy				
	PAK	*PAK-1*	*FREE*	*SUP*	*SUP + TARIFF*
Quantity imported (MMT)	1.7	1.5	1.4	1.4	0.6
Food import bill (million Rs.)	2792	2363	2232	2210	986
Exchange-rate risk[1]	37.4	26.9	24.6	27.3	6.1
Import subsidies (+) (million Rs.) or taxes (–)	+ 358	+ 303	0.0	0.0	– 198

[1]Probability that the food import bill would exceed Rs. 3,500 million.

Table 7–8
Alternative Food Policies in Pakistan: Effects on the Fiscal Budget

	Policy				
	PAK	*PAK-1*	*FREE*	*SUP*	*SUP+ TARIFF*
Quantity procured (MMT)	2.0	2.0	0	0	0
Government expenditures (million Rs.)					
Trade subsidies (+)	358	301	0	0	– 198
Consumers subsidies	1,017	38	0	0	0
Producers subsidies	0	0	0	29	102
Storage costs	362	364	0	342	384
Total	1,737	703	0	371	288

the beneficiary consumers to rise by 15 percent but would allow considerable savings in the fiscal budget and in the food import bill, without reducing by much the stabilizing effect on the subsidy program and its ability to prevent acute supply shortages.

Notes

1. Some policies have been changed in the early 1980s, and the description applies to policies that were in effect during most of the 1970s.

2. A study by Thobani (1983) suggests that an alternative policy of raising the procurement price from month to month between successive harvests according to the marginal interest and storage costs to the government could bring savings of up to Rs. 48 million annually (at 1981–1982 prices).

3. 1 maund = 37.324 kg.

4. Excluding noneconomic and fixed expenditures such as defense, internal security, and interest payments, these expenses accounted for over one-third of the remaining budget.

References

Gotsch, C., and Brown, G. 1980. Prices, taxes and subsidies in Pakistan agriculture, 1960–1976. World Bank Staff Working Paper No. 387, Washington, D.C.

McCarthy, F.D., and Taylor, L. 1981. Macro food policy planning: A general equilibrium model for Pakistan. *Review of Economics and Statistics:*107–121.

Squire, L.; Little, I.M.D.; and Durdag, M. 1979. Application of shadow pricing to country economic analysis with an illustration from Pakistan. World Bank Staff Working Paper No. 330, Washington, D.C.

Thobani, M. 1979. The effects of a change in wheat prices on incomes. *The Pakistan Development Review* 18:283–312.

———. 1983. Pakistan: An analysis of agricultural pricing policy. Unpublished ms.

Tolley, G.S.; Thomas, V.; and Wong, C.M. 1982. *Agricultural price policies and the developing countries.* Baltimore, Md.: John Hopkins University Press.

Index

About the Author

David **Bigman** is a senior lecturer and chairman of the Department of Agricultural Economics, Hebrew University of Jerusalem. He has worked at the Ministry of Finance in Israel, the World Bank, and the International Monetary Fund. He is the author and co-author of numerous articles in mathematical economics, international trade, and development. Together with T. Taya, he is the editor of the books *The Functioning of Floating Exchange Rates: Theory, Evidence and Policy Implications, Exchange Rate and Trade Instability: Causes, Consequences and Remedies;* and *Floating Exchange Rates and the State of World Trade and Payments.* He is the author of *Coping with Hunger: Towards a System of Food Security and Price Stabilization.*